READING ASSESSMENT

Also from JoAnne Schudt Caldwell

Comprehension Assessment: A Classroom Guide

READING ASSESSMENT

A Primer for Teachers in the Common Core Era

THIRD EDITION

JoAnne Schudt Caldwell

THE GUILFORD PRESS
New York   London

© 2014 The Guilford Press
A Division of Guilford Publications, Inc.
72 Spring Street, New York, NY 10012
www.guilford.com

Printed in the United States of America

This book is printed on acid-free paper.

Last digit is print number: 9 8 7 6 5 4 3 2 1

Library of Congress Cataloging-in-Publication Data

Caldwell, JoAnne (JoAnne Schudt)
    Reading assessment : a primer for teachers in the common core era / by
JoAnne Schudt Caldwell.
      pages cm
    Includes bibliographical references and index.
    ISBN 978-1-4625-1413-7 (pbk. : alk. paper)—ISBN 978-1-4625-1417-5 (cloth :
alk. paper)
    1. Reading—Ability testing.   I. Title.
    LB1050.46.C23 2014
    372.48—dc23
                                                          2013045879

About the Author

JoAnne Schudt Caldwell, PhD, is Professor Emerita at Cardinal Stritch University in Milwaukee, Wisconsin, where she also served as Associate Dean of the College of Education and Leadership. Dr. Caldwell is the author of *Comprehension Assessment: A Classroom Guide*. She is also coauthor (with Lauren Leslie) of the *Qualitative Reading Inventory, 5th Edition*, an informal reading inventory; of *Intervention Strategies to Follow Reading Inventory Assessment: What Do I Do Now?*; and (with Joyce Holt Jennings and Janet W. Lerner) of *Reading Problems: Assessment and Teaching Strategies*.

Preface

Much has changed since the publication of the second edition of this book in 2008. The importance of No Child Left Behind legislation has diminished as more and more states have received waivers, and response to intervention has become an accepted approach to determining a learning disability. However, as momentous as these initiatives were or continue to be, the publication of the Common Core State Standards (CCSS) for English Language Arts and Literacy in History/Social Studies, Science, and Technical Subjects represents "the most sweeping reform of the K–12 curriculum that has ever occurred in this country. . . . It is safe to say that across the entire history of American education, no single document will have played a more influential role over what is taught in our schools" (Calkins, Ehrenworth, & Lehman, 2012, p. 1). The Standards will affect what is published, what is taught, and, especially germane to this book, what is assessed.

The third edition of this book addresses changes in assessment that are the result of a focus on the CCSS. Previous editions focused on three key elements: the role of good reader behaviors as the basis for assessment, assessment as a four-step process, and the importance of assessment as a natural part of classroom instruction. These elements are still an integral part of the book. Although the reader may recognize content from previous editions, every chapter of the third edition contains new content, and two new chapters have been added. The sequence of the chapters has been altered, and the appendices at the end of chapters have also been revised to better fit the needs of teachers and coaches in this new educational environment.

- *Chapter 1: New Initiatives and New Concerns.* This new chapter sets forth the purpose and scope of the book, explains the four-step assessment process, and details key issues in reading assessment, such as the type of evidence we choose to assess reading and external influences on literacy assessment. It also explains the CCSS from the point of view of past research (Davis, 1968).

- *Chapter 2: Purposes of Reading Assessment.* As in the previous two editions, this chapter provides an interactive exercise to demonstrate to the teacher and coach what readers do as they read and comprehend text. New to this edition is an additional exercise that focuses on expository text. The chapter describes good reader behaviors and connects these behaviors to the CCSS. The chapter addresses new issues related to Standard 10, the expectation that students should be able to read grade-level text.

- *Chapter 3: Methods of Assessment.* This chapter is the old Chapter 9, reordered to provide information that is relevant to the understanding of succeeding chapters. It defines formal, informal, standardized, formative, and summative assessment. As in previous editions, it explains various forms of standardized scores and discusses the role of standardized assessments in today's schools.

- *Chapter 4: Assessment as Part of Instruction.* As in previous editions, this chapter explains the four-step assessment process using classroom examples; however, in this edition, the examples are based on assessment of the CCSS. The chapter contains a new section that explains how teachers and coaches can select teacher manual questions that match specific standards.

- *Chapter 5: The Informal Reading Inventory Process.* Although much of this chapter is the same as in previous editions, the role of the informal reading inventory process in relation to assessment of the Standards is discussed. In previous editions, an appendix listed and described published informal reading inventories. Because these inventories change rapidly and new editions appear regularly, Appendix 5.1 lists questions that a teacher or coach should ask about any published inventory that he or she may consider purchasing.

- *Chapter 6: Early Literacy.* This chapter is basically the same as in previous editions. It focuses on how early literacy should be assessed and how to engage in the running-record process. The role of the Reading Standards: Foundational Skills is addressed. In previous editions, an appendix listed specific examples of published early literacy assessments. Appendix 6.1 in this edition lists questions that a teacher or coach should ask before selecting any published instrument.

- *Chapter 7: Word Identification.* Much of the content of this chapter is the same as in previous editions. However, the miscue analysis process has been extensively revised in response to research conducted in relation to the piloting of the Qualitative Reading Inventory 5 (Leslie & Caldwell, 2011). The role of the Reading Standards: Foundational Skills is addressed, and Appendix 7.1 has been revised to list questions that a teacher or coach should ask before selecting any published instrument.

- *Chapter 8: Reading Fluency.* Although much of the chapter is identical to content in previous editions, issues with regard to the CCSS are addressed, specifically the place of fluency in close reading. Appendix 8.1 contains questions that teachers and coaches should ask about published fluency measures.

- *Chapter 9: Vocabulary Knowledge.* In previous editions, vocabulary assessment was included in the comprehension chapter. Because of its importance with regard to the CCSS, it deserved a chapter of its own in this edition. The chapter focuses on selecting words for assessment and on matching vocabulary assessment and instructional activities. As in previous editions, Appendix 9.1 lists questions that should be asked about published measures.

- *Chapter 10: Comprehension of Text.* Although some components of this chapter were present in previous editions, much of the chapter has been revised to address the demands of the CCSS. It contains a section on composing questions that match the Standards. With regard to instruction as a part of assessment, the chapter focuses on questions that suggest look-back strategies. It discusses the need to foster transfer to grade-level text in accordance with Standard 10 and suggests that much good instruction and subsequent assessment can occur during read-alouds, close reading, and summarization activities. Appendix 10.1 lists questions to ask about published instruments that assess comprehension.

- *Chapter 11: Schoolwide Reading Assessment.* This chapter is little changed from the previous editions.

Contents

READING ASSESSMENT

CHAPTER 1

New Initiatives and New Concerns

How Have They Influenced Reading Assessment?

Purpose and Scope of the Book

This book represents a first step in reducing some of the complexity that surrounds reading assessment. Like the first two editions, it is a primer and, as such, it offers an introduction to the subject of assessment as well as some guidelines for effective assessment of a student's reading ability. Reading is an extremely complex and multifaceted process, and assessing this process is also complex and multifaceted. However, a teacher or coach must start somewhere, and this primer offers a starting point.

Think about other complex processes. The first steps in learning are small. However, confidence grows with each "baby step" that is successfully mastered. With confidence comes the willingness to move on to more complexity and greater depth, such that the learner eventually takes giant steps. A beginning knitter does not attempt a complex pattern involving a variety of different stitches, but instead chooses a simple model. Later, after success with simple patterns, the knitter will competently handle complex designs. Learning to assess a student's growth as a reader is no different. The teacher or coach begins with small steps—with relatively simple strategies. These become the basis for developing increasing skill and competence in assessing reading.

This book describes a variety of beginning steps that a teacher or coach can take to develop expertise in the complex process of reading assessment. Some assessment strategies are described in detail, with instructions for implementing them in the reading classroom. Others are mentioned for the purpose of expanding the teacher or coach's knowledge base, but with no expectation that he or she will put them into practice at this stage of his or her career. They represent giant steps, and the premise of this book is that teachers and coaches must begin with the simple and move gradually to the complex. The primary purpose of this book is to guide the teacher or coach through the first steps in developing an effective system for assessing reading.

Description of the Assessment Process

This is a book about reading assessment, so it makes sense to describe first what I mean by *assessment*. Assessment is so much a part of our daily lives that we seldom think about it. We tend to take it for granted, and we just do it! When we assess, we acknowledge that there is something that we want or need to know. We then collect and analyze the evidence in order to make a judgment about it. This generally leads to a decision or to some form of action. For example, we assess the weather in the morning. Our evidence may be what we see as we look out the window, the local weather report, or a combination of the two. Based on this information, we decide to wear certain clothes or take an umbrella or (in some states) a shovel. We assess the amount and flow of traffic on the freeway, and perhaps turn off at the next exit. We assess the mood of our coworkers by listening to what they say, considering their tone of voice as they say it, and noting their body language. As a result, we either attempt to meet their needs, or we decide to avoid them for the rest of the day.

Assessment involves four steps. First, we identify what we want to assess. We usually do this in the form of a question. For example, as we move out of the driveway, we might ask, "Do I need to stop for gas before driving to work?" Second, we collect information or evidence. We check the gas gauge. If gas is low, we mentally determine how many miles we can drive before the tank hits empty. Third, we analyze the evidence. Perhaps gas is low and our mileage is limited but not enough to prevent us from getting to work. Fourth, as a consequence of our analysis, we make a decision. We would be late if we stopped for gas, and we have a conference with a concerned parent. We decide to fill up after work, not before.

Most of the time, the assessment process runs so smoothly that we tend to take it for granted. However, when the process fails us, we become very aware that something has gone wrong. We can run into problems with any of the four steps. Sometimes we are not specific enough about what we are assessing. "Do I have to stop at the supermarket on the way home?" is less specific than "Do I have what I need to prepare dinner tonight and lunch tomorrow?" Of course, the effectiveness of any assessment is heavily dependent upon the quality of the evidence we select; evidence can be insufficient or even inaccurate. A quick glance in the refrigerator offers less meaningful evidence than a careful examination of its contents based on a specific menu. Our analysis of the evidence may be faulty. We may, for example, assume that the block of white cheese is Gruyere, only to find out later that it is Parmesan and not what we needed for our recipe. Finally, we can make a wrong decision. We decide that a stop at the supermarket is not necessary, only to discover, as we begin to prepare dinner, that we should have done so.

Assessing a student's reading performance is no different. We ask a question about a student's reading. We select evidence that is appropriate for answering our question. We analyze the evidence and use it to make judgments about the student's strengths and needs. Then we take instructional action. At any point in the process, we can encounter the same problems we meet while assessing the weather, the state of our gas tank, or the contents of our refrigerator. However, reading assessment poses several additional issues.

Issues in Reading Assessment

Reading is an incredibly complex act, considerably more complex than checking the weather, estimating mileage, or preparing supper. Good readers engage in a variety of different activities as they read a selection. These activities are very different if the reader is a first grader who is just beginning to make sense of print, a fifth grader dealing with unfamiliar concepts in a social studies textbook, or an adult struggling with directions for filling out income tax forms. It is not enough to ask, "How well is the student reading?" That question is much too general. Instead, we need to know what specific behaviors indicate good and/or poor reading on the part of a student and at what level of development.

Types of Evidence

An important issue is the type of evidence we choose to assess reader behaviors. There are only so many options for assessing the weather or the state of our gas tank. However, there are many published instruments available for reading assessment and new ones appear every year. They take a variety of different forms: standardized, informal, group, individual, written, oral, constructed response, selected response, and more. In addition, we can (and should) construct our own assessments. It is difficult to sort through all the possible instruments, judge their quality, and determine if they are suitable for answering specific questions about a student's reading performance. And often, when we collect evidence, we do not know exactly what to do with it. If we note that the gas gauge is almost on empty, we know exactly what to do. It is quite another thing to deal with a variety of scores or observations, some of which may conflict with each other, and none of which suggest a clearly defined direction for instruction. We need guidelines for selecting evidence of reader behaviors and for using this evidence to design instruction.

We have tried to reduce the complexity of the reading process by breaking it into many little pieces, assuming that if we know the pieces, we will know the whole. Nothing could be farther from the truth! Have you ever attempted to put together a jigsaw puzzle without referring to the picture? It is extremely difficult to know where to begin or how to group the pieces. Do pieces of a similar color belong together, or do they form two separate areas in the puzzle? And the more pieces you have, the more difficult it is to see the whole. Reading is a very complex act, and we have attempted to understand it by dividing it into parts. But perhaps we have constructed too many parts and, as a result, have lost a sense of the whole.

For many years, reading instruction was driven by scope-and-sequence charts consisting of a multitude of different skills (Pearson & Hamm, 2005). A reader's understanding and use of phonics, for example, was separated into long lists of single consonants, consonant digraphs and blends, long and short vowels and r-controlled vowels and vowel combinations, and all were regarded as being of equal importance. Comprehension skills often looked very similar. For example, despite the fact that drawing an inference, making a judgment, and reaching a conclusion are more alike than different, they were considered separate skills to be assessed separately. Over time, educational terminology changed and student skills were referred to as "performance expectations" or "target behaviors." However, there was little decrease in the number of behaviors that should be monitored and assessed. States and/or districts constructed extensive lists of standards or outcomes that stipulated what students should be able to know and do at a particular grade level and in a specific content area. Although such standards were well intentioned, they tended to be very detailed and attempted to cover everything. In some cases, the standards were nothing more than the old scope-and-sequence chart served up in a different format.

One cannot quarrel with the purpose behind standards and lists of student performance expectations: to provide goals for teaching and learning. However, their sheer size and complexity could overwhelm a teacher or coach. Consider the example of a district that had carefully matched its pupil performance expectations for each grade to the state standards. At one grade alone, there were 50 different pupil expectations to be assessed! Let's do a bit of arithmetic and determine whether this is even possible. With one student and 50 expectations, the teacher or coach is responsible for assessing 50 items. With two students, the teacher or coach is responsible for 100 items. But with 25 students (the average size of many classrooms), the teacher or coach is responsible for instructing, assessing, and reporting on 1,250 reading behaviors! Is this even reasonable?

External Influences

Like any process, assessment is strongly affected by external influences. The price of gasoline can impact our decision about when and where to fill our tank. The price of ingredients and the amount of money in our food budget can affect our choice of menu. Similarly, influences external to the classroom and/or school district have affected reading assessment and continue to do so. For example, research conducted in colleges and universities often impacts what is assessed and how it is assessed. For instance, research in the 1970s indicated that prior knowledge was a critical component of reading comprehension; this led to a variety of prior knowledge assessments (Pearson & Hamm, 2005). Similarly, research that focused on phonological awareness, reading fluency, and narrative text structure resulted in the development of many formal and informal assessments that specifically addressed these components (Good, Kaminski, Smith, Laimon, & Dill, 2001; Rasinski, Reutzel, Chard, & Linan-Thompson, 2011; Stein & Glenn, 1979).

Classroom textbooks also affect reading assessment, as do district expectations about how these texts should be used. Textbooks not only provide the content that should be assessed, they also in many cases provide the assessments themselves. For example, many basal reading series include an extensive assessment system that includes initial screening measures, daily progress monitoring tasks, weekly quizzes, unit tests, and midyear/yearly assessments. Content textbooks also include a variety of assessment checkpoints and unit tests. A question is perhaps the basic unit of assessment, and textbooks explain what to ask, how to ask it, when to ask it, and how to evaluate student answers.

Concern about the quality of U.S. schools has influenced the design and usage of a variety of standardized measures. The National Assessment of Educational Progress (NAEP), often referred to as "The Nation's Report Card," conducts periodic assessments in reading, mathematics, science, writing, and other subjects and reports information about student performance at the national, state, and local levels (NAEP, 2011). Government mandates such as the now nearly defunct

No Child Left Behind (NCLB) Act and the newer response to intervention (U.S. Department of Education, 2004) also impact the nature of reading assessment. However, perhaps one of the most influential initiatives in the history of reading assessment is the Common Core State Standards for English Language Arts and Literacy in History/Social Studies, Science, and Technical Subjects (Common Core State Standards Initiative [CCSSI], 2010).

The Common Core State Standards

The Common Core State Standards (CCSS) were developed through the leadership of the Council of Chief State School Officers and the National Governors Association. Published in 2010, they "represent the most sweeping reform of the K–12 curriculum that has ever occurred in this country" (Calkins et al., 2012, p. 1). The intent of the Standards is to "ensure that all students are college and career ready in literacy" by the end of high school (CCSSI, 2010, p. 3). The Standards have been accepted by over 40 states and the District of Columbia, and two groups are presently developing computerized assessments for measuring student performance on the Standards: the Partnership for Assessment of Readiness for College and Careers (PARCC) and the Smarter Balanced Assessment Consortium (SBAC).

There are 10 "College and Career Readiness Anchor Standards for Reading" that apply to both informational text and literature. The basic content of the Anchor Standards is repeated and amplified in the Reading Standards for Literature K–5, 6–12, and the Reading Standards for Informational Text K–5, 6–12. In other words, "the informational reading and literature standards are both grounded in the same ten anchor standards and . . . each grade level's standard for informational reading has a mirror image in a standard for literature reading" (Calkins et al., 2012, p. 4). The Standards also include a list of "Foundational Skills" for levels K–5 that "are directed toward fostering student understanding and working knowledge of concepts of print, the alphabetic principle and other basic conventions of the English writing system" (CCSSI, 2010, p. 15).

The Standards emphasize much higher level comprehension skills than previous standards. They focus on "deep comprehension and high-level thinking skills" and demand student independence in grade-level text (Calkins et al., 2012, p. 25).

Refer to the 10 Anchor Standards listed on page 7 as I discuss how the CCSS differ from previous standards.

Gone are the extensive scope-and-sequence charts and the long lists of performance objectives for every content area. There are only 10 Common Core standards, and 9 of them refer to what students should be able to know and do.

COLLEGE AND CAREER READINESS ANCHOR STANDARDS FOR READING

Key Ideas and Details

1. Read closely to determine what the text says explicitly and to make logical inferences from it; cite specific textual evidence when writing or speaking to support conclusions drawn from the text.
2. Determine central ideas or themes of a text and analyze their development; summarize the key supporting details and ideas.
3. Analyze how and why individuals, events, and ideas develop and interact over the course of a text.

Craft and Structure

4. Interpret words and phrases as they are used in a text, including determining technical, connotative, and figurative meanings and analyze how specific word choices shape meaning or tone.
5. Analyze the structure of texts, including how specific sentences, paragraphs, and larger portions of the text (e.g., a section, chapter, scene, or stanza) relate to each other and the whole.
6. Assess how point of view or purpose shapes the content and style of a text.

Integration of Knowledge and Ideas

7. Integrate and evaluate content presented in diverse media and formats, including visually and quantitatively, as well as in words.
8. Delineate and evaluate the arguments and specific claims in a text, including the validity of the reasoning as well as the relevance and sufficiency of the evidence.
9. Analyze how two or more texts address similar themes or topics in order to build knowledge or to compare the approaches the authors take.

Range of Reading and Level of Text Complexity

10. Read and comprehend complex literacy and informational texts independently and with proficiency.

Note. From CCSSI (2010, p. 10).

Standard 10 refers to the level of skill expected of students. Is this moving from the sublime to the ridiculous? Can 9 standards truly capture the complex nature of the reading process? In the late 1960s, Davis (1968) used extensive factor analysis to identify eight separate subskills of the reading process: remembering word meanings; word meanings in context; understanding content stated explicitly; weaving together ideas in the content; drawing ideas from the content; recognizing the author's tone, mood, and purpose; recognizing literary techniques; and following the structure of the content. A glance at the Anchor Standards will confirm the close similarity between Davis's factors and the CCSS.

Anchor Standard 1

This standard clearly demonstrates the text-based nature of the Standards. The reader is expected to draw inferences from the text, not from prior knowledge or personal experience. The reader is expected to base conclusions and draw inferences on what the text says, not on what the reader already knows or believes. "In short, the Common Core deemphasizes reading as a personal act and emphasizes textual analysis" (Calkins et al., 2102, p. 25). This standard is closely aligned with Davis's factor of understanding content stated explicitly.

Anchor Standard 2

Determining the theme and/or central or main idea of a paragraph, multiple paragraphs, and/or an entire passage involves what Davis described as weaving together ideas in the content. Unfortunately, with regard to informational text, we have taught students that every paragraph contains a main idea usually contained in the first sentence. An examination of social studies and science textbooks points out the falsity of this assumption. A single main idea often stretches across multiple paragraphs. Main ideas are seldom stated explicitly and when they are, they are not always the first sentence in a paragraph or passage. Assessing a student's ability to determine main ideas has always been a focus of comprehension assessment and/or instruction. However, the Standards suggest the need to move main idea identification beyond a single paragraph. The Standards also indicate a need to assess a student's ability to write a coherent summary.

Anchor Standard 3

Analyzing how and why individuals, events, and ideas develop and interact over the course of a text is definitely a skill that moves beyond literal comprehension. A variety of question taxonomies (Bloom & Krathwohl, 1956; Mosenthal, 1996; Anderson & Krathwohl, 2001; Grasser, Ozuru, & Sullins, 2010) place "analyze" as a higher-level skill. With regard to the Standards, it is clear that all analyses are heavily dependent on the content of the text. Davis might describe this as drawing ideas from the content.

Anchor Standard 4

Interpreting words and phrases as they are used in a text matches nicely to Davis's factor of word meanings in context. The Standards are not concerned about word meanings known prior to reading; the focus is on the ability of students to determine word meaning from the context of the text. Many different kinds of reading assessment have focused on vocabulary knowledge. Generally students are asked to indicate word meaning, often by selecting one word out of four possible choices and/or by matching a word to a synonym or explanatory phrase. While some assessments place a word in the context of a sentence or paragraph, the focus is on selecting the correct meaning. Little if any assessment or instruction, for that matter, concentrates on how to use context to determine word meaning or which types of context provide the most or least information.

Anchor Standard 5

The Standard focuses on analyzing the structure of a text. In literature, this refers to the narrative structure of stories, poetry, plays, and the like. With regard to informational text, choice of structure involves several possible formats: description, cause–effect, sequence, problem solution, and compare/contrast (Caldwell & Leslie, 2013). Reading instruction has placed more emphasis on narrative structure with less assessment and instructional attention paid to the structure of expository text. Standard 5 allies with Davis's factor of following the structure of the content.

Anchor Standard 6

Assessing author point of view and/or purpose matches with Davis's factor of recognizing the author's tone, mood, and purpose. With regard to reading instruction, this standard may primarily relate to literature. Informational material in textbooks seems to be driven by the single purpose of informing or teaching. The point of view of the text author is seldom evident in social studies texts and few offer two author's versions of the same issue. Similarly, scientists believe that "school science time should not be devoted to critical analysis of science texts— texts that they note, are 'clearly authoritative'" (Shanahan, Shanahan, & Misischia, 2011 p. 422). This may change in the future as textbooks are rewritten to address the Standards.

Anchor Standard 7

Integration and evaluation of content presented in diverse media and formats may lend itself to assessment based on Standards 1 through 6, 8, and 9. That is, the student can be asked to draw inferences, determine main ideas, analyze how and why something occurs, and so on, with regard to diverse media and formats. The choice of Standard may be dependent on the function and purpose of the diverse media and format as related to the text. Does it clarify the text? Does it provide additional information? Does it present an opposing point of view?

Anchor Standard 8

Delineating and evaluating the arguments and specific claims in a text including the validity of the reasoning as well as the relevance and sufficiency of the evidence may address several of Davis's factors depending on the nature of the text: weaving together ideas in the content; drawing ideas from the content; recognizing the author's tone, mood, and purpose; recognizing literary techniques; and following the structure of the content. Actually, in order to meet Standard 8, a reader might employ all of Davis's factors.

Anchor Standard 9

Analysis of how two or more texts address similar themes or topics in order to build knowledge or to compare the approaches the authors take also seems to address several of Davis's factors: weaving together ideas in the content; drawing ideas from the content; recognizing the author's tone, mood, and purpose; recognizing literary techniques; and following the structure of the content. As was explained with regard to Standard 6, current textbooks seldom present two or more texts on the same theme or topic. This may change as textbooks are rewritten to address the Standards. Standardized assessment designed by PARRC and SBAC may well address this standard; however, until textbooks are changed, it will be up to the teacher to provide multiple texts on similar themes and topics in order to ascertain student ability to meet this standard.

Anchor Standard 10

Reading and comprehending complex text independently and proficiently basically means that students should be able to read text that is appropriate for their chronological grade level. For example, sixth graders are expected to "by the end of the year, read and comprehend literary nonfiction in the grades 6–8 text complexity band proficiently, with scaffolding as needed at the high end of the range" (CCSSI, p. 39). This represents a distinct change from our previous emphasis on instructional-level text, that is, text that a student can read with some comfort and success. The Standards "challenge teachers to provide scaffolded instructional support for every learner and to do so with complex and difficult text" (Fisher, Frey, & Lapp, 2012, p. 7).

Response to Intervention

Response to intervention (RTI) was born with the reauthorization of the Individuals with Disabilities Education Act in 2004, now known as the Individuals with Disabilities Education Improvement Act. This law states that a learning disability can be determined in two stages. First, does an individual respond appropriately to classroom instruction? Second, if this is not the case, does the individual respond to instruction that is focused on the student's specific needs? A student who does not make adequate progress after individualized and targeted instruction can then be considered for evaluation for a specific learning disability. Johnston (2010) explains the logic behind RTI as follows: because a learning disability may be the result of inadequate instruction as opposed to genetics, it is important to rule out the possibility that underachievement is the result of poor or inappropriate instruction.

RTI is generally viewed as encompassing three tiers of assessment and instruction (Johnston, 2010; Wixson, Lipson, & Johnston, 2010). Tier 1 instruction occurs in the regular classroom. Teachers use screening measures to identify students who are not making adequate progress and keeping up with their peers. These students move into Tier 2 instruction. In order to accelerate their progress, Tier 2 generally involves small-group instruction, added instructional time, and/or alternative forms of instruction targeted to specific instructional needs. Tier 2 does not replace or substitute for classroom instruction; rather, it is an addition to it. Those who still do not progress move into the Tier-3 level of instruction. This level can involve individualized instruction and possible evaluation for the existence of a learning disability.

The importance of assessment is clearly evident with regard to all three tiers. It is assessment that leads to placement in Tiers 2 or 3. The law requires that a student's response to instruction be carefully assessed through "data-based documentation of repeated assessments of achievement at reasonable intervals, reflecting formal assessment of student progress during instruction" (U.S. Department of Education, 2004). The nature and appropriateness of the assessment used is a critical component (Caldwell & Leslie, 2013). Short, easily administered assessments are popular; however, they may not be appropriate for monitoring progress in something as complex as literacy. Reading is a complex process and assessment is similarly complex. Assessment of oral reading fluency, for example, does not necessarily substitute for comprehension assessment even though fluency is often correlated with comprehension in the early grades. Dorn and Henderson (2010) recommend assessments that are "direct measures of specific skills and strategies needed for success in the general education setting" (p. 134).

The importance and relevance of the CCSS strongly suggest that RTI assessment and instruction should be examined and adapted in relation to the Standards. While the Reading Standards: Foundational Skills K–5 (CCSSI, 2010, pp. 15–17) provide guidelines for assessing and instructing print concepts, phonological awareness, phonics/word recognition, and fluency, the Standards focus on comprehension and define success "in terms of the knowledge and skills deemed necessary for college and career readiness rather than mastery of the school-like tasks that comprise current measures of achievement" (Wixson & Lipson, 2012, p. 389). This change has serious implications for RTI with regard to both assessment and instruction. Assessment and instruction in word identification and fluency has predominated in RTI. This emphasis may not be appropriate preparation for students to meet the Standards and demonstrate adequate performance on the state assessments designed by PARRC and SBAC. It is possible that many students who demonstrate acceptable scores in word identification accuracy and fluency as measured by current assessments may not perform adequately on Standards-based assessments and in grade-level text. The foundational skills of word identification and fluency may be the gateway to comprehension, but one cannot assume that assessment and instruction focused on these is a viable substitute for assessment that specifically concentrates on comprehension.

Summary

- Assessment is a four-step process: identifying what to asses, collecting evidence, analyzing the evidence, and making a decision based on the analysis.

- It is not enough to ask, "How well is a student reading?" We need to know what specific behaviors indicate good and/or poor reading and at what level of development.

- An important issue is the type of evidence we select to assess reader behaviors.

- Reading is a very complex activity and we have attempted to simplify it by breaking it down into smaller parts. For many years reading assessment was driven by lengthy scope-and-sequence charts consisting of a multitude of different skills. The size and scope of such charts were overwhelming for teachers.

- Assessment is strongly affected by external influences. Research strongly impacts what is assessed and how it is assessed. Many textbooks provide extensive assessment systems such as progress monitoring tasks, weekly quizzes, and unit tests.

- Concern about the quality of U.S. education has influenced the design and usage of standardized assessment measures such as the NAEP. Government mandates such as Response to Intervention (RTI) also influences reading assessment.

- The Common Core State Standards for English Language Arts and Literacy in History/Social Studies, Science, and Technical Subjects (CCSSI, 2010) represents a sweeping reform of the K–12 curriculum.

- Ten College and Career Readiness Anchor Standards for Reading apply to both literature and informational text. The Standards emphasize much higher-level comprehension skills than previous standards. They focus on the reading and comprehension of complex text and demand independence in doing so at a student's chronological grade level.

- The 10 Standards are closely allied with the factor analysis work of Davis (1968) who determined that the reading process could be broken into eight separate subskills.

- RTI involves three tiers of instruction: classroom instruction, small-group intervention, and individualized instruction. A student can be evaluated for a specific learning disability only if the student has failed to make progress in the regular classroom and in small-group instruction designed to meet his or her specific needs. RTI assessment of word identification and fluency should not substitute for assessment that is specifically focused on comprehension.

Activities for Developing Understanding

- Select something in your life that you assess frequently (grocery supplies, the organization of your desk, the state of your checkbook, etc.). Show how your actions fit into the four steps of assessment.

- Examine a classroom textbook. What types of assessment are recommended?

- Go on the web and examine the site that provides information on the National Assessment of Educational Progress (NAEP) (*http://nationsreportcard. gov*).

- Download the Common Core Standards (*www.corestandards.org*) if you have not already done so and examine how the 10 Anchor Standards are repeated and amplified in the Reading Standards for Literature and Informational text. Pay particular attention to your grade level.

- Go on the web and examine the site that provides information on RTI (*http://idea.ed.gov/explore/view*).

CHAPTER 2

Purposes of Reading Assessment

What Do Good Readers Do and How Can Teachers and Coaches Assess This?

Purposes of Reading Assessment

There are three basic purposes of reading assessment. First, a teacher or coach uses the assessment process to identify the good reader behaviors that a student displays and those that need instructional emphasis. Readers are not passive. They engage in a variety of activities as they construct meaning. Teachers and coaches must understand these processes, so they are equipped to select valid evidence that documents good reading. A teacher or coach must identify areas of strength and weakness with regard to the reader behaviors in order to align instruction with student needs. If the teacher or coach recognizes which good reader behaviors are absent or weak, he or she can design and focus instruction to introduce or strengthen them. The reader behaviors that are described in this chapter are closely aligned with the CCSS.

Second, teachers and coaches need to know how to determine a student's *reading level* —that is, the grade level at which a student can read in an acceptable fashion. The Standards set forth the goal of all students reading at their chronological grade level by the end of a grade, that is, by the end of fifth grade, a fifth grader should read and comprehend "at the high end of the grades 4–5 text complexity band independently and proficiently" (CCSSI, 2010, p. 14). Comparing a student's reading level with his or her chronological grade level can suggest the existence of a reading problem and the need for intervention instruction.

Third, teachers and coaches must assess progress. This involves noting progress in developing specific good reader behaviors as well as progress in moving toward competency in reading text at a student's chronological grade level.

Identifying Good Reader Behaviors and Areas of Weakness

What is this process called *reading*? What are readers doing as they read, and what do they have to learn? As teachers and coaches, what should we look for as we assess the developing literacy of our students? We have all been successful readers for many years. As a result, we seldom think about the act of reading; in fact, we tend to take it for granted. Let's engage in a short exercise to help us realize what we do so effortlessly every day of our lives as we read newspapers, magazines, grocery lists, road signs, novels, memos from the principal, and notes from a parent, to name only a few things. I am going to ask you to read a short selection, sentence by sentence, and to examine what went on in your mind as you read. Ready?

The Tale of Taffy and Diane

What did you do as you read this? You recognized the individual words, and you assigned some form of meaning to each one. You did this accurately and very quickly. You also recognized that this was a title and, based on the word *Tale*, you anticipate reading a story of some kind.

Diane wondered if she should keep Taffy. After all there were some advantages to having her around.

Again you recognized and assigned meaning to the individual words. You also inferred the existence of a problem with regard to keeping Taffy and you no doubt have questions. What kind of a problem? What will happen next? Will

Diane decide to get rid of Taffy? How will she do this? What will happen to Taffy? These questions lead you to read on, hopefully to find answers.

Taffy was very loving and seemed genuinely glad to be with her. She wasn't a whole lot of trouble and the expense was negligible.

Good readers synthesize information as they read and you connected the information in this sentence to the preceding one. However, you still have questions. Why did Diane want to get rid of Taffy if Taffy was loving and relatively trouble-free? Perhaps the word *negligible* gave you pause. It is not a common word and you may have had to think about its meaning. If it was an unfamiliar word for you, as a good reader, you used context and assigned a possible meaning. Given that it followed "wasn't a whole lot of trouble," you probably inferred that it meant insignificant or small. Perhaps *trouble* and *expense* raised an additional question. Who or what is Taffy?

But here was Taffy, pushing that darn thing back and forth, back and forth. She did this almost every day and Diane just couldn't break her of the habit.

At this point you are no longer aware of identifying and assigning meaning to words. For you, that is an automatic and effortless process. Your attention is focused on Taffy and Diane. Perhaps you have inferred that Taffy is an animal of some kind because she seems to enjoy pushing something (a toy perhaps) back and forth. What kind of animal? Perhaps a cat or dog but certainly not a goldfish or turtle. You have more questions than you did before, such as why would a pet's preoccupation with a toy lead her owner to consider getting rid of her? What kind of person is Diane? Perhaps you are now viewing her less favorably than before when you empathized with her difficult decision. You are using your prior knowledge and the clues in the text to predict possible answers to your questions. You are monitoring your comprehension. You know what you are unsure of. You are probably considering several possible interpretations—and, I might add, enjoying the suspense. Why do we stay up way past bedtime reading a book? It is because we have many questions about what will happen, and we want to find the answers. Otherwise, we know that sleep will elude us!

Taffy was making too much noise. That and the rebarbative movement were giving Diane a monstrous headache.

Good readers are aware of "roadblocks" to comprehension and I suspect you have now met one, the word *rebarbative*. What does it mean? What did you do?

I doubt that you reached for a dictionary. Caught up with the story action, you probably used the context of the story to assign a temporary meaning, such as *annoying* or *bothersome*. You then read on, eager to find out what will happen next.

> **Maybe she should get rid of Taffy but who would take her? Who would want her? And Diane knew she would feel guilty about it for the rest of her life if something happened to her pet.**

So Taffy is a pet. But what kind? At this point emotion enters the picture. If you are a pet owner, you can empathize with Diane's plight. You are caught up with what is happening! You are very aware of what you understand and of the questions you have. You want answers! You are probably even impatient with my comments. So let's move on.

> **Diane carefully examined her nails and shifted her position on the sofa. Taffy had finally finished. Diane sighed. She knew Taffy would head for the sofa and expect Diane to move so she jumped off.**

What picture is in your mind? Good readers engage in visual imagery as they read. You probably noted a contradiction. The picture of Diane examining her nails is meaningful, but the notion of a person jumping off a sofa introduces a somewhat discordant note.

> **Taffy watched her head for another chair. "Good kitty," she murmured and reached out to pet Diane.**

Were you surprised? And if you were, wasn't it fun? Had you considered the possibility that Diane was the pet, not Taffy? How did the names of Taffy and Diane lead you astray? And now you can probably say what Taffy was pushing back and forth: the vacuum cleaner. And you can go back and verify or change the meaning you assigned to *rebarbative* which means unpleasant, annoying, and/or irritating.

Let's summarize. What did you do as you read these few short sentences? First, you identified individual words. Most (if not all) were familiar to you, and you did not need to match letters and sounds. These words were what we call *sight words* —words that are recognized immediately without analysis. *Rebarbative* may have been unfamiliar, but as a good reader you were able to sound it out and pronounce it even though you had never seen it in print before. You assigned appropriate meanings to the words you identified. You connected the things you knew about pets with the information in the text. You made inferences based on your knowledge and the clues in the text. You asked questions and located their answers. You monitored your own comprehension or lack of it. In short, you were extremely active, and your sole focus was upon constructing meaning and finding out what was going on.

These key reading behaviors are the basis for reading assessment. We need to find out whether readers are able to do what you did so effortlessly. If they cannot, we need to teach them strategies for doing so. And it is not enough to identify which good reader behaviors to assess after reading a story. We need to assess these in different forms of text. You were extremely successful with the Taffy and Diane scenario, but would you have been as capable if you were reading an insurance form, a mortgage agreement, or a statistics textbook? Students who employ good reader behaviors when reading stories may become hopelessly confused in a social studies or science textbook. Let's see how reading a science text is somewhat different from reading a story.

Proving the Continental Drift Theory

Right away, you are aware that the following selection will not be a story. Even if you have no idea what the "continental drift" is, you know you are reading a science text probably because of the word *theory*. You realize that it will be very factual, that you will be expected to learn something, and that it probably will not contain "fun" surprises such as finding out that Diane was a cat. You may wonder what is meant by *drift*. Does it carry the same meaning as a snow drift, an aimless movement, or a thread of conversation? Much reading of informational text involves asking questions and reading to find an answer in subsequent text.

If you look at a map of the world, you may notice a strange phenomenon. The outlines of some continents seem as if they could fit together like a jigsaw puzzle.

As with the account of Taffy and Diane, you recognize and assign meanings to individual words. *Phenomenon* may be a new word but you can determine meaning from the context of the passage. Because it is preceded by *strange*, you probably assign a meaning of something that does not often occur. You are also aware that *outlines* do not refer to note-taking strategies involving Roman numerals and *jigsaw* does not refer to a tool of some sort. As a good reader, you understand that the common meaning of many words often change in science, social studies, and math texts.

In 1912 Alfred Wegener proposed the theory of the continental drift. He believed that the continents were once a single continent that broke and drifted apart to form today's continents.

Comprehending this passage is different from the passage concerning Taffy and Diane. You know that you are reading factual material that carries specific meaning. You also know that understanding each sentence is critical to understanding the whole. Have you ever deliberately skipped description in a story to focus on the characters' actions? Unlike a story where one can often skim over certain parts and still retain comprehension of the whole, you are aware that each sentence carries specific meaning that is critical to understanding of the passage.

What evidence was there for his theory? Identical plant fossils were found in all continents. The same reptile fossil was found in both South America and Africa. Rocks in the west of Africa matched those on the east coast of South America. Most scientists did not believe Wegener's theory. What force could be strong enough to move continents?

Can you begin to understand the complexity of expository text? The author lists evidence for Wegener's theory but does not explain why it is evidence. It is up to the reader to analyze why identical fossils and rocks suggest the existence of a single land form and why rocks found on the west coast of Africa and the east coast of South American are particularly telling. At this point, you are probably doing some careful rereading, what the Standards refer to as "close reading" (Coleman & Pimental, 2011).

When scientists were able to map the ocean floor, they discovered huge trenches and mountains. In 1960 Henry Hess suggested that they formed where magma pushed up through the ocean floor. This occurred when earth's plates moved apart.

New words continue to appear and more questions arise. Perhaps you know what *magma* means and perhaps you don't. Perhaps your concept of magma is fiery liquid flowing down the sides of a volcano, not up from the floor of the ocean. And while you are very much aware that earth's plates are not what you will use when eating dinner, you may not understand their specific meaning in reference to the ocean floor. You also have to identify what *this* in the last sentence refers to in order to make sense of the whole passage. You may be in the uncomfortable position of having to read on without clearly understanding the preceding text. This also may force you to reread. Expository text is seldom read in a continuous fashion. It generally takes the form of read, reread, read on, read back, read on, reread, and so on.

But what caused the plates to move apart? Hot currents in the mantle constantly rise, circle around, and fall in a process called convection. When the mantle moves, the plates floating on it also move.

Can you believe that you have only read a very small segment of science text? Consider all the unfamiliar concepts that you have encountered. Old vocabulary continues to appear in a new guise. *Mantle* is certainly not the ledge above a fireplace nor is it a cloak. What is *convection*? Can you begin to understand what students encounter and how even a good reader like you may feel overwhelmed?

Additional proof of the continental drift occurred when scientists studied the magnetism of rocks in the ocean that were formed from cooled lava of undersea volcanoes. Magnetic patterns indicated that the rocks formed at different times. This proved that the continental drift has occurred throughout Earth's history and is still occurring today.

More questions arise. Why are rocks in the ocean magnetic? How can magnetism tell their age? How is magnetism connected to currents in the mantle and the movement of continents? You are aware that you have to pull all this together, but you are also aware that you may need help to do so. As a good reader, you know when you comprehend and when you don't. As a good reader, you know exactly what you do not understand. If this text was assigned for a class, you would probably underline or highlight problematic parts to share with your teacher or classmates.

Consider some of the obvious differences between the account of Taffy and Diane and how Albert Wegener's theory was proven. We can empathize with Taffy and Diane, at least those of us who are pet owners can. We can laugh at being fooled by the surprise ending. We really did not learn anything, except that names can be a powerful influence in our interpretation of text. Reading the passage was relatively easy; it demanded little effort on our part. We were not expected to learn but to enjoy.

The account of the continental drift theory was totally different. It was packed with unfamiliar concepts. The author assumed that the reader could draw inferences about why fossils in different places provided some evidence for the theory. The author also assumed that you could arrive at a definition of *convection*. There were more unfamiliar words than in the Taffy passage and they carried very specific meanings. What may be the primary issue is the difficulty and unfamiliarity of the concepts in the science passage versus those in the account of the unhappy Diane.

If you were successful in comprehending either or both of the two passages, you did so by engaging in good reader behaviors. Consider the list on page 22.

GOOD READER BEHAVIORS

Use letter and sound patterns to pronounce words accurately and fluently.

Learn new words and extend the meanings of known words.

Determine what is important in the text.

Ask questions and read to find answers.

Draw inferences.

Recognize text structure.

Summarize, synthesize, reorganize, and evaluate ideas.

Form and support opinions.

Recognize the author's purpose/point of view/style.

Monitor comprehension and repair comprehension breakdowns.

Can you recognize when you engaged in these behaviors during your reading of the two passages?

The good reader behaviors are the basis of reading assessment. They are not something different from the CCSS. They just say the same things in different words and perhaps in a more user-friendly fashion. The following chart demonstrates how these good reader behaviors and the CCSS are related.

MATCH OF GOOD READER BEHAVIORS TO THE CCSS

Use letter and sound patterns to pronounce words accurately and fluently.
Reading Standards: Foundational Skills K–5 (CCSSI, 2010, pp. 15–17).

Learn new words and extend the meanings of known words.
Standard 4. Interpret words and phrases as they are used in a text, including determining technical, connotative, and figurative meanings and analyze how specific word choices shape meaning or tone (CCSSI, 2010, p. 10).

Determine what is important in the text.
Ask questions and read to find answers.
Draw inferences.
Summarize, synthesize, reorganize, and evaluate ideas.

Standard 1. Read closely to determine what the text says explicitly and to make logical inferences from it; cite specific textual evidence when writing or speaking to support conclusions drawn from the text.

And

Standard 2. Determine central ideas or themes of a text and analyze their development; summarize the key supporting details and ideas (CCSSI, 2010, pp. 15–17).

Recognize text structure.

Standard 2. Determine central ideas or themes of a text and analyze their development; summarize the key supporting details and ideas (CCSSI, 2010, pp. 15–17).

And

Standard 5. Analyze the structure of texts, including how specific sentences, paragraphs, and larger portions of the text (e.g., a section, chapter, scene, or stanza) relates to each other and the whole (CCSSI, 2010, pp. 15–17).

Form and support opinions.

Standard 8. Delineate and evaluate the arguments and specific claims in a text, including the validity of the reasoning as well as the relevance and sufficiency of the evidence (CCSSI, 2010, pp. 15–17).

Recognize the author's purpose/point of view/style.

Standard 6. Assess how point of view or purpose shapes the content and style of a text.

And

Standard 9. Analyze how two or more texts address similar themes or topics in order to build knowledge or to compare the approaches the authors take (CCSSI, 2010, pp. 15–17).

Monitor comprehension and repair comprehension breakdowns.

Required for meeting all of the Standards.

Determining Reading Level

The second purpose of reading assessment is to determine a student's reading level. This task involves estimating a student's ability to read and comprehend text at different grade levels. The basic question is: Can the student handle most of the selections that are used at his or her chronological grade level? The first indication of a reading problem is generally that a student cannot read as well as his or her classmates. If a third grader can read and comprehend selections that are appropriate for third grade, we say that this student is reading *at grade level*. A third grader who can read and comprehend selections appropriate for fifth grade is reading *above grade level*. One who is only comfortable with a first-grade selection is reading *below grade level*. An important category of reading assessment is determining what general level of text the student can read successfully.

Reading assessment often involves determining a student's instructional, independent, and frustration reading levels. The *instructional level* is the level of text that the student can read and comprehend with some assistance. *Independent-level* text is text that the student can read and comprehend without assistance. *Frustration-level* text is text that the student is not able to read with adequate word identification accuracy or comprehension. Unfortunately, for many students, their classroom text represents a frustration level.

However, nothing is ever as easy and straightforward as it may appear. Readers do not have a single instructional reading level. They may have a higher level when reading narrative text than when reading social studies or science text. Their instructional level for social studies text may be higher than for science text. What this means is that ideal assessment should pay attention to the different disciplines and realize that a competent reader of narrative fiction may experience difficulty reading social studies and science text at that level.

Determination of reading level is especially important given Standard 10 of the CCSS. Students are expected to read grade-level text, that is, text at their chronological grade level. To put it another way, according to the Standards, a student's instructional level should be the same as his or her chronological grade level. If it is not, the student should receive instruction for the specific purpose of raising the student's present level to his or her chronological grade level.

Unfortunately, the focus of intervention instruction has been to concentrate on instructional-level text with success measured as progress to the next level. It has not focused on helping a student attain a reading level that is appropriate for his or her own chronological grade level (Klenk & Kibby, 2000). The focus on instructional-level text in intervention settings is well-intentioned. Students are asked to read what they can handle with some support and, as a result, they are not placed in an uncomfortable situation. The avoidance of frustration-level text has been based on the premise that it leads to a negative emotional response in the reader. Frustration-level text is presumed to cause stress, decrease motivation, and reinforce bad habits such as lack of fluency. But, little research supports such assumptions. "Certainly students can be emotionally frustrated by difficult texts. However, they can also be highly motivated by these texts, depending on factors such as interest, prior knowledge and social considerations (Halladay, 2012, p. 60).

A focus on instructional-level text that is below a student's chronological grade level will not necessarily help the student to function in his or her classroom. It "may bar access to concepts and ideas otherwise acquired by reading grade level text. . . . Lack of exposure to grade level concepts, vocabulary and syntax may prevent children from acquiring information that contributes to their development of language, comprehension and writing" (McCormack, Paratore, & Dahlene, 2003, p. 119). However, it is still important to know a student's instructional level because it indicates the seriousness of a student's reading problem and the amount and intensity of the intervention instruction he or she should receive.

Determining Text Level

What makes a selection appropriate for one grade and not for another? In other words, how do we decide that a selection is at a specific grade level? In most cases teachers are given a textbook selected by the district and represented by the publisher to be at an appropriate grade level. Many classroom libraries are grouped according to the levels printed on the back of the book. Where do these levels come from, that is, how do publishers differentiate between a fourth-grade text and a fifth-grade one? Publishers use "readability formulas" to determine difficulty level. Readability formulas are based on the premise that longer sentences and longer words make text more difficult. These formulas count such things as the number of words in a sentence, the number of syllables in the words, and the number of words that are not considered common or frequent.

Readability formulas have serious limitations (Fisher et al., 2012). Various factors beyond sentence and word length interact to make a selection easy or difficult or appropriate for one grade level and not for another. Readability formulas do not take account of these factors. The presence or absence of pictures can make a text more easy or more difficult. Predictable text with often-repeated refrains or rhyme is generally easier and more appropriate for the lower grades. Text structure is another factor. Narratives are easier to understand than expository text. Page layout and the presence or absence of headings and other graphic aids are other considerations. Text coherence also influences difficulty level. Coherent texts are well organized, and authors clarify how each new piece of information is related to what they have already presented. They signal the introduction of new topics and organize ideas according to importance. Concepts represent different levels of difficulty. Reading about immigrants and the rise of the unions in late 19th-century America may be less difficult than reading about the structure of cells and organs. In addition, a reader's prior knowledge is a powerful determinant of text difficulty. A student who knows quite a bit about the topic of the text will find it easier to read and understand than an unfamiliar text at the same readability level.

Given all of these determinants of text difficulty, how do teachers or coaches choose appropriate texts for instruction? As mentioned previously, the recommendation was to provide students with text at their instructional reading levels, which was not easy to do. First, it presumed that the classroom teacher or coach knew each student's instructional level, which may or may not have been the case. Second, it presumed that texts at multiple levels would be available. While this was generally true for recreational reading, finding a variety of text at different levels on the same social studies and/or science topic was seldom possible. However, primarily in response to the Standards, we now realize that grade-level text can be appropriate for instruction of below-level readers if handled skillfully and sensitively. The focus of the CCSS on grade-level competence supports the use of grade-level text for all readers, and coordinating intervention instruction with classroom instruction represents a viable direction (Caldwell & Leslie, 2013).

Noting Student Progress

The overall purpose of instruction is to raise a student's instructional reading level. If the student's instructional level represents a match with his or her chronological grade level, we must guide the student to the next highest level. That is, if a fifth grader is reading at a fifth-grade level, we want that student to progress to the next level. If a student's instructional reading level is well below his or her chronological grade level, we must still focus on moving him or her to the chronological grade level although we know this may well represent a much harder task. The assessment process is thus centered on the determination of student progress. This is a critical component of response to intervention; the presence or absence of progress drives a student's movement through the tiers and possible assessment for a specific learning disability.

First, we assess what a student does well and what a student finds difficult, that is, we assess a student's proficiency with regard to specific good reader behaviors and/or Common Core standards. We do this for the specific purpose of designing instruction that matches the student's needs. As an integral part of instruction, we assess to note progress in one or more good reader behaviors and/or Standards.

Second, we assess a student's reading level with regard to level of text and type of text and ask the following questions. What level represents the student's highest instructional level? Does this level cross literature, social studies, and science or does the student exhibit different levels for different disciplines? What is the size of the gap between a student's instructional level and his or her chronological grade level? Again, once we have determined a student's reading level, we assess to note progress toward a higher level.

Throughout this book, we will be examining various forms of assessment that focus on the good reader behaviors and on student reading level.

Summary

• There are three main purposes of reading assessment: identification of the good reader behaviors, determination of a student's reading level, and assessment of progress in moving toward competency in reading text at a student's chronological grade level.

• Readers engage in a variety of good reader behaviors when they read. They use letter and sound patterns to fluently pronounce words. They attach meaning to words through context. They determine what is important in the text. They ask questions, find answers, and draw inferences. They recognize text structure and summarize text content. They form and support opinions and recognize an author's purpose. They monitor their comprehension and repair comprehension breakdowns.

• The good reader behaviors are the basis of reading assessment and they are closely related to the CCSS.

• Determination of reading level involves identifying a student's instructional reading level, that is, the level at which the student can read with some assistance. Determination of the instructional reading level is important given Standard 10, which states that students should be able to read text at their chronological grade levels. If the instructional level is below the chronological grade level, the student should receive instruction for the purpose of raising the present grade level to an appropriate level.

• An instructional focus on instructional level text may deny the student access to grade-level concepts, vocabulary, and syntax.

• Text leveling is based on readability formulas that are limited. They do not take account of text factors such as pictures, text structure, and page layout. They do not take account of text coherence and the difficulty level of the concepts.

• Assessment of progress involves a focus on the good reader's behaviors and the student's reading level.

Activities for Developing Understanding

• Select a short piece of text. Read it sentence by sentence. Stop after each sentence. What were you thinking of as you read each sentence? Use the list and chart in this chapter to identify your comprehension activities. Which good reader behaviors did you employ? Which Common Core standard did you meet? Share this exercise with a friend. Compare your thoughts, your good reader behaviors, and the Standards you met.

• Examine your own reading proficiency. What type of text probably represents your frustration level, your independent level, and your instructional level?

• Describe a time when you were required to read frustration-level text. How did you feel? What strategies did you engage in to make sense of the text?

• Compare three selections at the same grade level: a story, a selection for a social studies text, and a section from a science text. How are they alike? How are they different? Which one seems easier and why?

CHAPTER 3

Methods of Assessment

What Are the Different Kinds of Assessments and What Do They Tell Us about Reading Performance?

Many different measures can provide evidence of a student's reading performance. A teacher or coach can use published instruments or can construct his or her own instruments. Types of assessment are generally divided into different and often overlapping categories: formal and informal; norm-referenced and criterion-referenced; standardized and nonstandardized; and formative and summative. Interpretation of a student's score often depends on understanding the similarities and differences between these categories with regard to reading assessment.

Formal and Informal Assessments

Formal measures are usually commercial instruments prepared by publishers. Formal assessments are generally piloted prior to publication for the purpose of refining content and scoring procedures. The assessments of the CCSS developed by the Partnership for Assessment of Readiness for College and Careers (PARCC) and the Smarter Balanced Assessment Consortium (SBAC) are formal measures. Formal measures take many forms with regard to what they assess and how they go about it. Formal measures may assess early literacy, word identification, fluency, vocabulary knowledge, and/or comprehension. They may focus on a single age level such as the primary grades or they may span several levels. They may address a single reading behavior such as use of letter and sound patterns or many reading behaviors such as attaching meaning to words, comprehending what is explicitly stated in the text, and drawing inferences. Formal measures include detailed instructions on how to administer the test and how to score it. The meaningfulness and usefulness of test results depend on following the directions closely and exactly.

Informal measures include assessments developed by classroom teachers themselves who design the content and format of a test and how it is scored. Informal assessments can also be published. These include the informal reading inventory (IRI), discussed in Chapter 5, and assessments that are included in the teacher manuals of textbooks. The primary difference between formal and informal assessments is how they are used and scored. Teachers and coaches can decide whether to administer all or only part of an informal assessment. That is, a teacher can administer a chapter test from a social studies textbook but opt to delete certain items. As will become clear in Chapter 5, a teacher or coach can select what passage in an IRI to administer and what scoring options to use. The quality of an informal assessment of reading depends on its content as reflective of the good reader behaviors and perhaps, in the immediate future, the CCSS. It also involves examination of the nature of the questions that are asked and the clarity of directions for determining their accuracy. We will return to question formation in Chapter 10.

Informal instruments may be more authentic than formal measures, that is, they can be more similar to the actual task of reading. For example, reading a passage and retelling its contents are more authentic than reading a short paragraph and answering multiple-choice questions by filling in bubbles on a scan sheet or selecting an answer on the computer screen. Unfortunately, to some individuals, the term *informal* suggests assessments that are subjective or casual. Nothing could be farther from the truth! This book focuses primarily on the use of informal measures to gain the maximum amount of information about how a student reads different selections at different levels.

Formative and Summative Assessments

Informal measures can be formative or summative in nature. They can be used to assess what a student needs to know in order to design or adjust instruction (formative) or what a student has learned (summative). Formative measures involve frequent checks of student understanding and skills. Their purpose is to identify the learning needs of students so instruction can be adjusted. They "identify the gap between where students are and where they need to go in their reading development" (Roskos & Neuman, 2012, p. 534). In summary, "formative assessments are the forms of tests that can affect instruction and when used appropriately are associated with large student gains" (Risko & Walker-Dalhouse, 2010, p. 421). Summative measures generally result in a grade of some sort.

Unfortunately, formative classroom-based assessments often focus primarily on literal comprehension (Risko & Walker-Dalhouse, 2010). This can be a serious issue inasmuch as meeting the CCSS demands a high level of inferential comprehension on the part of the reader.

The overall purpose of formative assessments is to "provide information about student learning during instruction" (Risko & Walker-Dalhouse, 2010, p. 421). Throughout this book, I emphasize the necessity and effectiveness of combining assessment and instruction. A teacher should assess while teaching and teach while assessing. Formative and summative measures can take many forms: teacher observation of individual and group interactions; attention to comments made during discussion; various forms of written work; and student reactions to new classroom processes such as read-alouds, assigned projects, and various forms of classroom quizzes and tests. Unlike formal measures, they allow a teacher or coach to design or modify the assessment in order to collect the type of evidence that is needed. Informal formative and summative measures are extremely flexible; a teacher or coach can personalize assessment to the needs of the student and/or the whole class.

Norm-Referenced and Criterion-Referenced Assessments

When we use a norm-referenced test, we compare the student's score with the score of the norm sample—that is, the sample of students who were used to standardize the test. In criterion-referenced tests, we compare the student's score to a cutoff score (or criterion) set by the test authors.

How does norm-referencing work? Perhaps a simplified example will help. Let's say that fourth graders were field-tested across the country in October. They had an average score of 52 correct in reading. Since these fourth graders were in their second month of fourth grade, the score of 52 was set as 4.2 (fourth grade, second month). When your student, Sallie, got 52 correct, she was also assigned a score of 4.2.

Criterion-referenced tests describe a student's performance in terms of standards of excellence, using such terms as *pass, fail, basic, proficient,* or *advanced.* They describe "what a student can or cannot do with respect to a well-defined domain of knowledge or skill" (Sireci, 2005, pp. 115–116). When teachers assign 70–80% as representative of a grade of "C," they are basically assigning a criterion-referenced score. Some criterion-referenced measures base the cutoff score on a pilot sample of students; others, like the above example of assigning a specific percentage to a grade, do not.

A norm-referenced test would change when the test publishers again field-tested and sampled fourth graders across the country. The average score for these fourth graders might be 55 correct or 49 correct. Therefore, a higher or lower score for the number of correct items might result in the same designation of 4.2. A norm-referenced test fluctuates each time the test is normed. Norm-referenced tests are usually nationally normed; that is, the norm group represents students from regions throughout the nation. Some are locally normed as well. On the other hand, a criterion-referenced test might stay the same. The test makers might choose to retain the original 52 correct as the level of basic performance.

Standardized Assessments

What exactly does *standardized* mean? It means that the content of a test remains the same across administrations, and that the conditions of administration are identical for all test takers (Sireci, 2005). In other words, standardized tests "are designed and administered using uniform procedures" (Sireci, 2005, p. 113). Standardized tests are generally norm-referenced; they are measures of student achievement in which a student's score is compared to a standard of performance (Trice, 2000). When standardized tests are developed, they are field-tested on a large sample of students called a *norm group.* Scores of the norm group provide the standards for interpreting the scores of all other students who take the test, hence the name *standardized.* Basically, a student's score tells us how well a student did in relation to others, those in the norm group. Of course, it is important that the norm group be truly representative of the students it represents (e.g., fourth graders in the nation).

Standardized assessments take various forms. Some are multiple-choice, selected response measures, in which the student chooses one of four or five possible answers. Some combine multiple-choice sections with writing samples. Other standardized tests involve an oral question-and-answer format; the examiner asks a question and records the student's answer. Still others require the student to perform a task such as blending sounds to form words, reading a list of words, and orally reading a passage. The examiner records the student's performance in terms of accuracy, and sometimes in terms of the amount of time it took the student to complete the task. Some standardized tests can be administered to large groups. Others can only be administered to one individual at a time.

Standardized measures of reading are achievement tests, that is, they measure what students have learned. The popular Measure of Academic Progress (MAP; Northwest Evaluation Association, 2013) is a standardized test that describes a student's performance in terms of progress that was made. The tests constructed by PARCC and SBAC to evaluate the CCSS are standardized measures.

There are a variety of standardized test scores and it is important that you understand what they mean. Scores on standardized tests come in various forms: *grade equivalents, percentiles, stanines, standard scores,* and *RIT units.* Each one tells you the same thing in a slightly different way, and so it is easy to become confused about the differences.

Grade Equivalents

On the surface, grade equivalents seem easy to interpret, but unfortunately they are very often misinterpreted. Educators and parents frequently think of grade equivalent scores as similar to school grade levels, but they are actually very different. First, there is no such thing as a standard or identical level of achievement at a certain grade level. Reading achievement levels vary from school to school, depending on the curriculum and the student population. Third-grade students in a low-performing school may be reading at a level below their actual chronological grade level. Similarly, if students are in a high-performing district, a grade equivalent of 3.6 may woefully underestimate performance in the third-grade classroom. Grade equivalent scores simply indicate that a student's score is similar to the norm group's score at that grade level and on that test content.

Sometimes parents and educators interpret a grade equivalent score of 3.6 as indicating that the student can read at a middle third-grade level. Nothing could be farther from the truth! Suppose a third-grade student took the standardized test intended for third graders and attained a score of 5.7. This only means that the third grader obtained the same score that one would expect average fifth graders in April to obtain if they took the third-grade instrument. Grade equivalents only represent general estimates of achievement. They are best interpreted as rough estimates and never as absolute indicators of classroom performance. There is another problem with grade equivalents: they are based on the notion that learning is constant throughout the year—in other words, that it occurs in regular monthly increments. Any teacher or coach can recognize the fallacy of that premise!

In order to understand grade equivalents, a teacher or coach must consider where they come from. Remember that a student's performance on a standardized test is always compared to the scores of the norm group. Suppose that a large number of third graders in the norm group were tested in the sixth month of third grade (which would be February). Their average raw score (total number correct on the test) was 43 correct items. That score would be assigned a grade equivalent of 3.6, and any student who attained the same score would also receive a grade equivalent score of 3.6. Different individuals in the norm group are generally tested at different times during a school year to arrive at average scores that represent different months, such as 3.3 and 3.9. What happens if no norm samples are tested during some months? Test makers employ a variety of complex statistical manipulations to arrive at a full span of scores for any one grade level, ranging from 3.0 to 3.9.

How can teachers explain all this to parents? It sometimes helps to explain grade equivalents as representing "ballpark figures." For a third grader, a grade equivalent of 3.6 indicates that he or she is performing as an average third grader—but only in relation to the content of the test, not necessarily the curriculum of the school or classroom. A third grader with a score of 5.7 is not performing as a fifth grader, but is doing extremely well for a third grader (again, based on the content of the test). Grade equivalents are best interpreted as rough estimates of achievement, not as absolute indicators of classroom performance.

Percentile Scores

"A percentile score indicates the percentage of students [that a particular student] did better than" (Trice, 2000, p. 108). Percentile scores can range from 0 to 100. If a student scores at the 35th percentile, this means that he or she did better than 35% of the students in the norm group. Similarly, if a student scores at the 75th percentile, he or she did better than 75% of the norm group sample. Percentile scores are often confused with percent scores. A percent score of 50 usually means poor performance and a no-passing grade. A percentile score of 50 indicates average performance; the student did better than 50% of the norm group. Sixty-eight percent of the norm group scores tend to fall between the 15th and 84th percentiles; these scores are considered to indicate average performance. However, it is somewhat difficult to explain to a parent that a percentile score of 35 is not necessarily an indication of poor performance! In addition, a teacher or coach needs to realize that the difference between raw scores that convert to a percentile of 65 and a percentile of 75 may be very small. It is best to think of percentiles as broad indicators, like grade equivalents.

Stanine Scores

Stanine scores range from 1 to 9, with scores from 4 to 6 indicating average performance. Stanine scores tend to annoy people because they seem less precise than percentiles or grade equivalents. Some manuals caution that two scores should not be considered significantly different if they are in the same or adjacent stanines (Cangelosi, 2000). If we accept this notion, raw scores that convert to stanine scores of 5 and 6 would not be considered very different. Neither would raw scores that convert to stanine scores of 3 and 4. Like grade equivalents and percentiles, stanines tell us where a student scored in relation to the norm group for a specific test.

Standard Scores

It may be easiest to understand standard scores in relation to IQ. A student takes an intelligence test and achieves a raw score, a certain number of correct items. This raw score is converted to a standard score that has an average of 100 with a give-or-take of 15 points. (Statisticians call this give-and-take a *standard deviation*, but we do not need to go into that.) This means that any converted score that falls between 85 and 115 represents an average IQ. A score above 115 is considered above average, and a score below 85 is considered below average. All standardized tests convert raw scores to standard scores, but the average and the give-and-take may be different. A standard score of 100 on an achievement test may not be the same as a score of 100 on an intelligence test. The SAT college entrance examination has an average score of 500, with a give-and-take of 100. Colleges or universities that will not accept any student with a score lower than 400 are saying that, at the very least, they want average performers. A teacher or coach needs to determine what numbers represent the average and the give-and-take on a standardized test in order to interpret the scores correctly.

RIT Scale

The MAP (Northwest Evaluation Association, 2013) is a computer-administered, norm-referenced, standardized measure of student progress for grades 2 and above. Usually administered three times a year, the MAP provides student results based on their progress from administration to administration. It is an adaptive measure, that is, question difficulty is based on how well a student answers the previous question/s. If the student provides correct answers, the questions become more difficult. Similarly, inaccurate answers lead to easier questions.

MAP results are scored according to the RIT Scale, which is an equal-interval scale. This means that the units of difference between scores are the same whether a student achieves at the high, middle, or low end of the scale or whether the test is administered in the fall or the spring. How does this work? Perhaps you have used a tape measure stuck to a wall to determine the growth of your child. A tape measure is divided into feet and inches; it is an equal-interval scale. Your child may be short, tall, or of average height, but the units used to measure this (feet and inches) are identical. And if you check growth several months later, you are using the same units (feet and inches) that you used previously. This allows you to draw a valid comparison between the first and second measurement. RIT units work in much the same way.

Given a student's RIT score, MAP projects anticipated growth on the part of the student based on the norm group. Over time, MAP charts progress and/or lack of progress for an individual student, a class, a school, and/or a district. The RIT score is also connected to the Lexile range, which identifies reading material that represents an appropriate level of difficulty for the student. Accompanying charts indicate the specific skills that should be enhanced, developed, and/or introduced given a specific RIT score range. RIT scores are also reported in percentiles. As explained above, a percentile represents the percentage of norm-group students that an individual student matched or exceeded.

As a teacher or coach, how should you interpret scores for yourself and for parents? The important rule of thumb is to remember that all scores on norm-referenced tests represent comparisons to the scores of a norm group. It is important to use norm-group terminology with parents. For example, suppose you are telling parents that their daughter attained a percentile score of 65. Instead of saying, "Ellen did better than 65% of those who took the test," say, "Ellen's score was higher than the scores for 65% of the norm group—a national sample of students on whom the test was tried." Instead of saying that Harry's RIT score indicated acceptable progress, say "Harry's scores indicated acceptable progress as compared to the norm group." Scores must be interpreted in relation to the norm group, not in relation to students in a particular school or district (Cangelosi, 2000).

Avoid characterizing students as *average*, *above average*, or *below average*; always relate performance to the norm sample. Why is this important? Suppose that a student scores above average in relation to the norm group. This student may not be above average with regard to his or her own school or district. Using the term *above average* by itself without reference to the norm group can lead parents to make erroneous assumptions.

Emphasize that any test, standardized or nonstandardized, is only one test sample; it represents one day of performance. Always interpret the results of a standardized test in relation to classroom performance. Your assessment of a student's performance is more meaningful and more accurate than any standardized test can be. Focus on the good reader behaviors and/or the Standards. Explain what the student still needs to work on and describe how you intend to design instruction to accomplish this goal. You will find that this approach makes much more sense to parents.

The Role of Standardized Assessments in Today's Schools

Standardized achievement tests have been a part of the educational environment for a long time. Schools and districts administered them on a regular cycle, and days were routinely set aside for this task. The completed tests were then sent to the publisher for scoring, and results were returned usually months after the tests were completed. This process generally took too long to have any effect on classroom instruction, although the scores of individual children were regularly communicated to parents. Administrators rejoiced or groaned at the results, which usually became the topic of one or more staff meetings. Local newspapers sometimes published the results; if they did, there would be a flurry of interest or concern, and then things would return to "normal" until the next cycle of testing.

This all changed when the No Child Left Behind (NCLB) Act was signed into law in January 2002. It mandated that states create standards for what children should know and do in reading and math and measure student progress and achievement against these standards. In all cases, the measurement took the form of a standardized measure. At the present time, the majority of states have received waivers for NCLB on the basis of their agreement to annually participate in some form of rigorous standardized assessment. For most states, this will no doubt involve standardized assessment of the CCSS presently being designed by PARCC and SBAC.

States are also required to participate in testing as part of the NAEP, often referred to as "The Nation's Report Card" (NAEP, 2011). This testing, which focuses on math and reading, occurs every 2 years. The stated purpose of the NAEP is to compare state results to national results. If there is a large discrepancy between the two sets of measures, the state may be required to revise its standards and assessments.

Wow! All this certainly moves standardized achievement testing into the ranks of what is called *high-stakes testing*. High-stakes tests are "those with highly consequential outcomes for students, teachers and schools" (Afflerbach, 2004, p. 2), and they have always been with us. For example, college entrance exams are a form of high-stakes testing, with students' enrollment at a chosen college or university dependent on their test scores. Other types of high-stakes tests allow or deny students entrance into certain curricular options, such as gifted or honors programs. But at no time in our history have high-stakes tests taken such a prominent place, and they are likely to remain so for the foreseeable future. The measures designed by PARCC and SBAC will no doubt become high-stakes measures.

At the heart of any testing debate is the extent to which standardized tests actually measure reading performance. Afflerbach (2004) states that a single score only provides a limited snapshot of student performance and should never be used as the sole determinant of student achievement. Supporters of high-stakes tests agree in this respect. "If a single annual test were the only device a teacher used to gauge student performance, it would indeed be inadequate" (U.S. Department of Education, 2005). Goodman and Hambleton (2005) affirm that "it is not possible for one assessment to measure all the important skills and concepts that are taught over one or more years of instruction, and some processes may be better assessed in the context of the classroom" (pp. 92–93). In this respect, the issue may not rest with the testing itself, but with how it is used in a school or district.

So how do we educators deal with high-stakes testing? High-stakes yearly testing based on the CCSS is not going away. We can become angry and defensive, but it won't help. We cannot let such testing destroy our love of teaching, our commitment to our students, and our belief in the importance of our profession and our own effectiveness. How can we make the best of an unfortunate situation? Obviously, this involves accepting the responsibility to direct our best and most professional efforts to teaching.

Let me offer a few other suggestions. We should not take test results personally, even if it seems that administrators and the public think we should do so. In other words, test scores are not an indictment of our ability as teachers. If our students' test scores are low, we cannot accept the total blame or responsibility for this outcome. Unfortunately, if the scores are high, neither can we take full credit. Why? More factors enter into our students' grades than our effectiveness as teachers.

Popham (2001) makes a convincing argument that standardized tests measure three things: what students learned in school, the students' socioeconomic status (SES), and the students' inherited academic aptitude. Thus a teacher may teach exactly the same way over 2 years to two different classes and find that the test scores of the two groups are vastly different. This would not occur if the teacher's abilities were solely responsible for the scores.

Let's examine factors that affect test performance. Of course, student learning contributes to a test score. If we are successful in teaching students to engage in the good reader behaviors and/or the CCSS, they will do better on the test than if they are not able to do those things. They will also do better if our curriculum (as embodied by the good reader behaviors and the Standards) is clearly aligned to the test. So we can take some of the credit (or blame).

However, even after we allow for the powerful influence of good teaching and a carefully aligned curriculum, there are reasons why standardized test scores can never be used as an indictment of teacher competence. Items on standardized tests are sensitive to elements connected to student SES. In other words, certain items are more likely to be answered correctly by children from affluent or middle-class families who "grow up in a home environment rich in the sorts of materials and experiences that will substantially benefit them when it comes time to do battle with a standardized achievement test" (Popham, 2001, p. 57). We are talking about such things as access to and familiarity with reading materials, writing materials, and computer programs. We are also talking about travel experiences, such as trips to Disney World and other parts of the country. This should not be surprising. We have known for a long time that prior knowledge profoundly affects reading comprehension. It also affects the ability to answer questions correctly. There is another component besides prior knowledge that we must consider, and that is familiarity with and usage of Standard American English—the language that is utilized for item construction on such tests. Given all these factors, teachers who work with higher-SES students will probably see higher test scores than those who work with lower-SES students.

We must also consider our students' inherited academic aptitude. Children differ in their verbal, quantitative, and spatial potential, and their strength or weakness in each of these areas can affect test performance. Popham (2001) estimated that 40% of the items on a reading achievement test could well be influenced by inherited verbal ability and would be correctly answered by "kids who are born word-smart" (p. 68).

Other factors can affect standardized test scores. Test-taking skills play a part, as does attention to the task at hand. Because standardized measures are timed, student pacing is important. Staying with one test item for too long can interfere with completion of the test, and unanswered items can mean a lower score. Of course, a student can also just experience a bad testing day. A student who did not sleep well the night before, a child who has a stomachache or headache, or a child who is routinely excluded from games at recess or taunted by peers can perform poorly on a test for reasons other than reading ability or test-taking skills. The same behaviors can happen in the classroom. Teachers and coaches can offer many examples of good students who perform poorly on some measure of assessment. However, in the classroom, a teacher or coach can easily reevaluate student performance at another point in time. This is not an option for standardized tests. The student gets one chance, and one chance only, to demonstrate his or her ability.

Summary

- Formal assessment measures are usually commercial instruments prepared by publishers. They include detailed instructions on how to administer the test and how to score it. Their meaningfulness and usefulness depend on following the directions closely and exactly.

- Informal instruments include teacher-made instruments as well as the IRI and assessments included in teacher manuals. They may be more authentic than formal measures because of their similarity to the actual task of reading.

- Formative measures assess what a student needs to know in order to design or adjust instruction. Summative measures generally result in a grade of some sort.

- Norm-referenced tests are based on a comparison of the student's score to the score of the norm group, the sample of students used to standardize the test. Criterion-referenced tests describe a student's performance in terms of standards of excellence using terms such as *pass, fail, basic, proficient*, or *advanced*.

- In standardized assessment, the content of the test remains the same across all administrations and the conditions of administration are identical for all test-takers. Norm-group scores provide the standards for interpreting student scores.

- Standardized test scores include grade equivalents, percentile scores, stanine scores, standard scores, and RIT units.

- Standardized scores will continue to play an important role in today's schools given assessment of the CCSS and the requirements of NAEP.

- Standardized tests measure three things: what students learned in school, the students' SES, and the students' inherited academic aptitude.

- Different factors affect test performance: student learning, teacher effectiveness, curriculum quality, SES, prior knowledge, and familiarity with Standard American English.

Activities for Developing Understanding

- Go on the websites for PARCC and SBAC. How are these tests different from previously standardized achievement measures? What type of scores do they provide?

- Pretend you are planning for a conference with parents. Choose one form of score (grade equivalent, percentile, stanine, standard score, or RIT score), and plan what you will say to the parents about a high score and a low score.

• Interview several teachers regarding their perceptions of standardized assessment. To what degree do they feel that the tests accurately reflect the performance of their students? How do they use these results in the classroom?

• Interview several individuals who are not in the education profession. What are their perceptions about standardized tests?

• Interview several students regarding their perceptions of standardized tests. How do they feel about taking them?

CHAPTER 4

Assessment as Part of Instruction

How Can We Assess as We Teach?

The Four–Step Assessment Process in the Classroom or Coaching Session

Which comes first, assessment or instruction? Does instruction drive assessment, or does assessment drive instruction? There is a tendency to think of assessment as something that happens after instruction, something apart from instruction—such as asking students to answer questions after they have read a textbook chapter or a story. There is also a tendency to think of all assessment measures as paper-and-pencil tests. These tests represent very limited views of the assessment process. Good assessment is actually embedded in the process of instruction (Sweet, 2005). Assessment and instruction can happen at the same time.

Instruction and assessment cannot be separated; they are two sides of the same coin! The goal of any literacy lesson is the development of good reader behaviors and/or the CCSS. A teacher or coach who has identified a good reader behavior or a specific Standard as the focus of a lesson knows what to assess. However, if the teacher or coach is unsure about the lesson goal, assessment will probably be unfocused and ineffective. Teachers and coaches need to develop their own assessment systems according to their instructional goals.

Assessment can happen at any point in a lesson. It can be a planned and carefully thought-out procedure. It can also be unplanned. Sometimes the unexpected occurs. A teacher or coach who knows the goal of the lesson can use the unexpected as an added assessment tool.

Many sensitive and effective assessments do not look anything like a typical test. They do not necessarily involve a question-and-answer procedure or a paper-and-pencil format. For example, teacher observation of what students do and say in the reading classroom is a powerful assessment measure. In Chapter 1, I identified four steps in the assessment process. Let us reexamine these steps in terms of reading instruction.

Step 1: Identify the Good Reader Behaviors and/or Standards That You Are Teaching and Assessing

The first step is to identify what you are teaching and assessing (Au & Raphael, 2007). In other words, you must decide which good reader behaviors and/or which CCSS you want to develop in your students. The focus of all literacy lessons should be on the good reader behaviors and/or the Standards. These drive both the instruction and the assessment process. If you do not know what good reader behaviors or what Standards you are developing in your students, it will be difficult to select appropriate evidence for determining the quality of your students' reading behavior.

I remember teaching a novel to eighth graders. I really did not have any specific goals for my lessons. I didn't know anything about good reader behaviors and the importance of developing them in my students. I just wanted my students to understand the novel and (I hoped) enjoy it. Class discussion focused on literal understanding of what happened to the characters. I simply did not think about teaching my students to summarize or to move beyond the literal and draw inferences about the characters and the time in which they lived.

After we finished reading and discussing the book, I constructed a long and involved multiple-choice test. I corrected the test, turned my students' scores into letter grades, and entered them into my grade book. If you had asked me what I was assessing, I would have said, "Reading." But what did that mean? Some questions revolved around unimportant details. Some focused on more critical aspects of the plot. Others centered on vocabulary. I never attempted to separate these disparate elements. I never even considered whether a multiple-choice test was the best way to assess my students' comprehension. And because I did not allow them to look back in the novel to find the answers (I would have called that "cheating"), I actually didn't know whether I was assessing reading comprehension or student memory. Perhaps I was not even assessing anything at all related to reading! Perhaps I was simply assessing my students' motivation or persistence in completing such a lengthy task.

If I had focused my instruction on specific good reader behaviors and/or the Standards, I would have known what and how to assess. For example, if I had attempted to develop my students' ability to recognize an author's point of view or style, a multiple-choice test would have been a sorry assessment instrument. If I had focused on teaching my students to summarize, I could have asked them to write a short summary of a specific episode in the novel from the perspective of one of the characters. Knowing what good reader behaviors or what Standards you are teaching and assessing is the first step in the instruction/assessment process.

Perhaps, at this point, you would like to offer an argument. You may feel that the good reader behaviors and the Standards are too general. Shouldn't teachers and coaches specifically address all those different pupil expectations that made up the scope and sequence charts and district literacy standards? Given the research of Davis (1968) that I explained in Chapter 1, the CCSS do a pretty good job of covering the reading process and so do the good reader behaviors. All those skills or pupil expectations may not necessarily be separate entities. There are other difficulties with long lists of pupil expectations or skills. On a list, they all tend to take on equal importance. However, they may not be equally crucial to successful reading performance that leads to readiness for college and career competence as required by the Standards. For example, some lists of pupil expectations include "identifies mood. " Is this as important as "summarizes information?" It is difficult to believe that it is. Some pupil expectations lend themselves to rich instructional and assessment options; others do not. One of the advantages of the good reader behaviors and CCSS is that they focus on clearly defined and important reading behaviors.

If assessment is to be effective, it must be manageable. For this reason, it is crucial to have a realistic starting point. The good reader behaviors and/or the Standards provide this starting point. By focusing on them, a teacher or coach can realistically and adequately design an assessment and evaluate it effectively. We know that the reading process is much more than the sum of the good reader behaviors and the CCSS, but these allow us to realistically handle the instruction and assessment of an extremely complex process.

Should we worry about the fact that good reader behaviors and the Standards may or may not be separate activities? I do not think so. The good reader behaviors and the Standards are guidelines that help you as a teacher or coach select an instructional focus. Chances are that in developing one good reader behavior, you are developing others. If you show students how to determine the meaning of unfamiliar words from context (Standard 4), you are probably also helping them to draw inferences based on the text (Standard 1). If you guide them in recognizing the structure of a text, you may be also helping them to identify and/or phrase the central idea. The good reader behaviors and the CCSS provide you with a manageable frame of reference for designing instruction and assessing reading. In short, they drive instruction and assessment!

Step 2: Collect Evidence That Is Related to the Good Reader Behaviors and/or the CCSS

If you know what good reader behaviors and/or Standards you are teaching and assessing, you have a better chance of selecting meaningful evidence. Evidence should be relevant; that is, the evidence should be clearly related to the good reader behaviors or the Standards that you have chosen as your focus. If, for example, you are teaching students how to analyze text (Standard 3), your evidence will be the analyses they draw and the text elements that that they used to do this. Of course these can be either oral or written. If written, you can correct at your leisure; if oral, you will need some form of checklist to record the adequacy of answers offered in a class discussion or in response to a question on your part. The classroom or tutoring session is a busy place! As a teacher or coach, you have to pay attention to many things at once. You cannot trust your memory. If your evidence comes from observation of students' activities or comments, you need to set up some manageable system for recording what they say and do, so you won't forget it. You also need to maintain some record of individual student progress.

The following account of Adam's instruction and assessment suggests how all this gathering of evidence may be accomplished. Adam chose the following good reader behaviors as the focus of his lesson: recognizing the structure of the text (Standard 5) and determining central ideas (Standard 2). Adam decided to use focused group discussion to develop and assess his sixth graders' understanding of informational text structure and the central idea. Prior to assigning a selection in their science text, Adam divided his class into five groups.

Adam explained that informational text was generally written following one of five different structures. The students briefly discussed the differences between the structures, and Adam used everyday examples to explain and clarify the meaning of cause–effect, problem–solution, and so on. Adam also explained that the central idea of a selection is closely tied to the structure; that is, the author chooses the most appropriate structure to develop his or her main idea.

Identifying the central idea and the text structure helps students to understand, organize, and remember the content.

Adam divided the chapter into sections according to chapter headings: he and the students then orally read a section at a time. This ensured that all students, even the less able, had access to the content. After a section was read, the students formed into their groups and spent some time discussing the central idea or purpose of the author and the structure the author employed. Adam moved around to the different groups, answering questions, clarifying areas of confusion, offering suggestions, and reinforcing student comments. Each group then shared the results of their discussion with the class. Following this sharing, the class read the next text segment with Adam and gathered again in groups to determine the central idea and appropriate structure.

During group and whole-class discussion, Adam collected evidence about the students' understanding of text structure and its central idea. He used a simple checklist to keep an ongoing record of both group and individual comments. See Adam's Checklist on page 48. The checklist had two columns: one marked "structure" and one marked "central idea." If a group provided an appropriate choice of structure with valid reasons for its selection, Adam placed a check under "structure" next to the group. If the group's identification of the central idea and reasons for its choice was acceptable, Adam placed a check under the column marked "central idea." Adam was also concerned about the performance of individual students during the discussion. If a student made a particularly relevant remark, Adam put a check next to his or her name. If a student made a comment that suggested confusion or lack of understanding, Adam placed a question mark next to the student's name. During the discussion, Adam was both instructing his students in and assessing their understanding of expository text structure and the central idea. Admittedly, using a checklist takes discipline and practice on the part of the teacher. However, if Adam had not kept some record of the discussion, he might not have remembered individual students who experienced difficulty and/or displayed good reader behaviors. The classroom is a busy place, and forgetting occurs very easily in the best of circumstances!

In summary, Adam followed the first two steps of the assessment process. He identified what he was teaching and assessing by selecting good reader behaviors and/or CCSS as his focus and by choosing appropriate instructional activities to develop them. He then collected evidence that was related to the good reader behaviors and the Standards using a checklist to record student performance.

Such checklists are really works in progress; that is, as you use them, you will change and adapt them to your specific needs. You may, for example, just choose to focus on students that you are concerned about. You may find that the use of specific headings such as Adam's focus on two standards are too cumbersome for

Adam's Checklist

Good Reader Behavior _Standard Standard 2, Standard 5_

Date _____ Selection _What Makes Up Earth's Layers?_

Activity _Discussion_

	Standard 2: Central Idea	Standard 5: Informational Text Structure
Group 1	✓ ??	✓ ✓
Lakendra	✓	✓ ✓
Lorne	???	?
Marta	?	✓
Willy	✓ ?	✓
Group 2	??✓	✓ ✓
Shane	✓	
Paola	?	✓ ✓
Rosa	?	?
Harry	✓ ?	
Group 3	✓ ??	✓ ✓ ✓
Kendall	?	?
Brett		✓
Altonia	?	✓
Brenda	✓	?
Group 4	??✓	✓ ✓
Rosa	✓	✓ ✓
Jackie	?	
Jon	?	✓
Allie		
Group 5	✓ ??	✓ ?
Allison	?	✓
Dan	?	
Mackenzie		✓
Pedro	✓	✓

you and just work with checks applicable to the overall lesson. There are various ways in which you can use and adapt assessment checklists.

Marva uses a checklist during the word-sorting activity in her primary classroom. As her students sort word cards to demonstrate similar letter–sound patterns, she employs the checklist to keep track of their progress. Her checklist does not have specific headings related to sorting patterns. She simply uses a plus mark to indicate that a student has no difficulty in forming meaningful sorts. If the student needs some small help or suggestion, she assigns a checkmark. Students who are unable to sort receive a minus sign, and Marva pays particular attention to their needs during the next session. Often Marva groups her students for word sorting, but she still uses the checklist to keep track of individual participation in the group activity.

Dan uses the checklist during vocabulary discussions that focus on the use of context to determine meaning (Standard 4). If students demonstrate understanding of specific context usage, he marks them with a plus sign. If they are not able to recognize or use context, he uses a minus sign. In some cases, a student's comments suggest some knowledge of context use, albeit incomplete; in these cases, he assigns a question mark. If he notes that a specific form of context (definition, syntax, morphology, or semantics) is more problematic for students, he simply notes this on the checklist.

Robert uses the checklist when he teaches his middle school students how to read expository text by noting topics and expanding these into central ideas (Standard 2). Because the discussion is quite fast-paced, Robert checks two possibilities: *On Target* and *Off Target*. If a student participates in the discussion and demonstrates understanding of the reader strategies that Robert is modeling, he or she receives a checkmark under *On Target*. Robert places a checkmark under *Off Target* for students who do not participate or who offer erroneous or confusing comments.

Anna uses the checklist during sustained silent reading—a time when she spends time with individual students. She asks them to read a short portion of their chosen book and summarize the content up to that point (Standard 2). She assigns a plus or minus as she evaluates each.

Step 3: Analyze the Evidence on the Good Reader Behaviors and/or Standards

In an attempt to make sense of students' reading performance, teachers and coaches must interpret the evidence they have collected about the good reader behaviors and/or Standards (Valencia, 2007). Adam's checklist offered evidence about his students' understanding of informational text structure. He realized that capturing the central idea was still somewhat problematic, and he identified students like Lorne and Rosa who might need additional support. After several sessions focusing on central idea and text structure, Adam also asked his students to summarize a selected part of the text by identifying the central idea and using an appropriate text structure (Standards 2 and 5). Each group collaborated to write a summary on a designated piece of text. What did this add to Adam's knowledge about his students' understanding of informational text structure and central idea? This is where a rubric comes in.

What Is a Rubric?

A *rubric* describes student performance according to various levels of proficiency. In other words, it offers guidelines for analyzing the evidence. For example, in Chapter 1, I talked about deciding whether you should stop to fill your gas tank. The evidence you would collect is obviously your gas gauge. However, how do you analyze the state of your gauge? What guideline or criterion do you use for filling up? Do you fill your tank if you are at the halfway mark? Do you fill it if you are three-quarters down? I have a friend who never stops for gas until the gauge reads practically empty! On the other hand, I get very nervous when the gauge hits half-empty. Each of us is using different criterion for stopping for gas, and the criterion we are using is a type of rubric—a guideline for analyzing the evidence.

A rubric is a tool for examining student work and for judging the quality of that work. I remember assigning projects and, when it came time to give a grade, choosing the better students' work to examine first. I then used their performance as a guide for evaluating the others. I suppose this was a form of a rubric, but not a very efficient or thoughtful one. Prior to assigning the project, I should have listed what I wanted the students to include in the project and what I expected the project to look like. In other words, I should have constructed a rubric. Then not only would I have had a guideline for evaluation, but I could have shared this guideline with my students—who then would have known exactly what was expected of them.

Why should a teacher or coach take the time to construct and use a rubric? First, a rubric clarifies the process of analyzing evidence of good reader behaviors. It provides guidelines for judging quality (Au & Raphael, 2007). Second, if a rubric is shared with students, it can improve the students' performance by making the expectations of the teacher or coach quite clear. Students can use the rubric as a guide for completing the task and for evaluating themselves. Self-assessment can be a powerful instructional tool, and a rubric can both instruct and assess!

A rubric can be written, but it does not have to be. My friend and I use mental rubrics or guidelines to determine whether we should stop for gas. I stop when the gauge reads half-empty; she stops when it is almost on empty! As another example, think about preparing for a vacation. Some of us make lists of what we must pack and what we must do before we leave. We check each item off. Did we notify the post office to stop mail? Yes. We check it off. Did we take a bathing suit? Yes. We check it off. This list is a simple form of written rubric. Others of us use a mental rubric, checking off in our heads what we have completed and what still needs to be done.

Constructing a Rubric

As a teacher or coach, how do you construct a written rubric? There is one primary guideline: keep it simple! Teachers and coaches rarely have time to construct involved rubrics. They do not have time to score long and complex ones. You want a rubric that is easy to use and is focused upon specific good reader behaviors and/or the CCSS. If the rubric is too complex, you will eventually discard it (and probably feel guilty for doing so!). Avoid the guilt and emphasize simplicity.

A rubric is made up of two elements. It lists criteria for what should be included in a piece of work, and it articulates levels of quality from excellent to poor. Let's construct a simple rubric so you can get an idea of how to work with these two components. Let's build a rubric for assessing a salesperson. We have all had experiences with very efficient and helpful salespeople. We have also had shopping experiences ruined by bad-tempered salespeople who would not or could not answer our questions or provide the help we needed.

First, we need some criteria for what makes a good salesperson. Think about salespersons that you would describe as good or excellent, and use what you remember about their behavior to generate some criteria. For example, a salesperson should be friendly. This seems self-evident; nobody appreciates a grouch! A salesperson also should know his or her merchandise. Nothing is more annoying than to ask questions about a possible purchase and not receive an answer (or receive the wrong answer). A salesperson should be attentive and not ignore you by chatting with other sales personnel or arranging merchandise. A salesperson should listen to your needs and not try to talk you into buying something you don't want. A salesperson should be helpful—that is, willing to make suggestions and offer you alternatives if the merchandise you originally wanted is unavailable. We could probably generate many more criteria, but let's keep it simple. We now have five criteria: A good salesperson is friendly, knows the merchandise, is attentive, is a good listener, and is helpful. We have the first element of our rubric: criteria for performance.

Let's move to the second part: levels of quality. Each criterion needs to be ranked in some way. The simplest ranking is a yes–no rating; for example, the salesperson was either friendly or not friendly. Another form of ranking involves numbers such as 4, 3, 2, and 1, with 4 standing for highest quality. Young children can understand yes–no ratings and numbers very well. Other rankings are more descriptive. Some rubrics use one or two statements to describe each ranking, and this is a point you may eventually reach. In the beginning, however, strive for simplicity. If you want to move beyond yes–no ratings and numbers, use only one or two words to describe your gradations of quality. In assessing a salesperson, you might use these terms: "Very effective," "Effective," "Somewhat effective," and "Not effective." Suppose you are interested in assessing knowledge and understanding. Your descriptors might be "Full understanding," "Some understanding," "Incomplete understanding," and "Misunderstanding." If you are interested in how often something occurs, you might use "Frequently," "Usually," "Sometimes," and "Never."

So, after listing criteria and deciding upon how to rank them, we put the two criteria together to form a simple rubric for assessing a salesperson.

A Good Salesperson . . .	4	3	2	1
Is friendly				
Knows the merchandise				
Is attentive				
Is a good listener				
Is helpful				

How can you, as a busy teacher or coach, find the time to construct a rubric? You find the time by making it part of your instruction. You don't stay after school to create rubrics on your own! You don't construct them over the weekend! You create rubrics collaboratively with your students. This is a powerful vehicle for sharing good reader behaviors and/or the expectations of the Standards. Explain the assignment to the students, and ask them what would make a good rubric. Guide them to choose suitable criteria. Work with them to select realistic descriptors. Deciding on important criteria and choosing descriptors for quality are effective activities for developing the students' understanding and appreciation of good reader behaviors and/or the Standards. Involving the students will also help you to keep the rubric simple. You want a rubric that the students understand as well as you do because they are going to use it too. Once a rubric is created, use it again and again. If it needs to be revised, involve the students in the revision. In fact, it has been my experience that students often take the initiative in revising or expanding rubrics.

Some districts have constructed their own rubrics, and teachers or coaches are required to use them. There are also published rubrics (Burke, 2005, 2006; Billmeyer, 2001; Glickman-Bond, 2006), and the web is full of rubrics for myriad tasks. If such measures are helpful, by all means use them. If they seem overwhelming, use parts of them. Start with what you can realistically handle. As you and your students become more experienced in the instruction and assessment of good reader behaviors, your rubrics will naturally become more complex. Allow yourself to grow into the process.

Adam and his class worked together to construct a short individual rubric to use for evaluating the students' summaries. They decided on a simple yes–no rating. They agreed that four or six checks would indicate a very good job in summary writing. After the students finished their summary, they filled out the rubric and evaluated themselves. Adam collected these filled-out forms, wrote his own evaluations on the same papers, and then returned the papers to the students.

Adam's Rubric

Name _____   Date _____

Text to be summarized _____

___ I began with an introductory sentence.

___ The introductory sentence stated the central idea of the summary.

___ I identified the text structure used by the author of the text.

___ I included at least three examples that followed the structure.

___ I included examples that were important to the central idea.

___ I summarized what the author wrote, not what I thought.

Score

4–6 checks: I did a very good job!

3 checks: I did okay.

1–2 checks: I need to think harder about how to write a good summary.

Step 4: Make an Instructional Decision about the Good Reader Behaviors and/or Standards

You identified the good reader behaviors and/or Standards that you are assessing; you collected evidence, and you analyzed it by using a checklist and a rubric. You know which good reader behaviors and/or Standards were evident and which were not. The fourth step is to decide what you are going to do with this information. How will the evidence and your analysis of it indicate future instructional directions? Unfortunately, teachers and coaches often ignore this last step. After they have analyzed the evidence, they record it in a grade book and plan another lesson totally unrelated to what went on before!

Teachers and coaches make several kinds of instructional decisions. One decision involves choosing the focus of the next lesson. What good reader behavior and/or Standard will a teacher or coach emphasize next? Another decision relates to instructional format. Will the next lesson be presented to the class as a whole? Does the class need to be grouped in some way? What kind of grouping will best achieve the teacher's or coach's objectives? Should the teacher or coach set up some form of collaborative or cooperative grouping, in which students with different abilities work together on a common project? Or should the teacher or coach form groups composed of children with similar abilities and offer differentiated instruction? Another instructional decision relates to individual students. Which individuals need additional support? How best can that support be given?

Based on assessment, Adam made two types of instructional decisions. First, he made a decision that focused on the entire class. His analysis of students' comments and written summaries led him to plan more activities for developing an understanding of central idea, text structure, and summarization. His analysis also focused on individual students. This evaluation of individual progress resulted in a decision to provide additional small-group instruction for several students while other students collaborated in groups.

Another decision that you as a teacher or coach must make after instruction involves grading. If the instruction culminates in an assignment or project of some sort or a form of test, you must decide how to score it and assign a grade. A rubric can make this much easier. If you know exactly what you are looking for, it will not be difficult to differentiate work that deserves an A from work that merits a C.

Matching Assessment and Instruction to the CCSS

A teacher or coach may have multiple textbook series for reading, language arts, social studies, and/or science. Teacher manuals allied to these series offer many instructional suggestions. They recommend a variety of teaching strategies, offer numerous ideas for student activities, provide a plethora of questions for students to answer, and include a variety of assessments in the form of short comprehension checks and/or more complex unit tests. However, at the present time, this poses a problem with regard to the CCSS. Textbooks that are presently in use were written before the Standards were published, and they will need to be rewritten to align with the Standards. The authors of the Standards have published criteria to guide publishers and curriculum developers in performing this task (Coleman & Pimental, 2011). Unfortunately, these revisions are not going to happen quickly; it takes a long time to design and prepare a textbook series. In addition, even if the publishers distribute new series within a year or two, school districts will probably not be able to afford a complete change of textbooks across the different content areas. So, until the publishers prepare and publish new textbooks and until districts are able to replace them, you are basically on your own with regard to matching teacher manual suggestions to the Standards. This involves determining what Standard or Standards are developed and/or assessed by an activity recommended in the teacher manual. Of course, you can construct your own questions and activities, but doing so can be extremely time-consuming. However, if you choose to do this task, the following guidelines are also applicable.

You need to develop a deep understanding of the Standards so you can match questions and activities to specific Standards. In some cases, it will be quite easy. A question labeled cause–effect fits neatly under Standard 5. Similarly, a question that asks students to identify the main idea provides an obvious match to Standard 2. In cases, however, the match to the Standards may be less obvious. In these situations, you may have to construct questions and design activities that match the Standards and ignore those in the teacher manual that do not seem to be a good fit.

The CCSS, like questions and activities in your teacher's manual, are driven by words that indicate what an individual should do. We are talking about question words like *what*, *where*, and *why* and direction words such as *summarize*, *compare*, and *analyze*. If you understand the specific meanings of these words, which ones mean basically the same thing, and which ones represent different conceptual entities, matching instructional and assessment activities to the Standards will not pose a problem. (The meaning of specific question stems is more fully discussed in Chapter 10.) Let us closely examine the Anchor Standards for reading. Exactly what do they say students should do? What guidelines can we use to match an activity in the teacher's manual to a specific Common Core standard?

Anchor Standard 1

Read closely to determine what the text says explicitly and to make logical inferences from it; cite specific textual evidence when writing or speaking to support conclusions drawn from the text.

"What the text says explicitly" and "specific textual evidence" are key components of this Standard. Basically Standard 1 is the literal comprehension standard.

"The absolute first order of business is that students need to be able to grasp what a text actually *says and suggests*" (Calkins et al., 2012, p. 39). Standard 1 is perhaps the first rung on the ladder. If students are not able to comprehend what the text explicitly says, they will not be able to engage in the activities described in Standards 2 through 9. The Standards are text-based. That is, the text is the source of information, not prior knowledge, readers' personal opinions, or readers' individual life-style experiences.

Literal questions in a teacher's manual or activities that draw on literal text components represent a match with Standard 1. Such questions ask students to locate answers in the text or use what the text says to complete an activity. Some inference questions also represent a viable match with Standard 1 but only if the basis for the inference is the text.

Anchor Standard 2

Determine central ideas or themes of a text and analyze their development; summarize the key supporting details and ideas.

This standard matches well with teacher manual questions and activities that ask students to identify the main idea (informational text) and the theme (literature). Some manuals ask students to summarize segments of text and this matches with Standard 2, but only if the summary is text-based. Summary contents must be drawn specifically from the text, not from student's prior knowledge and/or personal opinions. Research that asked students from grade 4 through high school to summarize text revealed that many students built their summaries around personal opinions (Leslie & Caldwell, in press)—that is, they did not meet the requirements of Standard 2.

Anchor Standard 3

Analyze how and why individuals, events, and ideas develop and interact over the course of a text.

The ability to match teacher manual questions and activities to Standard 3 depends on what is meant by *analyze*. Synonyms for *analyze* include *examine, evaluate, scrutinize,* and *probe,* words seldom seen in teacher manuals. Analysis has always been considered a high-level cognitive activity and the well-known Bloom's taxonomy places analysis after knowledge, comprehension, and application and before synthesis and evaluation (Bloom & Krathwohl, 1956). A later revision of Bloom's work places analysis after remembering, understanding, and applying and before evaluating and creating (Anderson & Krathwohl, 2001).

Standard 3 requires higher-level thinking akin to Ciardiello's (1998) convergent questions, which begin with why, how, and in what way and ask students to explain procedures, state relationships, and make comparisons. Analysis also aligns with the question levels of Grasser et al. (2010) that focus on comparisons, causes, consequences, goals, instruments, and procedures. Mosenthal's (1996) highest question level includes identification of cause, effect, reason, result, explanation, and similarity.

Given the above, questions that include words such as *why, how,* and/or *in what way* can be matched to Standard 3. Activities that ask students to state causes or consequences, explain procedures, and make comparisons can be considered as representative of Standard 3. However, there is one caveat. The analysis must be text-based, that is, the causes, effects, procedures, and comparisons must be drawn from the text. How is this different from Standard 1 that also requires answers to be text-based? For Standard 3, the reader must use the phrasing of the question to infer what the answer involves: causality, consequence, a procedure, a comparison, or the like. For example, if the question uses "how" as a question stem, the reader is probably expected to describe a process of some sort. If the question includes "why," the reader is expected to locate reasons or causes. If the question asks the reader to compare, the reader must locate how two things are alike or different. In order to answer such questions, the reader must identify relevant text components, some of which may be found in different parts of the text. The reader must understand, for example, that analyzing why something occurs, how it occurs, or its relationship to other entities requires different types of information. Effective analysis requires very close reading of the question and of the text.

Anchor Standard 4

Interpret words and phrases as they are used in a text, including determining technical, connotative, and figurative meanings and analyze how specific word choices shape meaning or tone.

At first glance, this seems to represent an easy match from a teacher manual to a standard as there are many vocabulary questions and activities in teacher manuals. However, matching a question or activity to Standard 4 depends on the source of information. Suppose a student is asked to look up a word in the dictionary. Is this a match to Standard 4? No, it is not. The key phrase in Standard 4 is "used in the text." If you go beyond the Anchor Standards and examine the Reading Standards for Literature and Informational Text, you will note that the emphasis is placed on the text as a source of specific word meaning. The reader must use the text to determine the meaning of figurative, connotative, and technical language as well as to analyze the effect or impact of specific word choices on text meaning.

If you select vocabulary words emphasized in your teacher manual, you may have to change the focus of the question or activity. For example, if the manual asks students to locate word meaning from the dictionary or glossary, you will have to add to that activity by asking the students to explain why the definition fits within the context of the passage and/or why it represents a viable word choice. Just selecting a relevant meaning will not meet the intent of Standard 4; the text-based relevance must be examined and/or explained.

Anchor Standard 5

Analyze the structure of texts, including how specific sentences, paragraphs, and larger portions of the text (e.g., a section, chapter, scene, or stanza) relate to each other and the whole.

Standard 5 focuses on analysis of structure in literature and exposition. A variety of different structures characterize literature: narratives, essays, plays, poetry, and so on. Within these structures are smaller structures such as sentences, paragraphs, chapters, scenes, and stanzas. Expository text also has different structures: newspaper columns, magazine articles, directions for assembling something, and opinion pieces, to name a few. An important form of expository text is the textbook chapter, the overall purpose of which is to inform and teach using five general structures: description, comparison, sequence, cause–effect, and problem–solution. These structures can involve entire chapters or sections of a chapter, or they can involve just a single paragraph.

Teacher manuals vary as to how they label the questions and activities they recommend. In several history and science texts that I have examined, a focus on structure is often evident. If, for example, cause–effect is attached to a question, it may well be a match for Standard 5 but only if answering the question or engaging in the activity is based on the content of the text.

Anchor Standard 6

Assess how point of view or purpose shapes the content and style of a text.

Standard 6 primarily focuses on the point of view of the author. In narrative text, the focus may be on a character's point of view as described by the author. This Standard represents a bit of a problem with regard to informational text such as social studies and science. The purpose of these texts is to teach, and seldom is the point of view of the author apparent. For example, social studies texts do not present two authors' versions of the same issue. Instead they describe events and issues in a somewhat neutral fashion. Similarly, science texts are very factual and do not allow for contrasting points of view or purposes; the presentation is clearly authoritative.

We can address this Standard in social studies by focusing on the different points of view of individual historical figures, political parties, government policies, and so on, and some teacher manuals include questions and activities that ask students to do this. How this Standard is instructed and assessed in science may have to wait until the new textbook series are published. It may be that they will include contrasting points of view regarding science issues such as climate change, organic farming, and alternative medicine, but at the present time science texts seldom do this.

Anchor Standard 7

Integrate and evaluate content presented in diverse media and formats, including visually and quantitatively, as well as in words.

This Standard is an easy one to match with a teacher's manual. If a question and/ or activity refers to a picture, chart, graph, or the like, it is a match.

Anchor Standard 8

Delineate and evaluate the arguments and specific claims in a text, including the validity of the reasoning as well as the relevance and sufficiency of the evidence.

This Standard is not acceptable for literature (CCSSI, 2010); it only applies to informational text. At K–5 levels, students are expected to identify reasons that the author gives to support specific points in the text. At levels 6–12, students are expected to evaluate such arguments and claims. This Standard is a follow-up to Standard 6 in that point of view must be identified before it can be evaluated. It is doubtful that present teacher manuals include questions and activities that address Standard 8. As mentioned previously, informational textbooks tend to be neutral in their presentation of content; they do not focus on evaluation of the textbook author's reasoning and/or claims. You may find a question and/or activity in a social studies manual that presents the viewpoint of historical figures, and they could allow for some discussion of their validity. Admittedly, this Standard presents a bit of a dilemma. What is the source of criteria for judging argument validity? The text-based nature of the Standards seems to suggest that something more than personal opinion is in order, such as the opinions and actions of others, historical events, and specific contexts that influence behavior.

Anchor Standard 9

Analyze how two or more texts address similar themes or topics in order to build knowledge or to compare the approaches the authors take.

In order to assess this Standard, two similar texts are necessary. Although present teacher manuals present a variety of selections, seldom do they present two texts on the same topic or theme. This drawback means you may be on your own with regard to locating such material until social studies and science textbooks specifically address this Standard.

Sharing Good Reader Behaviors and the CCSS with Students

Who should know about good reader behaviors and/or the Standards, the lesson focus, and the assessment evidence to be collected? Should it be just the teacher or coach? Or should students also be aware of these issues? Think about how eager students are to participate in sports. Motivation is rarely an issue. Of course, playing basketball or soccer may be more fun than many classroom activities. However, I suspect that part of students' motivation has to do with their understanding of the game, their knowledge of its rules, and their awareness of what they need to learn in order to play well.

Do students have that understanding of the reading process? Do they know what good readers do? If an athletic coach requires a specific drill for developing free-throw shooting, students generally know what the coach is doing and why. Do students know why a reading teacher or coach asks them to write a summary, identify text structure, or determine the central idea? I recall a third grader who was busily employed in filling out a worksheet. When he finished, he put down his pencil and announced, "There! It's done. I don't know what it means, but I did it." How sad!

Do students know about the CCSS? Do they understand how these standards may be very different from what has gone before? Do they understand each standard? For example, consider Standard 6. Do they understand what is meant by "point of view" and how the purpose of an author can shape how a text is written? Do they know that informational text can be structured in five different ways but narrative text employs a single basic structure?

It is important to develop students' awareness of their own thought processes during the reading process. The good reader behaviors and the Standards are the vehicles for doing this. From the very first day of class, students need to know about them. Put the good reader behaviors and Standards on bulletin boards and talk about them every day. Model them for the students. Share the lesson focus with the students. Share how you are assessing their development as good literacy learners. Construct rubrics collaboratively with the students and use this collaboration as a way to further develop their understanding of the good reader behaviors and the Standards. Finally, ask students to describe their own good reader behaviors and have them evaluate which Standards they find difficult.

In the past, assessment was the sole prerogative of a teacher or coach, and to students it was often a mysterious and confusing process. Have you ever received a grade and had no idea why you received it? Teachers or coaches assessed and assigned grades, but the students often had no idea what they did or did not do to earn the grades. Assessment should be a more collaborative venture. Students must take control of their own learning and teachers must design effective instruction. Without assessment, this is not possible.

Making Reading Assessment Manageable

Classrooms and coaching sessions are very busy places. As a teacher or coach, you do not have unlimited time to plan and assess instruction. Even if you tie your instruction to good reader behaviors and the Standards, it is easy to become hopelessly bogged down in planning instruction, assessing student behavior, recording evidence, designing and scoring rubrics, and making decisions about the next steps. Some shortcuts are available to teachers or coaches, however, and you should use them. Teacher and coach burnout is a very real thing; it often occurs because individuals attempt to do too much and, as a result, have no sense of accomplishing anything. Take as many shortcuts as you can to achieve that balance!

- *First, don't feel that you have to assess everything students do.* Teachers and coaches often go on guilt trips if they don't correct every paper, look at every worksheet, and keep track of every discussion. Why should you? There are some activities that students do just for practice. They don't need more than your awareness that the students actually worked on them. There are some activities that develop classroom climate and student collaboration. Again, they do not need detailed analysis. And there are some activities that are just plain fun and make the reading classroom or tutoring session a happy place to be.

- *Choose important activities to assess.* It takes time to develop a rubric, use it for scoring, and record the results. One or two thoughtfully chosen pieces of evidence will give you more input than six or eight hastily developed ones. You have 9 months of school, which translates into approximately 36 weeks. If you assess one or two activities each week, you will have more than enough data to document individual progress.

• *Choose a small number of students to focus on each day.* If you have 25 students in your classroom, directing specific attention to each of them on a daily basis may be very difficult. Cunningham (1992) suggests dividing the number of students in your class by 5. Each day, pay special attention to 5 students as opposed to 25. On Monday, focus on the Monday students. Examine their work very carefully. Spend individual time with them. Watch them and write notes about their behavior and performance. On Tuesday, focus on the Tuesday students; on Wednesday, focus on the Wednesday students; and so on. This practice allows you as a teacher or coach to concentrate on a realistically manageable number of students each day.

• *Involve students in self-correction and self-assessment.* Have students correct their own work whenever possible. This works well for worksheets, homework assignments, and similar activities. However, don't give the students an answer key. Nobody ever learned anything using an answer key. Students concentrate on matching their answers to the key and pay little or no attention to why an answer was right or wrong. Instead, put the students in small groups. Have them compare their answers without an answer key and come to some agreement. After they have determined an answer that all group members can agree on, then allow them to compare this answer to the answer key. Also involve self-correction with examination of the text. Ask the students to indicate what text information they might have missed or how the text could be changed to provide a clearer answer.

• *Set up simple procedures for recording your observations.* For example, use a common template (such as the one provided on p. 63) for recording observations about student performance. Adam's checklist used a such a template. Place the names of your students in the first column on the left. Divide the rest of the sheet into four or five columns. Leave a blank space at the top of the template for writing in the good reader behavior and/or the Standard that is your focus. Write student names in the first column. You can then duplicate multiple copies of this template, or place it on your pad. Whenever you want to observe your students or evaluate their work, fill in the Good Reader Behavior/Standard blank and the blank column heads, and you are ready to go!

Dealing with Report Cards and Grade Books

Teachers and coaches rarely have input into the format of the report card. The school or district makes this choice, and the teachers or coaches are required to use the format whether or not they agree with it. Many report cards have very limited formats. They require a single letter grade for reading and offer minimal space for a teacher's or coach's comments. A teacher or coach may feel that it

Sample Template

Good Reader Behavior/Standard _____

Date _____

Selection _____

Activity _____

offers little in the way of substantive information to the parents or the students. If this is so, the teacher or coach may want to insert a checklist with the report card. The checklist could list the good reader behaviors and/or Standards that were stressed during the grading period.

Some teachers or coaches may prefer a narrative report. Be aware, however, that these reports can be very time-consuming. If you choose to write a narrative, it helps to divide the report into categories of reading behavior and/or the Standards. Keep the same categories for all students and, above all, make the process manageable.

Reporting each student's progress in developing good reader behaviors and/or the Standards can seem a monumental task if your grade book does not lend itself to such assessment. I suspect that many teachers and coaches still do what I did some years ago, whether they are using a paper or electronic grade book. I entered a lot of grades into my grade book, and I did this on the same page in the order in which they occurred. At the end of the grading period, I averaged the grades and transferred this to the report card. I hesitate to admit this, but I gave all grade book entries the same weight. A workbook page counted as much as a written summary!

It makes more sense to divide your grade book into pages or sections for each good reader behavior and/or Standard that you emphasize. This method allows for a more fine-tuned evaluation of a student's performance. Instead of assessing "reading" in a vague and general way, as I once did, you can see a pattern of student strengths and weaknesses with regard to a good reader behavior or Standard. These observations can be easily translated into a report card checklist or narrative.

Grade books should not just contain number grades or percentages. This system tends to limit the kind of information that you can include. How can you describe the quality of a summary in terms of a number? Describing student performance in terms of letters such as A, B, C, and D can also be somewhat limiting. Do you really want to evaluate a student's participation in discussion with a letter grade? Consider using a simple coding system as an alternative to numbers and letters: a plus mark means good performance, a checkmark means adequate performance, and a minus mark signals below-average work. If your rubrics include a point system, record the student score with the total number of points that could be earned. For example, if a rubric has a total of 10 points, and a student achieved 6, do not take the time to translate this rubric into a percent score. Simply record it as 6/10. Or record rubric ratings that are descriptive as opposed to numerical. For example, if you used "Very effective," "Effective," "Slightly effective," and "Not effective" on a rubric, abbreviate these ratings and record them in your grade book. This method allows you to record many more good reader and writer behaviors in your grade book—and, as a result, to arrive at a more complete picture of a student's strengths and weaknesses.

In this computerized age, electronic grade books have become quite popular. Unfortunately, some are very limiting. They restrict teachers to number grades that cannot be divided into sections, and they do not allow for checkmarks or designations such as "Very effective." This is because the system does the computing for the teacher and arrives at a single grade composite for all numerical entries. (A single grade for a process as complex as reading is really a contradiction in terms!) Unfortunately, some schools have mandated such systems. I can think of only one alternative to such a requirement: use the electronic system for those grades that fit a numerical grading system, and use a paper grade book for all others. And work diligently to change the system by explaining to whoever will listen that numbers are not the only way to assess performance and may even be unsuitable for doing so in some cases.

Making Time for Individual Reading Assessment

Assessment is the basis for making decisions about the whole class as well as individual students. At the close of an instructional activity, a teacher or coach generally has an idea of the progress of the class and can pinpoint which students are having difficulty. The problem is finding time in a busy day to assess those individuals who are struggling, to determine what is the problem, and to decide how it can be remedied. How can a busy teacher or coach concentrate on one student? What about the rest of the class? Won't they get out of control? These are very valid questions, whether you are talking about a class of 27 students or a group of 5. An important component of assessment is establishing methods of classroom management that give teachers and coaches time to deal with individuals. Although there are no easy answers, teachers and coaches can provide time for individual assessment by setting up the practice of individual silent reading.

If all the students are engaged in silently reading books of their own choosing, a teacher or coach can use this time to work with a single student. Unfortunately, many students are not used to reading on their own. They may sit still for a short period of time, but then they begin to act up. The teacher or coach becomes the disciplinarian who maintains order, and thus has no time to work with individuals. You can avoid this problem if you include individual silent reading as a daily activity, beginning with the very first day of class. Set up rules for acceptable behavior during this period and enforce them. If your students are not used to reading for long periods, begin with very short time segments and then gradually increase these. For example, Glenn began with 5-minute silent reading periods for his third graders because a very short period was all they could manage. He gradually increased the time, and by November the students were happily occupied for 20 minutes at a time.

Stock your room with all sorts of reading materials at all sorts of difficulty levels. Students who might not read a book may become engrossed in magazines, store catalogues, brochures, programs from sports events, comic books, or newspapers. And don't forget the computer and all the materials that students can find to read on the web. Allow students to choose what they want to read. Perhaps there is a wonderful book that you loved and nobody has picked it up. Or perhaps your students are reading some books that you find trivial, and you feel driven to move them to more challenging material. Resist the temptation to force a change, however. Just be happy they are reading! Offer and promote other books as choices, but allow the students to say "no." When students are ready for more challenging material, they will take that step on their own. The whole point is to have students quietly occupied in a worthwhile endeavor to give you some time for interacting with individual students.

Summary

- Assessment and instruction cannot be separated. Both are based on an understanding of good reader behaviors and/or the CCSS.

- A teacher or coach identifies what is being taught and assessed (i.e., the goal of the lesson) in terms of good reader behaviors and/or the Standards. A reading selection is not the goal of a lesson; it is the tool that the teacher or coach uses to develop good literacy behaviors. The teacher or coach identifies, collects, and records evidence about student performance relevant to the good reader behavior and/or Standard that is the focus of the lesson.

- Rubrics are procedures used to analyze evidence; they function best if they are simple in design and application. Teachers and coaches should construct rubrics with their students or, at the very least, make certain that the rubric is clearly understood by the students. As a result of analyzing evidence, a teacher or coach makes instructional decisions about future class activities and about the progress of individual children.

- Instructional suggestions, student activities, and questions in a teacher's manual can be matched to the CCSS. The Standards are driven by words that indicate what an individual should do. Question words include *what, where*, and *why*; direction words include *summarize, compare*, and *analyze*. Some teacher manual questions or activities provide a direct match; others may need to be amended. In some cases the teacher or coach will have to construct questions that match the Standards.

• The teacher or coach should share good reader behaviors and the Standards, the lesson focus, and the assessment with students.

• There are various ways of making assessment manageable. For example, instead of assessing everything students do, a teacher or coach can assess only important activities and limit these to two or three a week. Simple procedures can be used for recording these observations. Assessment is an ongoing process.

• If a report card format is limiting, a teacher or coach should consider adding a checklist or a narrative report. A grade book can be organized according to good reader and writer behaviors.

• A teacher or coach can arrange time for individual assessment by setting up daily individual silent reading.

Activities for Developing Understanding

• Choose a selection in a reading, social studies, or science textbook. Use the four-step process to design and assess a lesson based on a CCSS. Implement the lesson. How could it be revised to become more efficient or manageable?

• Choose a unit in a reading, social studies, or science textbook. Examine the various instructional activities and questions provided in a teacher manual. Identify some that are a match with specific Standards.

• Choose a reading, social studies, or science unit. Select some teacher manual activities that you do not believe are a match to the Standards. Can you adapt or add to them so they become a match? If not, explain why.

• Design a rubric for assessing a good reader behavior and/or a Standard.

• In what ways will the CCSS affect your teaching?

• Identify a CCSS that will need your special attention to develop, that is, assess and teach. Why is this Standard particularly problematic?

CHAPTER 5

The Informal Reading Inventory Process

How Does It Address the Purposes of Reading Assessment?

Overview of the IRI Process

Teachers and coaches have always listened to students read orally. They have always asked questions after silent reading to decide whether the students understood what they read. In fact, it would be difficult to imagine a reading classroom where teachers or coaches did not listen to their students read and did not evaluate their comprehension.

Joy called Billy, a second grader, to sit next to her at a cozy table tucked into a corner at the front of the room. The other children were all busy at various tasks.

Some were illustrating a story that the class had composed that morning. Others were engaged in reading books. Still others were occupied at various learning centers. The classroom aide moved around answering questions, making suggestions, and helping individual students as needed. This gave Joy an opportunity to focus on an individual child.

Joy asked Billy to read aloud a second-grade selection from a published IRI "The Family's First Trip" (Leslie & Caldwell, 2011). After Billy finished, Joy asked him to retell what he had read, thanked him for reading to her, and sent him back to join his classmates.

A similar scenario occurred in David's fifth-grade classroom. The children were independently reading books of their own choice, a daily event. As they did so, David moved around the room stopping occasionally to chat with a student. He paused at Cissy's desk and inquired whether she was enjoying her book, *Walk Two Moons* by Sharon Creech (1994). She enthusiastically said that she was. David then told her to continue silently reading the next several pages. When she finished, he asked Cissy to retell the events on those pages, thanked her for talking with him, and moved on to another student.

Larissa met with Carl, a seventh grader, during his study period. She chose an upper middle school selection from a published IRI (Leslie & Caldwell, 2011). She asked Carl to read aloud a selection entitled "Biddy Mason," a true account of an enslaved woman who gained her freedom and became a wealthy and respected citizen. After asking Carl questions to evaluate his comprehension, Larissa chose an easier passage and repeated the process.

These are not unusual situations to encounter in a reading classroom or intervention setting. In fact, listening to students read and asking them about their reading are very common occurrences. Why are they so common? Because teachers and coaches realize that these are powerful assessment tools that can offer valuable information on the three purposes of reading assessment discussed in Chapter 2: determining a student's reading level, identifying good reader behaviors and areas of weakness, and documenting evidence of progress on the part of the student.

Joy and Billy

Let's return to Joy and Billy. What was Joy assessing as Billy orally read the selection "The Family's First Trip"? There were several things. Joy was interested in Billy's accuracy in pronouncing words. Was he able to pronounce words appropriate for second grade? Joy was also concerned about his fluency. Did he read the selection not only accurately, but at an appropriate pace and with some expression? Finally, and perhaps what's more, she wanted to know whether Billy was able to understand what he read.

What criteria did Joy use to evaluate Billy's fluency? She paid attention to his rate of reading and his voice intonation. Although Billy paused before some words, most of his reading was smooth and expressive and he paid attention to punctuation signals. Did Billy make the text sound meaningful? He did. Was he enjoyable to listen to? He was.

What about Billy's pronunciation accuracy? Let's look at how Billy read the text. First I provide the original text; then I show how Billy read it. To make it easy for you to notice the difference between the actual text and Billy's reading, I have underlined mispronunciations and additions and crossed out omissions.[*]

Text	Billy's Reading
The Family's First Trip	*The Family's First Trip*
Thomas lived in a small town with only 2,000 people. It was June 12th and Thomas was excited. His family was planning a trip to Atlanta to visit his aunt. Unlike his home town, Atlanta is a big city. Thomas had never traveled to a big city before. He had to decide what to bring. It was a two-day car trip. So, he needed to take along things to keep him busy in the car. He was reading a book and decided to bring it. But, he realized that he couldn't read all the time in the car. If he read too much he would get dizzy. He had to think of something that wouldn't use his eyes. He decided to bring his CD-player and favorite CDs.	Thomas lived in a small town with only 2,000 people. It was June 12th and Thomas was excited. His family was planning a trip to <u>Atlantica</u> to visit his <u>auntie</u>. <u>Uncle</u> his home town, Atlanta is a big city. Thomas <u>was</u> had never traveled to a big city before. He had to <u>dakide</u> <u>that</u> to bring. It was a two-day car trip. So, he needed to take along things to keep him busy in the car. He was reading a book and <u>discovered</u> to bring it. But, he <u>really</u> that he couldn't read all the time in the car. If he read too much he would get dizzy. He had to think of something that <u>would</u> use his eyes. He <u>deeded</u> to bring his CD-player and <u>favored</u> CDs.
Thomas knew that they would be going out to dinner. Another night they were going to a country music show. He brought long pants and a shirt for going out to dinner. But the music show would be outside. He brought a pair of shorts and a tee shirt for that. He had enough clothes, books, and CDs. What else did he need? He almost forgot his toothbrush	Thomas knew that they would be going out to dinner. Another night they were going to a <u>court</u> music show. He <u>bought</u> brought <u>along</u> pants and a shirt for going out to dinner. But the music show would be outside. He brought a pair of shorts and a tee shirt for <u>the</u>. He had ____ clothes, books, and CDs. What else did he need? He almost forgot his

[*] The selection read by Billy, "The Family's First Trip," is from Leslie, L., & Caldwell, J. S. (2011). *Qualitative Reading Inventory 5* (p. 201). Boston: Pearson. Copyright 2011 by Pearson. Adapted by permission.

and pajamas! He would have been embarrassed if he had forgotten them!

The first day of driving went quickly for Thomas as he read and listened to his CDs. His parents were looking for a hotel to stay in. Thomas and his sister begged their parents to find a place with a swimming pool. Luckily they had remembered to pack their swimming suits. Their parents found a small hotel with a heated pool. Thomas and his sister got in their suits and spent an hour in the pool before dinner. The first part of their trip was fun. They looked forward to seeing their aunt the next day.

toothbrush and <u>pananas</u>! He would have been <u>embraced</u> if he had forgotten them!

The first day of driving <u>want</u> went <u>quick</u> for Thomas as he read and listened to his CDs. His parents were looking for a hotel to stay in. Thomas and his sister <u>began</u> their parents to find a place with a swimming pool. <u>Lucky</u> they had <u>reminded</u> to pack <u>they</u> their swimming suits. Their parents found a small hotel with a <u>hetten</u> pool. Thomas and his sister got in their suits and spent an hour in the pool before dinner. The first part of their trip was fun. <u>There</u> they looked forward to seeing their aunt the next day.

What criteria did Joy use to assess Billy's accuracy in reading the selection? As Billy read, Joy recorded his errors on her copy of the text. After Billy returned to his computer activities, Joy counted the number of words in the selection. There were 304. She also counted Billy's mispronunciations, word omissions, and word additions. Billy made a total of 26 errors. Joy translated this into a percentage. She subtracted 26 from 304 and then divided 278 by 304. Billy's percentage of accuracy on this second-grade selection was 91%. Based on this percentage, Joy determined that this selection and others like it probably represented an instructional reading level for Billy. That is, Billy could read second-grade words, but not independently. He would need some instructional support if second-grade material were to represent a truly meaningful and enjoyable experience for him.

Joy also noted some good reader behaviors on Billy's part. For example, many of Billy's errors reflected his understanding of the text. His mispronunciation of *uncle* for *unlike* implies that he expected some involvement of an uncle given that the trip was to see his aunt. His mispronunciation of *discovered* for *decided* suggested that Billy expected the following text would refer to the contents of the book he was reading. His error of *bought* for *brought* implies an assumption that Thomas might need new clothes for the trip. Similarly Billy's error of *began* for *begged* indicated an expectation that Thomas and his sister were going to prepare for the end of the trip or initiate some suggestions for finding a hotel. He was not a wild guesser who offered any alternative for an unknown word. His mispronunciations contained many of the same letters and sounds as the original word such as *Atlantica* for *Atlanta, discovered* for *decided, court* for *country*, and *pananas* for *pajamas*.

After Billy read, Joy assessed his comprehension. She asked him to retell the selection and took brief notes on what he said. Here is Billy's retelling.

"Well, they were going on a trip to see their aunt in a big city. And he took along books and CDs and clothes and stuff. They would go to shows and eat dinner in a restaurant. And when they got there or almost got there, they stayed in a motel with a pool and had a lot of fun."

Joy felt that Billy demonstrated acceptable understanding of the selection. He described the intent of the trip, listed what he took along, mentioned what they would do when they arrived, and described the stop at a motel with a pool.

Joy spent approximately 15 minutes listening to Billy read. She spent another 10 minutes counting errors, determining a percentage, reviewing his errors, and rereading his retelling. What did Joy gain from these 25 minutes? She had an approximate reading level for Billy—second grade. She could compare this level with later efforts in order to document progress. She also noted some important good reader behaviors on Billy's part.

David and Cissy

What did David learn about Cissy's reading as a result of his brief pause at her desk during independent reading? The book that she was reading, *Walk Two Moons* (Creech, 1994), was part of the classroom library. No grade level was attached to the book, but David considered it appropriate for fifth graders, many of whom had already read and enjoyed it. Cissy was reading chapter 15 when David asked her to retell what she had read. As Cissy retold events that spanned several pages, David skimmed these same pages as he listened to Cissy.

> "They were sitting in the river because it was real hot and this boy told them it was private property and he was kind of like threatening them. Then a snake bit Gram. It was a water moccasin. And Gramps cut the bite and the boy helped to suck out the poison. They went to the hospital and Gramps gave the boy some money. Gramps stayed with Gram right in the hospital bed. And Sal and the boy start making up to be friends."

David asked Cissy how she would have felt at that point. She replied that she couldn't understand how Gram could be so calm and keep holding the snake. She also predicted that Gram might die, and that would be terrible for Sal, who loved her grandparents so much. She obviously wanted to keep on reading, so David thanked her and moved on to another student. In the few minutes that David spent with Cissy, he learned that she could silently read text that was appropriate for fifth grade; that she understood what she read; and, perhaps most important, that she was deeply involved with the characters in the novel.

Larissa and Carl

What did Larissa want to learn about Carl's reading? Carl was not doing well in many of his classes, and Larissa wanted to determine whether this problem could be due to difficulties with reading. Like Joy, Larissa noted Carl's fluency. For the most part, Carl read very slowly, stopping often to figure out unfamiliar words. He read in a low monotone and often ignored punctuation signals. Larissa was also interested in his ability to identify words at an upper middle school level. Like Joy, she marked Carl's word pronunciation errors, word omissions, and word additions on her copy of the text. She used the number of words in the selection and the number of Carl's errors to arrive at an accuracy level. Carl made a total of 95 errors while reading a 750-word passage. His accuracy level was 87%, considered to be a frustration level. This suggested to Larissa that Carl could not yet successfully handle upper middle school text. Carl's comprehension after reading also verified that this level of material was too difficult for him. He was only able to answer 3 of 10 questions correctly, for a comprehension score of 30%. Few good reader behaviors were evident as Carl struggled with "Biddy Mason." For this reason, Larissa decided to repeat the process with an easier selection. Larissa had indeed discovered that reading difficulties were probably contributing to Carl's problems in school. Now she had to determine the level of text that Carl could read and understand.

Joy, David, and Larissa all used elements of what is known as the informal reading inventory (IRI) process to assess their students' reading growth. Each teacher asked the student to read, orally or silently; each asked the student to retell or answer questions about the reading; and each used criteria to evaluate fluency, word pronunciation, and comprehension.

The IRI process is generally used with an individual student. The student reads a passage at a specific grade level, either orally or silently. For example, Billy read second-grade text, Cissy read text appropriate for fifth grade, and Carl struggled through an upper middle school selection. If the student reads orally, the teacher or coach records and counts any oral reading errors, as Joy and Larissa did. After reading, the student retells the gist of the selection and/or answers questions about its content. Both Joy and David employed retelling, and Larissa asked specific questions.

The IRI process is what its full name implies—an informal assessment tool. Therefore, it allows for flexibility on the part of teachers or coaches, who can adapt administration to meet their needs. The IRI process can be an effective and sensitive measure for collecting evidence about a student's reading. A teacher or coach can use the process to address all three purposes of reading assessment. First, the teacher or coach can determine the level of text that a student can read successfully. Both Joy and David were able to do this, and when Larissa discovered that Carl was unable to read at his middle school level, she had to probe further. Second, the IRI process can also be used to suggest areas of strength and weakness. Both Joy and David observed good reader behaviors in their students, while Larissa did not because of the difficulty level of the text. Finally, the IRI process can be used to measure an individual student's progress. It allows a teacher or coach to compare student performance at different points in time, such as before teaching/coaching begins and later on during the process. The IRI process can be used in RTI programs, both for identifying students who need additional help and for verifying progress.

Differences between the IRI Process and an IRI

We must distinguish between the IRI process and an IRI itself. The IRI process can be used with any passage to determine whether a student can read and comprehend it. A teacher or coach can use selections from a published IRI, as Joy did, or a trade book, as David did. The teacher or coach can also use selections from a basal reading series or content textbooks. The IRI process holds much potential for assessing the CCSS. Standard 10 requires students to read at their chronological grade level. The IRI process can help teachers and coaches determine the extent to which students can do this. It allows a teacher or tutor to evaluate a student in an authentic reading situation. The student can be asked to read selections that he or she encounters daily in the classroom.

An IRI is a published instrument that consists of a variety of passages at different grade levels. Both Joy and Larissa used a published IRI to assess their students' reading level. Each passage is followed by questions to ask the student. IRI grade levels usually span preprimer, primer, and first through sixth or eighth grades. Some IRIs contain high school passages. All IRIs offer detailed directions for recording and scoring student responses.

You can use the IRI process with a published IRI, as Joy and Larissa did, or you can use it with a passage that you select, as David did. You may find that a published IRI is more convenient. It includes a copy of the passage for the student to read and a copy for you to write on. It provides scoring guidelines on each teacher copy. On the other hand, using the IRI process with selections that you choose yourself allows you to evaluate a student's performance on the basis of the materials you are actually using in your classroom. Graded passages from an IRI may or may not parallel your classroom materials. For example, the "Biddy Mason" passage that Carl read was probably representative of the general difficulty level of upper middle school selections. However, it may not have been similar in content and format to the literature selections that Carl was expected to read and understand.

The IRI process has been validated by practice over many years of literacy assessment. It is part of many published assessment batteries. It is a process that teachers and coaches have used over and over again—asking students to read in order to determine their performance and progress.

Published IRIs offer different assessment options. Some provide graded word lists. Others include procedures to determine whether the passage is about a familiar topic. Most IRIs offer some process for analyzing the oral reading errors that a student makes. Some IRIs assess comprehension by scoring the student's retelling as well as scoring answers to questions. As you become more familiar with the IRI process, you will be able to use these options with any passage as a possible source of evidence about a student's reading. The more options you use, the more you learn. Unfortunately, it is also true that the more options you use, the more time these take. A short focused assessment may offer more information than a detailed series of IRI options. If you intend to purchase an IRI, Appendix 5.1 lists questions to ask about published IRIs as well as a list of current IRIs.

The IRI Process and the CCSS

The IRI process can be used to assess a student's ability to read grade-level text. Standard 10 of the College and Career Readiness Anchor Standards for Reading stipulates that students are expected to "read and comprehend complex literary and informational texts independently and proficiently" (CCSSI, 2010, p. 10). "The grade-specific iterations call, more specifically, for students to read what the CCSS refer to as grade-level complex texts and to do so with independence" (Calkins et al., 2012, p. 32). Basically, this means that students should be reading text at their chronological grade level. Third graders are able to read third-grade text, sixth graders are able to read sixth-grade text, and so on.

Using the IRI process allows you to determine a student's level in relation to his or her chronological grade level. That is, you ask a student to read actual textbook segments and answer questions allied to a specific Standard. Admittedly, using an IRI is much easier in that the text and questions are provided. If you use the IRI process with textbooks, you will have to select a passage and choose questions from the teacher manual or compose your own. Of course the best scenario would be to select and/or construct questions that address specific Standards. I discuss question formation in Chapter 10.

The Informal Reading Process and RTI

The IRI process can be a meaningful assessment to determine a student's movement into or out of a specific tier. It can be applied using a published inventory or regular classroom material. Many RTI assessments focus on word identification and fluency. The advantages of the IRI process is that the teacher or coach can evaluate these components in the context of a specific passage and combined with a focus on meaning.

Using the IRI Process to Determine Reading Levels

Can a student successfully read the content-area textbook used in his or her classroom? Can the student read a selection from a basal anthology or a novel that is part of the class curriculum? These are important questions in today's classrooms given the demands of the CCSS. The IRI process allows you to determine whether a student can successfully read and comprehend the material used in his or her classroom. You can ask the student to read a representative selection from the textbook, anthology, or novel, and use the IRI process to find out whether he or she is successful in doing so. Until published IRIs address the specificity of the Standards, you may find using your textbook and writing questions allied to the CCSS a more efficient use of your time and a more valid form of assessment.

The IRI process also allows you to determine whether a student can read and comprehend passages at higher or lower levels of difficulty than the classroom materials. You can use the IRI process to determine the highest level of text that the student can handle successfully. Many students can read material that is more difficult than their classroom texts. Unfortunately, many others can only handle passages that are much easier than their classroom materials. It is important for you as a teacher or coach to know this information. It helps you to decide whether a student has a reading problem. Students who are unable to read selections appropriate for their grade level may have difficulties with reading that can have a negative impact on their overall school performance. Knowing your students' reading levels also allows you to effectively group students of similar ability.

There are basically two purposes for using the IRI process. Most teachers and coaches use the IRI process to find out whether students can read and comprehend material at their chronological grade level. A teacher or coach chooses a selection that is appropriate for that grade level and uses the IRI process to determine whether a student can handle it successfully. The second purpose is to determine the highest level that a student can manage. Of course, asking a student to read several passages of different difficulty levels takes much more time, and busy teachers or coaches often leave this more detailed assessment to reading specialists or other diagnosticians in their school or district. However, it is important for teachers and coaches to understand the full scope of the IRI process.

The IRI process provides two possible scores: a score for word identification accuracy when the student reads orally and a comprehension score. Word identification accuracy scores and comprehension scores are then used to determine three possible levels for the student: the independent level, the instructional level, and the frustration level. The *independent level* is the grade level at which a student can read without teacher or coach guidance. You are probably reading at an independent level when you choose a novel for pleasure reading. *Walk Two Moons* (Creech, 1994) probably represented an independent reading level for Cissy. The *instructional level* is the level at which a student can read with teacher or coach support. Second-grade text was an instructional level for Billy. Usually the instructional level is the level used for reading instruction. Perhaps sections of this book represent your instructional reading level. They may contain some concepts that are new to you. Because of their unfamiliarity, you may need to reread certain pages at a slower pace and pose questions about their content. The *frustration level* is the level that is too difficult and results in a frustrating experience for the student. I would guess that the directions for an income tax form or the contents of an insurance policy represent a frustration level for you, as they do for me.

If a student reads a passage orally, the IRI process provides two scores: an independent, instructional, or frustration level for word identification accuracy, and an independent, instructional, or frustration level for comprehension. If the student reads the passage silently, there is only one score: an independent, instructional, or frustration level for comprehension.

Most published IRIs use similar scoring criteria. A word identification accuracy score of 98–100% represents an independent level. If all word identification errors are counted, as Joy and Larissa did, a score of 90–97% represents an instructional level (Leslie & Caldwell, 2011). If only errors that change meaning are counted, 95–97% represents an instructional level. A score below 90%

IRI PROCESS LEVELS

Independent: The student can read and comprehend without assistance.

Instructional: The student can read and comprehend with assistance.

Frustration: The student is unable to read with adequate word identification accuracy and comprehension.

indicates a frustration level. For comprehension, a score of 90–100% on the questions suggests an independent level, and a score of 70–89% represents the instructional level. A score below 70% signals a frustration level.

Where do the numbers above come from? You get the numbers for word identification accuracy by counting the number of errors (often called *miscues*) the student makes while orally reading the passage. You get the numbers for comprehension by counting the number of questions that the student answers correctly. If you ask a student to retell, as Joy and David did, you do not get a numerical score from the retelling; you must evaluate the quality of the retelling on your own.

How does the IRI process play out? To determine whether a student can read classroom materials, choose a representative passage from your content textbook, your basal anthology, or trade books used for instruction. If the student is successful in identifying words and comprehending the selection, you have your answer. If, on the other hand, the student is unsuccessful, you know that classroom materials may be too difficult.

SCORING GUIDELINES FOR THE IRI PROCESS

Word Identification Accuracy

Independent level:

98–100% word identification accuracy

Instructional level:

90–97% word identification accuracy if all errors are counted

95–97% word identification accuracy if only meaning change errors are counted

Frustration level:

Less than 90% word identification accuracy if all errors are counted

Less than 95% word identification accuracy if only meaning change errors are counted

Comprehension

Independent level: 90–100% accuracy in answering questions

Instructional level: 70–89% accuracy in answering questions

Frustration level: Less than 70% accuracy in answering questions

Dennis was in third grade and newly arrived in his school. His teacher wanted to determine whether he could handle materials that were used in the classroom. She asked him to orally read several pages of a third-grade selection from the school's basal reading anthology. She recorded his word identification errors. When he finished reading, she asked him several questions about the selection. Denis was successful, scoring at an instructional level for both word identification accuracy and comprehension. What does this mean? Denis would probably be able to keep up with his peers.

Perhaps you are interested in finding the highest level that a student can read successfully. Choose a beginning passage. If this passage represents an independent level for the student, move to the next higher passage. Keep moving up until the student reaches a frustration level. This does not take as long as you might think. Usually two or three passages are sufficient to establish the highest instructional level. Determining the highest level usually requires that you use a published IRI that provides multiple passages at different grade levels.

After several weeks of school, it became evident to Holly's teacher that she was not able to keep up with her third-grade peers. The teacher asked Holly to read a short third-grade selection. Holly scored at a frustration level for both word identification accuracy and comprehension. The teacher then chose a second-grade selection for Holly to read. Holly scored at a frustration level for word identification accuracy and at an instructional level for comprehension. The teacher

---

FINDING THE HIGHEST INSTRUCTIONAL LEVEL

Choose a passage of suitable length.

If the student reads orally:

> Record word identification errors.
>
> Record comprehension.
>
> Determine independent, instructional, or frustration levels for word identification accuracy, for comprehension, and for the total passage.

If the student reads silently:

> Record comprehension.
>
> Determine independent, instructional, or frustration levels for comprehension.

If the student scores at an instructional level, move up to the next highest level.

If the student scores at a frustration level, move down to the next lowest level.

Continue until the highest instructional level is reached.

then chose a first-grade passage. Holly was successful at this level, scoring at an instructional level for word identification accuracy and at an independent level for comprehension. Holly's teacher placed Holly at a first-grade reading level. This represented a difference of 2 years from Holly's chronological grade placement, and her teacher immediately contacted the school reading specialist to arrange for additional reading instruction.

As you can see, one purpose of the IRI process is to determine whether a student can read and comprehend material that is appropriate for his or her grade level. This is a key issue with regard to the Standards. A second purpose is to have the student read increasingly difficult passages to find his or her highest instructional level.

Scoring Word Identification Accuracy

In order to score word identification accuracy and arrive at an independent, instructional, or frustration level, you must know the number of words in the passage. If you have a passage of 100 words and the student makes five errors, his or her word identification score is 95%—an instructional level. Unfortunately, few passages are so considerate as to have exactly 100 words. If you are using a published IRI, the number of words in each passage is stated. If you are using your own passage, you have to count the number of words. When you are scoring word identification accuracy, the first step is to subtract the number of errors from the total number of words to arrive at the total number of correct words. Then divide the number of words read correctly by the total number of words. For example, Gloria read a 243-word passage and made 26 errors. She read 217 words correctly. Dividing 217 by 243 gives us .89, or 89%, a frustration level.

Types of Oral Reading Errors

What kind of errors do students make? They substitute or mispronounce words. For example, Ellie read *He helped to fix the bus* as *He hoped to find the bus*. Ellie made two errors, substituting *hoped* for *helped* and *find* for *fixed*. As noted earlier, such errors are often called miscues. Sometime these miscues are nonwords, such as *aminals* for *animals* or *hovy* for *heavy*. Students often omit or add words. Glen read *They like to be in the sun* as *They like the sun* omitting three words: *to, be,* and *in*. Each omission counts as an error. Later on, he read *There are fish in lakes* as *There are a lot of fish in lakes*. Glen added three words: *a, lot,* and *of*. Each addition counts as an error. Each substitution, mispronunciation, omission, or addition counts for 1 point.

Counting Errors That Do Not Change Meaning

What if a substitution, omission, or addition does not alter the meaning of the passage? For example, a student reads *They saw a hen and cows* as *They saw hens and cows*. Is the omission of *a* and the substitution of *hens* for *hen* errors? The meaning of the passage is not really distorted. Some people also feel very strongly that you should only count those errors that do change passage meaning, such as substituting *looked* for *liked* in the sentence *They liked petting the kittens*. Some people feel that you should not count any errors that are self-corrected. You have to decide how you feel about this choice. I recommend that you count all deviations from the text even if they do not change the meaning. First, this method represents a faster and more reliable scoring system. Deciding whether a miscue really changes meaning can take more time than you might like to expend. And two people can violently disagree! What about self-corrections? Again, whether you count these is up to you. I generally count them as errors because each represents an initial misreading of a word.

If you only count meaning-change errors, you have to adjust your scoring system. An instructional level for meaning-change errors is signaled by scores between 95 and 97%. What if Joy had only counted errors that changed meaning? Billy made a total of 26 errors. Four did not change meaning and he corrected 4. If you do not count these errors, Billy made 18 errors for an accuracy score of 94%. So Billy is very close to the independent range. Only counting errors that change meaning, generally does result in a higher score, and I tend to take a cautious approach. I would rather underestimate a student's level than overestimate it. However, as I said above, that is your decision.

Recording Oral Reading Errors

How do you record errors or miscues on your copy of the student's text? The easiest and fastest way is simply to make a checkmark when a miscue occurs. If the student omits two words, use two checkmarks; if a student adds three words, make three checkmarks; and so on. This will give you the total number of miscues. Examples of coding miscues with checks and using traditional coding follow. As you can see, the traditional coding is more descriptive, but both forms of recording miscues serve the purpose of determining a student's reading level for a specific piece of text.

Billy's Reading

The Family's First Trip

Thomas lived in a small town with only 2,000 people. It was June 12th and Thomas was excited. His family was planning a trip to <u>Atlantica</u> to visit his <u>auntie</u>. <u>Uncle</u> his home town, Atlanta is a big city. Thomas <u>was</u> had never traveled to a big city before. He had to <u>dakide</u> <u>that</u> to bring. It was a two-day car trip. So, he needed to take along things to keep him busy in the car. He was reading a book and <u>discovered</u> to bring it. But, he <u>really</u> that he couldn't read all the time in the car. If he read too much he would get dizzy. He had to think of something that <u>would</u> use his eyes. He <u>deeded</u> to bring his CD-player and <u>favored</u> CDs.

Billy's Errors Marked with Checks

The Family's First Trip

Thomas lived in a small town with only 2,000 people. It was June 12th and Thomas was excited. His family was planning a trip to Atlanta to visit his aunt. Unlike his home town, Atlanta is a big city. Thomas had never traveled to a big city before. He had to decide what to bring. It was a two-day car trip. So, he needed to take along things to keep him busy in the car. He was reading a book and decided to bring it. But, he realized that he couldn't read all the time in the car. If he read too much he would get dizzy. He had to think of something that wouldn't use his eyes. He decided to bring his CD-player and favorite CDs.

Billy's Reading

The Family's First Trip

Thomas lived in a small town with only 2,000 people. It was June 12th and Thomas was excited. His family was planning a trip to <u>Atlantica</u> to visit his <u>auntie</u>. <u>Uncle</u> his home town, Atlanta is a big city. Thomas <u>was</u> had never traveled to a big city before. He had to <u>dakide</u> <u>that</u> to bring. It was a two-day car trip. So, he needed to take along things to keep him busy in the car. He was reading a book and <u>discovered</u> to bring it. But, he <u>really</u> that he couldn't read all the time in the car. If he read too much he would get

Billy's Errors Marked with Traditional Coding

The Family's First Trip

Thomas lived in a small town with only 2,000 people. It was June 12th and Thomas was excited. His family was planning a trip to *Atlantica* Atlanta to visit his *auntie* *uncle* aunt. Unlike his home town, Atlanta is a big city. Thomas *was* had never traveled to a big city before. He had to decide *dakide* *that* what to bring. It was a two-day car trip. So, he needed to take along things to keep him busy in the car. He was reading a book and *discovered* decided to bring it. But, he *really* realized that he couldn't read all the time in the car. If he read too much he would get dizzy. He had to think of something that <u>would</u> use his eyes. He <u>deeded</u> to bring his CD-player and <u>favored</u> CDs.

dizzy. He had to think of something that wouldn't use his eyes. He decided to bring his CD-player and favorite CDs.

(margin notes: would / deeded / favored)

Which system of recording errors is better? If you use checkmarks, should you feel guilty about not using a more descriptive recording system? I do not think so. Use the system that makes you comfortable. You have an entire professional career to grow into a descriptive recording system. The important thing is that you use the IRI process often. If you are uncomfortable or unsure of yourself, you probably won't. And you will miss an important method of assessing reading.

Students do other things while reading orally. They often repeat a word. Sometimes they hesitate before pronouncing a word. They often ignore punctuation. Should you code these mistakes as errors? Some published IRIs suggest that you should, but I do not agree. They do not alter the text, so they really do not represent errors (McKenna, 1983). You may note them if you wish, but you do not want the IRI process to become so detailed that you avoid using it. Arranging time for the IRI process with an individual student is often very difficult, so you want a process that is both effective and efficient.

Scoring Comprehension

The scoring process for comprehension questions is quite easy. Mark each question as correct or incorrect. Find out the total number correct, and divide by the total

---

MISCUE CODING SYSTEM

Omissions: Circle.

It was a (cold) winter day.

Insertions: Insert the added word above a caret.

all
John looked at˰ the toys in his room.

Substitutions or mispronunciations: Write above the word.

well
He knew the mouse lived in the wall.

Self-corrections: Mark with a C.

holding   C
He was having a birthday party.

number of questions. Karla answered seven questions correctly out of a possible eight. This translated into a score of 87%—an instructional level. Sometimes a student will answer part of a question. For example, Jake was asked to name two ways in which a virus differs from a cell. He was only able to name one. Should he receive half credit? Again, in the interests of an efficient IRI process, I suggest that you score an answer as either correct or incorrect and do not score partial credit. Of course, the best way is to avoid asking questions that require multiple answers!

Scoring Listening Comprehension

One of the most critical factors that contributes to the development of reading is oral language. Because oral and written language share the same systems of sound, vocabulary, and structure, once words have been pronounced, the ability to comprehend written language is heavily dependent upon an oral language base. The level of a student's oral language base can be estimated by using the IRI process. Instead of reading a passage, the student listens to one, and listening comprehension level is determined from the number of correct answers to questions following listening.

Why would a teacher or coach be interested in level of listening comprehension? Listening comprehension is often regarded as a measure of a student's comprehension potential in the absence of decoding problems (Gough & Juel, 1991; Stanovich, 1991). Let us suppose that a student's reading level is at third grade based on numerous pronunciation errors and a low score in comprehension. Perhaps if the student were asked to listen to a third-grade passage, he or she might demonstrate better comprehension in the absence of having to pronounce words. Perhaps the student might be able to comprehend fourth- or fifth-grade passages. For students who have difficulties with decoding, it is often a good idea to estimate their listening comprehension—the level they can comprehend with ease if word identification is not a problem. For students whose reading level is below that of their classmates, listening comprehension level can suggest whether these students can profit from orally presented material at their chronological grade level (Leslie & Caldwell, 2011).

Issues Regarding the IRI Process

Different Levels for Word Identification Accuracy and Comprehension

Students often score at different levels for word identification accuracy and comprehension, so a teacher or coach needs to determine what is the total passage level. For example, recall that when reading second-grade material, Holly scored at a frustration level for word identification accuracy and at an instructional level for comprehension. In first-grade text, her level was instructional for word identification accuracy and independent for comprehension. When this happens, choose the lower level, as Holly's teacher did, determining that second grade represented a frustration level for Holly and first grade represented an instructional level.

It is always better to underestimate a student's reading level than to overestimate it. If you assign a level that is too high, you may miss the existence of a reading problem. For instance, Jerome consistently scored higher on comprehension than on word identification accuracy. If his teacher had assigned the comprehension level as his overall level, Jerome would have been placed as reading at his chronological level of fourth grade. However, he was at a frustration level for word identification accuracy in second-grade text. Assigning a fourth-grade level would have masked Jerome's very real problem with word identification.

There is another reason for underestimating reading level. You may be choosing instructional materials based on that level. If a student cannot read the chosen material, substituting an easier book can be quite embarrassing to the student. It is much nicer to be able to say, "This book is too easy for you. Let's try one that is more difficult." The problem of under- or overestimating levels will not be an issue if you assign total passage levels based on the lower level attained in word identification accuracy and comprehension. It is my experience that this results in a realistic reading level in most cases.

Familiarity of Topic

The IRI process, like many assessment practices, is heavily influenced by topic familiarity. You can expect that the student will not perform as successfully when reading selections on unfamiliar topics. For example, Rosemary attained a strong third-grade level when reading about a birthday party. She did less well when reading an expository third-grade selection about the procedure of carding and spinning wool. Similarly, students tend to do better when reading stories or narratives than when reading textbooks or other expository materials. For these reasons, you cannot expect that a score derived from a narrative on a familiar topic will carry over to all text. I realize this complicates the matter, but a student may have multiple reading levels depending on what was read. Caldwell and Leslie (2004) found that good eighth-grade students did well when reading narrative text. They were less successful in social studies text and demonstrated very poor performance in science text. Narrative selections on familiar topics will probably represent your student's highest reading level. Of course there is a caveat attached to this. You should not assume that this narrative level will transfer to science and social studies. It probably will not.

How can you tell whether a passage is about a familiar topic? Preprimer, primer, first-grade, and second-grade selections tend to be written on topics familiar to that age group. This is true of published IRIs as well as textbooks written for younger students. By third grade, however, more and more unfamiliar topics are introduced to students. Many IRIs suggest various prereading procedures, such as asking a student to define key concepts or to predict from the title what the selection will be about. Sometimes the easiest way is simply to ask the student what he or she knows about the topic. When asked what she knew about sheep and wool, Rosemary responded, "Not very much. I know a sheep is an animal, and I think wool goes into a sweater." Often a teacher or coach will know a student so well that it will be easy to select a passage on a familiar topic.

The CCSS do not address the issue of prior knowledge. They focus on a student's ability to engage in close reading of all text, both familiar and unfamiliar. They expect readers to use the text for answers. In a way, we may have overemphasized prior knowledge. Teachers spend quite a bit of time preparing students to read a specific text. They prepare advance organizers and engage in a variety of procedures for increasing students' knowledge of the text topic prior to reading. It is difficult to quarrel with this procedure. However, what happens when the student meets unfamiliar topics in college textbooks and/or workplace manuals? There will be no one to prepare them for this unfamiliar content. There will be no one to provide information that will facilitate understanding of unfamiliar text. What the Standards seem to suggest is that teachers should guide students on how best to deal with unfamiliar text; they should not provide this information for them. The authors of the Standards' Appendix A (CCSSI, 2010) state that current standards and curricula have not done enough to foster independent reading of complex texts.

Length of Passage

If you are using a published IRI, the length of the passage is not an issue. However, if you are selecting a passage from a trade book or a basal reading textbook, you need to be conscious of how long it is. As always, classrooms are busy places, and you will not have unlimited time for individual assessment! It is probably better to choose only part of a selection for the IRI process instead of the entire selection. How much should you select? A long passage requires more administration time, and some students are threatened by having to read lengthy selections on their own. On the other hand, too short a selection does not provide enough evidence to make valid instructional decisions. The accompanying box suggests guidelines for selecting passages of appropriate length. These are not

GUIDELINES FOR PASSAGE LENGTH

Preprimer level: 40–60 words

Primer level: 60–100 words

First-grade level: 100–200 words

Second-grade level: 200–300 words

Third-grade level and above: 300–400 words

rigid guidelines. Remember that the IRI process is an informal procedure, and you are free to adapt it to your own needs.

Materials and Preparations for the IRI Process

You will need a student copy of the selection and a copy for you to record word identification errors and answers to comprehension questions. If you are using a published IRI, examiner copies are provided for you to duplicate. If you are using your own selection, you will need to duplicate the student's copy. Published IRIs provide questions for you to ask, with space for you to record the student's answers. If you are using your own selection, you should write or select the questions beforehand.

Many teachers and coaches like to record IRI sessions, so they can go back and verify their marking of students' errors and answers to questions. I have used the IRI process many times, and I still find that this method is helpful. Does this make a student nervous? An explanation that you are recording because you can't remember everything often helps to reduce any concern on the part of the student. If you place the recorder off to one side, students quickly forget about it.

Where should you test a student? Obviously a quiet place is most desirable. Noise can be distracting to both you and the student. Many teachers and coaches test students at the back of a classroom while the other students are engaged in relatively quiet activities. How long does the process take? This varies quite a bit from student to student, depending on your purpose for using the IRI process. If you are using the process to determine whether a student can read a specific text, it probably won't take too long. If you are attempting to find the student's highest reading level, it will take longer. Sometimes you only need to administer one or two passages in order to find that level. Sometimes you will have to administer more. The nice thing about the IRI process is that you can adapt it to your needs. There is no reason why you can't stretch the process over several short sessions. In fact, for some students, that might be most desirable.

Using the IRI Process to Identify Good Reader Behaviors and Areas of Weakness

Fluency

As noted in Chapter 2, good readers read fluently—that is, accurately, quickly, and expressively. A teacher or coach who asks a student to read orally presents a wonderful opportunity for evaluating the presence or absence of fluency. Students who are not fluent are choppy readers. They pause often, repeat words, and stumble over them. They read in a monotone and use little expression. Other students race through the text, ignoring punctuation marks and sentence breaks. Their goal seems to be to complete the reading as soon as possible. You can judge the presence or absence of fluency simply by listening to a student read orally. You will know a fluent reader when you hear one! Another opportunity offered by the IRI process to evaluate fluency is to determine reading rate as measured by words per minute. Determining rate of reading is discussed in Chapter 8.

Retelling

Some published IRIs ask a student to retell the contents of the selection before answering questions. They generally provide scoring grids of some sort, where the examiner marks the ideas that the student recalled. You can use this option with any passage. After the student has finished reading either orally or silently, ask the student to tell you all that he or she can remember. Underline on your copy the parts that the student remembered. If you have recorded the session, you can listen to the retelling to verify your initial impressions. How should you evaluate a retelling? You can do this by asking yourself several questions about the retelling. Was it complete? In other words, did the student remember the important ideas? You can't expect a student to remember everything, but he or she should be able to recall the main points. In the case of narratives, the student should remember the main character, the problem, and how the problem was resolved. In the case of expository text, the student should remember the main ideas and a few supporting details.

A retelling can suggest the presence of good reader behaviors. For example, good readers determine what is important in the text; they summarize and reorganize ideas in the text; and they make inferences and predictions. The focus of Standard 2 is summarization. Usually a retelling does not add a lot of time to the IRI process. A retelling is certainly more authentic than answering questions because it represents what people actually do when they read. Using simple checklists, such as the ones provided on page 90, to evaluate retelling helps to remind you what you are looking for.

Retelling Checklist for Narrative Text

_____ Identified main character (or characters)

_____ Identified the character's problem

_____ Identified the setting

_____ Described the resolution

_____ Included steps for arriving at the resolution

_____ Made inferences

_____ Retold sequentially

_____ Retold accurately

_____ Offered personal reaction

From _Reading Assessment, Third Edition: A Primer for Teachers in the Common Core Era_ by JoAnne Schudt Caldwell. Copyright 2014 by The Guilford Press. Permission to photocopy this form is granted to purchasers of this book for personal use only (see copyright page for details).

Retelling Checklist for Expository Text

_____ Identified main ideas

_____ Identified supporting details

_____ Made inferences

_____ Retold sequentially

_____ Retold accurately

_____ Offered personal reaction

From _Reading Assessment, Third Edition: A Primer for Teachers in the Common Core Era_ by JoAnne Schudt Caldwell. Copyright 2014 by The Guilford Press. Permission to photocopy this form is granted to purchasers of this book for personal use only (see copyright page for details).

Look-Backs

In many published IRIs, the student is expected to answer the comprehension questions without looking back in the text. However, for students who are in third grade or above, this assumption might underestimate their comprehension ability. Think about why a student might not be able to answer a question. Perhaps the student did not comprehend during reading. On the other hand, perhaps the student comprehended but then forgot what he or she read. Using look-backs can help you distinguish between the two. If a student does not know an answer or provides an incorrect one, ask him or her to look back in the text to locate the missing information. If a student can do this, you can assume that the initial error was due to forgetting, not lack of comprehension. However, if the student is unsuccessful in looking back, the problem is probably lack of comprehension. Good readers use look-backs most of the time. In particular, look-backs reflect the good reader behavior of monitoring comprehension and repairing comprehension breakdowns. Rarely are people expected to read something once and then answer questions without access to the text. Even on standardized tests, students are allowed to look back in paragraphs while they choose their answers. The Common Core standards focus on the student using the text in order to summarize, support and draw inferences, analyze text, determine word meaning, and identify and evaluate arguments in the text. To be successful in this process, a reader must reread probably multiple times. For this reason, I suggest that you employ look-backs as a regular part of the IRI process.

Using the IRI Process to Determine Progress

In order to determine whether a student has made progress, you need a starting point. You need to know the student's beginning level so you can compare this with the student's level at a later time. Many districts are designing intervention programs for students who are having difficulties in reading as part of the RTI initiative. The IRI process can be used for an analysis of reading status prior to an intervention program and of gains made following the program. The IRI process can also be used by a classroom teacher to measure growth throughout the school year. Several studies suggest that the IRI process is sensitive to both immediate and long-term change.

You can use the IRI process in two ways to measure student growth. One way is to administer the same passage for the pre- and postintervention assessment. The teacher or tutor should find the student's highest instructional level and then readminister the same passage later. A second option is to use two different passages that are as similar as possible. The passages should be at the same readability level, have the same structure (narrative or expository), and be of the same level of familiarity.

Some school districts use the IRI process to measure individual growth at the beginning of the year, at the midpoint, and at the end. Admittedly, this takes a lot of time on the part of classroom teachers, but the benefits are well worth it. Some schools use creative ways to find time for the IRI process. For example, combining two classrooms for a project of some sort frees one teacher to work with individual students. Some districts have trained parents or aides to administer the passages and ask the questions. In one school, university undergraduates in a reading practicum course administered the IRI process to students.

Like present classroom textbooks, published IRIs are not aligned with the CCSS. They ask questions that focus on literal aspects of the text. They also include inference questions but the quality and depth of these are suspect (Applegate, Quinn, & Applegate, 2001). If you are using a published inventory, you have to carefully examine the questions to determine their alignment to the Standards and you may have to create your own questions. Forming questions is discussed in Chapter 10.

Group Administration of the IRI Process

The IRI process is primarily used with individuals; however, it can be adapted for group use. A teacher or coach will not find it as sensitive a process when employed with groups, but it can provide information about students' probable reading levels.

Jeanne, an enterprising fourth-grade teacher with a large class, knew that she would have to find some sort of shortcut in order to evaluate the progress of all her students. She did not have an aide, and there were few parent volunteers in her classroom. Also, there was no support system in the school to help her with the IRI process. She reasoned that if students could silently read a passage and successfully answer questions on their own, she could assume that they were reading at an instructional level. Accordingly, in September, Jeanne duplicated a passage at the fourth-grade level and a list of questions for the entire class. She asked her students to read the passage silently, look back to find answers to the questions, and write down their answers. Jeanne scored the questions, and a few days later she repeated the process. However, some children were given higher-level passages, and some were asked to read an easier passage. She continued in this way until she had determined the highest instructional level for each child at the beginning of the school year.

Jeanne did not totally abandon working with individuals. She spent some time with the children who did not succeed with the fourth-grade passage, asking them to read orally so she could evaluate their word identification accuracy and fluency. Jeanne repeated this process in January and at the end of the school year. Each time, she compared an individual child's levels and noted the amount of growth. Parents were very appreciative of her efforts, and the students were proud of how much they had grown. This group adaptation of the IRI process considerably lessened the amount of time Jeanne had to spend with single students. She admitted that she would have preferred to spend individual time with each student, but in the absence of any school support, she did the best she could. She felt that the results presented a valid picture of her students' progress across a school year.

Another group adaptation involves oral reading. Linda chose a second-grade selection and divided it into five relatively equal parts. She counted the number of words in each part. Linda then assembled a group of five second graders and told them that they would be taking turns reading orally and answering questions. Each child read in turn, and Linda recorded errors on her copy of the text. After each child finished reading his or her part, Linda asked two or three questions to evaluate comprehension and then moved on to the next child. Linda used the number of errors that each child made to assign a probable reading level for word identification accuracy. Linda knew that this was perhaps a poor substitute for an individual IRI process assessment, but she felt it was better than nothing. She repeated this process regularly throughout the school year, using different levels of text.

Summary

• The IRI process is an individual assessment that allows a teacher or coach to determine reading level, to identify good reader behaviors and areas of weakness, and to determine individual progress.

• An IRI is a published instrument containing passages at different grade levels.

• The IRI process provides two possible scores: a score for word identification accuracy and a score for comprehension. The scores are then used to determine a student's independent, instructional, and frustration reading levels.

• Word identification accuracy scores are determined by counting the number of oral reading errors or miscues that a student makes while reading orally. Comprehension scores are determined by counting the number of questions that are answered correctly.

• Students may have different levels for word identification accuracy and comprehension on the same passage. The teacher or coach should assign a total passage level by choosing the lower of the two.

• The IRI process can be used to identify several good reader behaviors: reading fluently and expressively, determining what is important in the text, summarizing ideas in the text, making inferences and predictions, and monitoring comprehension. Fluency evaluation, answering questions, retelling, and look-backs are ways of assessing these behaviors.

• The IRI process can be used to determine student progress at different points in time. The teacher or coach compares levels prior to instruction with levels attained after instruction.

• The IRI process can be used to determine if a student is able to read grade-level text. It is an assessment that can determine a student's placement and progress in RTI.

• The IRI process can be used to assess the CCSS. However, until published informal reading inventories are aligned to the Standards, the teacher will have to write or select questions that address the Standards.

• The IRI process can be amended for group administration; however, this provides a less sensitive measure of student ability.

Activities for Developing Understanding

• Use Appendices 5.2 and 5.3 for practice in using the IRI process with a selection from a basal reader (Appendix 5.2) and with a published IRI (Appendix 5.3).

• Use a published IRI listed in Appendix 5.1 and administer the passages to find a student's highest instructional level. Score oral reading, comprehension, and retelling according to the IRI guidelines.

Questions to Ask about Published IRIs

Published IRIs are very similar in some ways. They all contain graded passages, a process for recording oral reading errors, a system for assessing reading rate, and questions for evaluating comprehension. However, they also differ, and each one has some special items that distinguish it from other inventories. They may differ in the type and number of passages that are included. They may include other assessments such as tests of phonics and sight-word reading. They may have a variety of instructional options. The teacher or coach should examine what is included in a particular IRI and ask specific questions in order to determine which one best fits his or her needs.

• To what extent was this inventory piloted? For example, are the passages at each specific level of equal difficulty? Was the instrument administered to students of various ages and were passages and/or questions adjusted accordingly? You want an informal instrument that is as valid and reliable as it can possibly be. Extensive and specific piloting ensures this outcome.

• What levels does this inventory address? Do the levels that are assessed meet your needs?

• What is the nature of the passages? Do they include both narrative and expository text? How many passages are present at each level? Multiple passages allow you to assess progress over time.

• What is the source of the passages? Were they written by the authors? Were they taken from representative textbooks? How close are they to what your students meet during their reading and content-area instruction?

• What types of questions are asked? Question types can suggest how the authors define comprehension. Are questions primarily literal in nature or do they ask students to draw and/or justify inferences?

• What added assessments are present such as word lists, phonics tests, retelling assessments, and so on? Are these something that you yourself would use?

• How much time will it take you to learn how to administer and score the instrument? Of course it will take time, but it helps to estimate what is involved just in the basic scoring (oral reading errors, fluency, and comprehension), not necessarily the scoring of added features.

• Skim the directions. Are they clearly stated or do you have to reread them several times?

• To what extent does the inventory reflect the Standards? Is there any match between the questions asked and the nine standards? Do questions address text structure, analysis, recognition of central idea, author point of view, and so on?

The following is a list of current IRIs that are described on their publisher websites as currently in print. The list is not all-inclusive. New editions appear frequently. However, older IRIs that have not been updated can be located on *Amazon.com*.

Analytical Reading Inventory
Woods, M. L. J., & Moe, A. J. (2011)
Pearson

Bader Reading and Language Inventory
Bader, L. A., & Pearce, D. L. (2013)
Pearson

Basic Reading Inventory
Johns, J. L., & Elish-Piper, L. (2012)
Kendall/Hunt

Classroom Reading Inventory
Wheelock, W. H., Canpbell, C. J., &
Silvaroli, N. J. (2011)
McGraw-Hill

Ekwall/Shanker Reading Inventory
Shanker, J. L., & Cockrum, W.A. (2014)
Pearson

Qualitative Reading Inventory 5
Leslie, L., & Caldwell, J. (2011)
Pearson

Practice in Scoring Word Identification Accuracy and Comprehension Using the IRI Process

Donny read the following second-grade selection from an IRI.[*] Two copies of this selection have been provided. On the first copy, score Donny's performance using checkmarks. Then, on the second copy, score his performance using the traditional coding system. Decide whether Donny's word identification accuracy suggests an independent, instructional, or frustration level for second-grade material. After you have finished, compare your scoring to mine. Then go on to evaluate Donny's retelling. Compare your evaluation to mine.

Donny's Reading

Marva Finds a Friend

One rainy day Marvin hard a funny sound.

He looks out the window and saw a little cat with white fur.

It was white and it looked hungry.

Marvin went out and picked up the cat.

They then he she brings it in.

She and her mother took a soft yool and they dry it.

Mother gives the cat some fancy feast.

And the cat eats it all!

Marva said, "I will name this cat Boots. I will take care of it."

"I hope you don't belong to anyone," Marva said.

"No, Marva, this cat might belong to someone," her mother said. Marva felt bad.

She said to Boots, "But I want you to be my cat."

That night Marva's mother looked at the news.

She saw an aid that said, "Lost. Gray cat with white feet. Call 376-2007."

Marva starts to cry.

"But I want to have Boots," she said.

"It's not right, Marva, we have to call," said her mother.

Marva knows her mother is right.

The next day a woman and a girl come to her home.

---

[*] The selection "Marva Finds a Friend" is from Leslie, L., & Caldwell, J. S. (2011). *Qualitative Reading Inventory 5* (pp. 177–179). Boston: Pearson. Copyright 2011 by Pearson. Reprinted by permission.

The girl saw Boots and she cried, "That's my cat, Boots!"

"But I named her Boots too," Marva said.

The girl took Boots in her arms.

She thanks Marva and her mother for taking care of the cat.

Then she said, "I live on the next street.

Why don't you come over and play with me and Boots?"

Marva was mad to give up Boots, but she was happy that she did make a new friend.

Marva's mother now know what to get Marva for her birthday!

Your Recording Using Checkmarks

Marva Finds a Friend

One rainy day Marva heard a funny sound.

She looked out the window and saw a little gray cat with white feet.

It was wet and it looked hungry.

Marva went out and picked up the cat.

Then she brought it inside.

She and her mother took a soft towel and dried it.

Mother gave the cat some food.

And the cat ate it all up!

Marva said, "I will name this cat Boots. I will take care of it."

"I hope you don't belong to anyone," Marva said.

"Now, Marva, this cat may belong to somebody," her mother said. Marva felt sad.

She said to Boots, "But I want you to be my cat."

That night Marva's mother looked in the newspaper.

She saw an ad that read, "Lost. Gray cat with white feet. Call 376-2007."

Marva started to cry.

"But I want to keep Boots," she said.

"It's not right, Marva, we have to call," said her mother.

Marva knew her mother was right.

The next day a woman and a girl Marva's age came to the house.

When the girl saw Boots she cried, "That's my cat, Boots!"

"But I called her Boots too," Marva said.

The girl took Boots in her arms.

She thanked Marva and her mother for taking care of Boots.

Then she said, "I live on the next street. Why don't you come over tomorrow and play with me and Boots?"

Marva was sad to give up Boots, but she was happy that she'd made a new friend.

Marva's mother now knew what to get Marva for her birthday!

264 Words

Number of errors: _____

Subtract the number of errors from 264: _____

Divide this number by 264 to arrive at a percentage for word identification accuracy: _____

Level (circle one):   Independent,   Instructional,   Frustration

Your Recording Using the Traditional Coding System

Marva Finds a Friend

One rainy day Marva heard a funny sound.
    She looked out the window and saw a little gray cat with white feet.
    It was wet and it looked hungry.
    Marva went out and picked up the cat.
    Then she brought it inside.
    She and her mother took a soft towel and dried it.
    Mother gave the cat some food.
    And the cat ate it all up!
    Marva said, "I will name this cat Boots. I will take care of it."
    "I hope you don't belong to anyone," Marva said.
    "Now, Marva, this cat may belong to somebody," her mother said. Marva felt sad.
    She said to Boots, "But I want you to be my cat."
    That night Marva's mother looked in the newspaper.
    She saw an ad that read, "Lost. Gray cat with white feet. Call 376-2007."
    Marva started to cry.
    "But I want to keep Boots," she said.
    "It's not right, Marva, we have to call," said her mother.
    Marva knew her mother was right.
    The next day a woman and a girl Marva's age came to the house.
    When the girl saw Boots she cried, "That's my cat, Boots!"
    "But I called her Boots too," Marva said.
    The girl took Boots in her arms.

She thanked Marva and her mother for taking care of Boots.

Then she said, "I live on the next street. Why don't you come over tomorrow and play with me and Boots?"

Marva was sad to give up Boots, but she was happy that she'd made a new friend.

Marva's mother now knew what to get Marva for her birthday!

264 Words

Number of errors: _____

Subtract the number of errors from 264: _____

Divide this number by 264 to arrive at a percentage for word identification accuracy: _____

Level (circle one):   Independent,   Instructional,   Frustration

My Recording Using Checkmarks

Marva Finds a Friend

One rainy day Marva heard a funny sound.

She looked out the window and saw a little gray cat with white feet.

It was wet and it looked hungry.

Marva went out and picked up the cat.

Then she brought it inside.

She and her mother took a soft towel and dried it.

Mother gave the cat some food.

And the cat ate it all up!

Marva said, "I will name this cat Boots. I will take care of it."

"I hope you don't belong to anyone," Marva said.

"Now, Marva, this cat may belong to somebody," her mother said. Marva felt sad.

She said to Boots, "But I want you to be my cat."

That night Marva's mother looked in the newspaper.

She saw an ad that read, "Lost. Gray cat with white feet. Call 376-2007."

Marva started to cry.

"But I want to keep Boots," she said.

"It's not right, Marva, we have to call," said her mother.

Marva knew her mother was right.

The next day a woman and a girl Marva's age came to the house.

When the girl saw Boots she cried, "That's my cat, Boots!"

"But I called her Boots too," Marva said.

The girl took Boots in her arms.

She thanked Marva and her mother for taking care of Boots.

Then she said, "I live on the next street. Why don't you come over tomorrow and play with me and Boots?"

Marva was sad to give up Boots, but she was happy that she'd made a new friend.

Marva's mother now knew what to get Marva for her birthday!

264 Words

Number of errors: _45_

Subtract the number of errors from 264: _219_

Divide this number by 264 to arrive at a percentage for word identification accuracy: _83_

Level (circle one):   Independent,   Instructional,   (Frustration)

My Recording Using the Traditional Coding System

Marva Finds a Friend

Marvin hard
One rainy day Marva heard a funny sound.

He looks
She looked out the window and saw a little (gray) cat with white *fur* feet.

white
It was wet and it looked hungry.

Marvin
Marva went out and picked up the cat.

When^c he^c
Then she brought it inside.

tool   *they dry*
She and her mother took a soft towel and dried it.

gives   *fancy feast*
Mother gave the cat some food.

eats
And the cat ate it all (up!)

Marva said, "I will name this cat Boots. I will take care of it."

"I hope you don't belong to anyone," Marva said.

No *might* *someone*
"Now, Marva, this cat may belong to somebody," her mother said. Marva
had
felt sad.

She said to Boots, "But I want you to be my cat."

at *news*
That night Marva's mother looked in the newspaper.

said
She saw an ad that read, "Lost. Gray cat with white feet. Call 376-2007."

starts
Marva started to cry.

have
"But I want to keep Boots," she said.

"It's not right, Marva, we have to call," said her mother.

knows *is*
Marva knew her mother was right.

come *her home*
The next day a woman and a girl (Marva's age) came to the house.

and
(When) the girl saw Boots she cried, "That's my cat, Boots!"

named
"But I called her Boots too," Marva said.

The girl took Boots in her arms.

thanks *the cat*
She thanked Marva and her mother for taking care of Boots.

Then she said, "I live on the next street. Why don't you come over (tomorrow)
and play with me and Boots?"

mad
Marva was sad to give up Boots, but she was happy that she'd made a new
friend.

knows
Marva's mother now knew what to get Marva for her birthday!

264 Words

Number of errors: _45_

Subtract the number of errors from 264: _219_

Divide this number by 264 to arrive at a percentage for word identification accuracy: _83_

Level (circle one):   Independent,   Instructional,   (Frustration)

Your Evaluation of Donny's Retelling

Retelling Checklist for Narrative Text

_____ Identified main character (or characters)

_____ Identified the character's problem

_____ Identified the setting

_____ Described the resolution

_____ Included steps for arriving at the resolution

_____ Made inferences

_____ Retold sequentially

_____ Retold accurately

_____ Offered personal reaction

Evaluating Retelling

Use the retelling guidelines to evaluate Donny's retelling. Then compare your evaluation to mine.

Donny's Retelling

"Marva found this cat. It was wet and hungry and she wanted to keep it. She called it Boots. But it belonged to someone else, and the girl came and took it away and asked Marva to play with her and the cat and Marva was mad. And that's all I remember."

My Evaluation of Donny's Retelling

Retelling Checklist for Narrative Text

✓ Identified main character (or characters)   *Marva and the girl*

✓ Identified the character's problem   *Marva wanted to keep the cat.*

___ Identified the setting

✓ Described the resolution   *The girl took the cat.*

___ Included steps for arriving at the resolution

___ Made inferences   *Inferred Marva was mad, which was inaccurate*

✓ Retold sequentially

✓ Retold accurately   *Except for Marva being mad*

___ Offered personal reaction

Practice in Scoring Word Recognition Accuracy and Comprehension Using a Published IRI

Paul read the following fourth-grade selection from a published IRI.[*] His errors are recorded, and his retelling and answers to the questions are included. Count his errors and determine his level for word identification accuracy. Score his answers to the questions and determine his level for comprehension. Then use the Retelling Checklist and evaluate his retelling. What good reader behaviors did you note? Then compare your scoring and evaluation to mine.

This IRI allows for two word identification accuracy scores: one for all errors (called Total Accuracy) and one only for errors that change meaning (called Total Acceptability). I placed an X in the margin for errors that I did not believe changed meaning. Then I figured out both scores.

You will note that this IRI evaluates topic familiarity before the student reads the passage by asking several questions about the concepts in the passage. Answers are scored on a 3-point scale. Paul's answers suggested familiarity with the topic of the passage.

You will also note that there is a place for the teacher or coach to record the student's performance following a look-back. When Paul was asked to look back in the text for an answer, I recorded this task by writing in *Look-Back*.

---

[*]The scored selection and checklists (except for the Retelling Checklist) are adapted from Leslie, L., & Caldwell, J. S. (2011, pp. 268–270). *Qualitative Reading Inventory 5*. Boston: Pearson. Copyright 2011 by Pearson. Adapted by permission. As noted within the Appendix, the "Johnny Appleseed" selection itself is from Armbruster, B. B., Mitsakos, C. L., & Rogers, V. R. (1986). *America's history* (p. 204). Lexington, MA: Ginn. Copyright 1986 by Ginn. Reprinted by permission of the publisher.

Your Scoring of Paul

Level: Four

Narrative

Concept Questions:

Who was Johnny Appleseed?

he went west and planted apple trees

(3-2-1-0)

Why do people plant fruit trees in certain places?

they look good there or they grow best there

(3-2-1-0)

Why do people plant apple trees?

they like apples — you get food

(3-2-1-0)

What does "making apple cider" mean to you?

just making it from apples

(3-2-1-0)

Score: 10 /12 = 83 %

✓ FAM _____ UNFAM

Prediction:

_____

_____

Johnny Appleseed

John Chapman was born in 1774 and grew up in Massachusetts. He became a farmer and learned (how) to grow different kinds of crops and trees. John especially liked to grow and eat apples. Many people were moving west at that time. They were heading for Ohio and Pennsylvania. John knew that apples were a good food for settlers to have. Apple trees were strong and easy to grow. Apples could be eaten raw and they could be cooked in many ways. They could also be dried for later use. So in 1797, John decided to go west. He wanted to plant apple trees for people who would build their (new) homes there.

John first gathered bags of apple seeds. He got many of his seeds from farmers who squeezed apples to make a drink called cider. Then, in the spring, he left for the western frontier. He planted seeds as he went along. Also, he gave them to people who knew how (valuable) apple trees were.

John walked (many) miles in all kinds of weather. He had to cross dangerous rivers and find his way through strange forests. Often he was hungry, cold, and wet. Sometimes he had to hide from unfriendly Indians. His clothes became ragged and torn. He used a sack for a shirt, and he cut out holes for the arms. He wore no shoes. But he never gave up. He guarded his precious seeds and carefully planted them where they had the best chance of growing into (strong) trees.

Level: Four

John's <u>fame</u> spread. He was nicknamed Johnny Appleseed. New <u>settlers</u> welcomed him and ~~gratefully~~ *grat ply* accepted a gift of apple seeds. Many ~~legends~~ *leg ons* grew up about Johnny Appleseed that were not (always) true. However, one thing is true. Thanks to Johnny Appleseed, apple trees now grow in parts of America where they (once) never did. (308 words)

From *America's History* by B. B. Armbruster, C. L. Mitsakos, and V. R. Rogers (1986). Copyright © 1986 by Ginn. Reprinted by permission of the publisher.

Number of Total Miscues
(Total Accuracy): _____

Number of Meaning-Change Miscues
(Total Acceptability): _____

Total Accuracy		Total Acceptability
0–7 miscues ____ Independent	____	0–7 miscues
8–32 miscues ____ Instructional	____	8–16 miscues
32+ miscues ____ Frustration	____	17+ miscues

Rate: 308 × 60 = 18,480 / *204* seconds = _91_ WPM

Retelling Scoring Sheet for Johnny Appleseed

Setting/Background
____ John Chapman was born
____ in 1774.
____ He became a farmer
____ and grew crops.
____ John liked
____ to grow

____ and eat apples.
____ People were moving west.
____ Apples were a good food
____ for settlers to have.

Goal
____ John decided
____ to go west.
____ He wanted
____ to plant apple trees.

Events
____ John got many seeds
____ from farmers
____ who squeezed apples
____ to make a drink
____ called cider.
____ He left
____ for the frontier.
____ He planted seeds
____ as he went along.
____ He gave them away.
____ John walked miles.
____ He crossed rivers
____ and went through forests.
____ He was hungry
____ and wet.
____ He had to hide
____ from Indians
____ unfriendly Indians.
____ His clothes were torn.
____ He used a sack
____ for a shirt
____ and he cut out holes
____ for the arms.
____ He wore no shoes.

Resolution
____ John's fame spread.
____ He was nicknamed
____ Johnny Appleseed.
____ Settlers accepted seeds
____ gratefully.
____ Thanks to Johnny Appleseed,
____ apple trees grow

It's about this guy who went west. He liked to eat apples so he planted them. He had problems like he was hungry and he crossed rivers and hid from Indians and he planted seeds as he went. He went across forests and he use sacks for shirts and he got famous.

Level: Four

____ in many parts
____ of America.

Other ideas recalled, including inferences:

Questions for Johnny Appleseed

1. What was John Chapman's main goal?
   Implicit: to plant apple trees across the country

   plant a lot of apple
   trees all over the west

2. Why did John choose apples to plant instead of some other fruit?
   Implicit: the trees were easy to grow; the fruit could be used in a lot of ways; he especially liked apples

   he liked apples

3. Where did John get most of his seeds?
   Explicit: from farmers or from people who made cider

   farmers

4. Why would John be able to get so many seeds from cider makers?
   Implicit: cider is a drink and you don't drink seeds; apples have a lot of seeds and you don't use seeds in cider

   there aren't seeds in
   cider

5. How do we know that John cared about planting apple trees?
   Implicit: he suffered hardships; he guarded the apple seeds carefully

6. How did John get to the many places he visited?
   Explicit: he walked

   walked

7. Name one hardship John suffered.
   Explicit: being hungry, cold, wet, lost, in danger from unfriendly Indians

   Indians who were unfriendly —
   he was cold — he didn't
   have clothes

8. Why should we thank Johnny Appleseed?
   Explicit: apple trees now grow in parts of America where they once never did

   why would we want to
   thank him — he's dead

Without Look-Backs

Number Correct Explicit: ____

Number Correct Implicit: ____

      Total: ____

    ____ Independent: 8 correct

    ____ Instructional: 6–7 correct

    ____ Frustration: 0–5 correct

With Look-Backs

Number Correct Explicit: ____

Number Correct Implicit: ____

      Total: ____

    ____ Independent: 8 correct

    ____ Instructional: 6–7 correct

    ____ Frustration: 0–5 correct

Retelling Checklist for Narrative Text

____ Identified main character (or characters)

____ Identified the character's problem

____ Identified the setting

____ Described the resolution

____ Included steps for arriving at the resolution

____ Made inferences

____ Retold sequentially

____ Retold accurately

____ Offered personal reaction

My Scoring of Paul

Level: Four

Narrative

Concept Questions:

Who was Johnny Appleseed?

he went west and planted apple trees

(③-2-1-0)

Why do people plant fruit trees in certain places?

they look good there or they grow best there

(③-2-1-0)

Why do people plant apple trees?

they like apples — you get food

(③-2-1-0)

What does "making apple cider" mean to you?

just making it from apples

(3-2-①-0)

Score: ___10___ /12 = ___83___ %

✓ FAM _____ UNFAM

Prediction:

Johnny Appleseed

John Chapman was born in 1774 and grew up in Massachusetts. He became a farmer and X learned (how) to grow different kinds of crops

and trees. John especially liked to grow and eat *espickly* apples. Many people were moving west at that *the* X time. They were heading for Ohio and Pennsylvania. John knew that apples were a good food for settlers *sett ling ers* to have. Apple trees were strong and easy to grow. Apples could be eaten raw and they could be cooked in many ways. They could also be dried *drod* for later use. So in 1797, John decided to go west. He wanted to plant apple trees for people who would build *were building* XX their (new) homes there. X

John first gathered *gattered* bags of apple seeds. He got many of his seeds from farmers who squeezed *squashed* apples to make a drink called cider. X

Then, in the spring, he left for the western frontier *front*. He planted seeds as he went along. Also, he gave them to people who knew how (valuable) apple trees were.

John walked (many) miles in all kinds of X weather. He had to cross dangerous *dan grous* rivers and X find his way through strange forests. Often he was hungry, cold, and wet. Sometimes he had to hide from *some* unfriendly Indians. His clothes X became ragged *raggy* and torn. He used a sack for a shirt, and he cut out holes for the arms. He wore no shoes. But he never gave up. He guarded *garted* his precious *pregnant* seeds and carefully planted *put* them where they had the best chance X of growing into (strong) trees. X

Level: Four

John's fame spread. He was nicknamed Johnny Appleseed. New settlers welcomed him and gratefully *grat ply* accepted a gift of apple seeds. Many legends *leg ons* grew up about Johnny Appleseed that were not (always) true. How-X ever, one thing is true. Thanks to Johnny Appleseed, apple trees now grow in parts of America where they (once) never did. (308 X words)

From *America's History* by B. B. Armbruster, C. L. Mitsakos, and V. R. Rogers (1986). Copyright © 1986 by Ginn. Reprinted by permission of the publisher.

Number of Total Miscues
(Total Accuracy): _____24_____

Number of Meaning-Change Miscues
(Total Acceptability): _____11_____

Total Accuracy		Total Acceptability	
0–7 miscues ____ Independent		____ 0–7 miscues	
8–32 miscues _24_ Instructional		_11_ 8–16 miscues	
32+ miscues ____ Frustration		____ 17+ miscues	

Rate: 308 × 60 = 18,480/*204* seconds = _91_ WPM

Retelling Scoring Sheet for Johnny Appleseed

Setting/Background

____ John Chapman was born
____ in 1774.
____ He became a farmer
____ and grew crops.
✓ John liked
____ to grow

✓ and eat apples.
____ People were moving west.
____ Apples were a good food
____ for settlers to have.

Goal

____ John decided
✓ to go west.
____ He wanted
____ to plant apple trees.

Events

____ John got many seeds
____ from farmers
____ who squeezed apples
____ to make a drink
____ called cider.
____ He left
____ for the frontier.
✓ He planted seeds
____ as he went along.
____ He gave them away.
____ John walked miles.
✓ He crossed rivers
✓ and went through forests.
✓ He was hungry
____ and wet.
✓ He had to hide
✓ from Indians
____ unfriendly Indians.
____ His clothes were torn.
✓ He used a sack
✓ for a shirt
____ and he cut out holes
____ for the arms.
____ He wore no shoes.

Resolution

✓ John's fame spread.
____ He was nicknamed
____ Johnny Appleseed.
____ Settlers accepted seeds
____ gratefully.
____ Thanks to Johnny Appleseed,
____ apple trees grow

It's about this guy who went west. He liked to eat apples so he planted them. He had problems like he was hungry and he crossed rivers and hid from Indians and he planted seeds as he went. He went across forests and he use sacks for shirts and he got famous.

Level: Four

___ in many parts
___ of America.

Other ideas recalled, including inferences:

Questions for Johnny Appleseed

C 1. What was John Chapman's main goal?
   Implicit: to plant apple trees across the
   country

   *plant a lot of apple
   trees all over the west*

C 2. Why did John choose apples to plant instead of some other fruit?
   Implicit: the trees were easy to grow; the
   fruit could be used in a lot of ways; he especially liked apples

   he liked apples

C 3. Where did John get most of his seeds?
   Explicit: from farmers or from people who
   made cider

   farmers

C 4. Why would John be able to get so many
   seeds from cider makers?
   Implicit: cider is a drink and you don't
   drink seeds; apples have a lot of seeds and
   you don't use seeds in cider

   *there aren't seeds in
   cider*

C 5. How do we know that John cared about
   planting apple trees?
   Implicit: he suffered hardships; he guarded
   the apple seeds carefully

   *he went through a lot — he
   didn't give up*

C 6. How did John get to the many places he
   visited?
   Explicit: he walked

   walked

C 7. Name one hardship John suffered.
   Explicit: being hungry, cold, wet, lost, in
   danger from unfriendly Indians

   *Indians who were unfriendly —
   he was cold — he didn't
   have clothes*

✓ 8. Why should we thank Johnny Appleseed?
   Explicit: apple trees now grow in parts of
   America where they once never did

   *why would we want to
   thank him — he's dead*
   Look back: C

Without Look-Backs	
Number Correct Explicit:	3
Number Correct Implicit:	4
Total:	7
___ Independent:	8 correct
✓ Instructional:	6–7 correct
___ Frustration:	0–5 correct

With Look-Backs	4
Number Correct Explicit:	4
Number Correct Implicit:	8
Total: ___	
✓ Independent:	8 correct
___ Instructional:	6–7 correct
___ Frustration:	0–5 correct

Retelling Checklist for Narrative Text

✓ Identified main character (or characters)

✓ Identified the character's problem

✓ Identified the setting

____ Described the resolution

✓ Included steps for arriving at the resolution

____ Made inferences

✓ Retold sequentially

✓ Retold accurately

____ Offered personal reaction

CHAPTER 6

Early Literacy

What Do We Need to Know about Beginning Readers?

Overview of Early Literacy

A few years ago, I ran into a friend and her young son, Steven, at a local store. Steven was happily engaged in picking out school supplies, and he had amassed a rather formidable pile of notebooks, tablets, pencils, crayons, scissors, and glue sticks. When I arrived, he was attempting to decide on a book bag to hold all his treasures. The presence of different cartoon characters and movie heroes on the bags was making this a difficult choice. When Steven finally selected his book bag, I asked him whether he was excited about school, and he solemnly assured me he was. I asked him why. Without hesitation, Steven mentioned new friends and riding the school bus as reasons for his positive anticipation. Then he exclaimed, "And I'm going to learn how to read all by myself! I won't have to ask

Mom or Jessie [his sister] to read to me. I can't wait!" Like Steven, many people think that learning to read begins in school, but this represents a limited concept of early literacy (or what has come to be called *emergent literacy*).

The development of literacy begins long before a child enters a classroom or tutoring session. It begins with the development of oral language. Spoken language and written language are much alike. They share the same sound system, the same vocabulary, and the same structure. For example, the sounds that form the spoken word *dog* are the same sounds that are represented by the letter sequence *d -o -g*. The meaning of the word *dog* is the same, whether we are talking, writing, or reading. The structure of sentences in spoken and written language remains basically the same. The spoken sentence "I saw a big dog" will be represented in print in the same way (*I saw a big dog*). It will not be twisted or altered to another form, such as *dog big saw I a*. This means that if children are to learn to read and write their language, they must first acquire that language. They must learn the sounds that stand for meaning. They must learn the underlying concepts. They must learn how to string sounds together to form words and words together to form sentences. They must learn certain language conventions, such as adding *-ed* to signify what happened in the past.

Any language represents an extremely complex system. Think about all the grammar books that have been written. Consider the size of an unabridged dictionary. These books are attempts to describe a system that children seem to learn quite effortlessly. Why and how do they do this? Children learn almost immediately that language brings rewards. It brings attention. It brings food and toys. It brings comfort and knowledge. It helps to establish and maintain relationships that can be very satisfying. Perhaps the most important thing is that language brings meaning into their world. Language allows them to describe their feelings and experiences and share them with others. Language in childhood develops through interaction with parents, caregivers, siblings, and peers. Language expands when parents and caregivers talk with a child, encourage the child's verbalizations, and use language to support problem-solving efforts (such as deciding whether to go to the zoo on Saturday or discussing what present to take to a party).

Oral language is absolutely necessary for literacy development, but it is not sufficient. There are children with adequate oral language skills who unfortunately lack a basic requirement for learning to read and write. That basic requirement is preschool literacy experiences. The amount and quality of literacy experiences in a preschooler's life will positively or negatively affect later literacy development. What do we mean by *literacy experiences*? Let's go back to Steven. Steven's home environment is filled with a wide variety of books, magazines, newspapers, and other examples of print. Steven's parents and grandparents all enjoy and value reading. Steven was given books from the very beginning of his life—sturdy books that defied destruction by chewing, bending, or tearing.

Steven also had pencils, crayons, and paper. He was encouraged to write, even if that writing looked more like scribbles. He played with alphabet blocks, magnetic letters, and computer games based on letters and sounds. He listened to songs and nursery rhymes, and he watched computer videos that visually portrayed his favorite stories. And what is probably most important, Steven's parents, grandparents, and sister read to him every day almost from the time of his birth.

"The single most important activity for building the knowledge and skills eventually required for reading appears to be reading aloud to children" (Adams, 1990, p. 46). Effective storybook reading involves the child and the reader in a conversation about the book, the characters, and the plot. The reader and the child ask questions together. They relate the book to their own lives. The reader offers information to the child and responds to the child's questions and comments. The reader draws the child out, encourages verbalization, and expands on the child's comments. Children learn a lot about their language and about literacy from storybook reading. They learn new vocabulary words and new concepts. They learn new sentence structures and new ways of saying things. They learn new language conventions, such as question words, dialogue patterns, and word endings like -er, -est, and -ly. They learn that print matches the sounds of speech, and that reading is a meaningful and enjoyable activity.

In summary, literacy development begins when oral language development begins. Literacy development is fostered by active oral language interactions with parents and caregivers. It is further supported by caregivers who value and model literacy activities, and who make literacy materials such as books and writing easily accessible (Pressley, 2006).

What Children Need to Know about Language

Engaging in oral language and participating in many and varied literacy experiences help a child to become aware of such language elements as words, syllables, and phonemes or sounds (Adams, 1990). Children must pay attention to these elements if they are to succeed as readers and writers. Some children develop this awareness on their own. Others need more structured experiences with individual sounds. It is impossible to identify and spell words without a consciousness of words as individual units composed of syllables and phonemes. Let's briefly examine each.

Word and Syllable Awareness

As proficient readers, we know that any utterance is made up of different words, and if we were asked to, we could count and keep track of the number of words in any spoken message. Of course, we probably would not comprehend very much while doing this, because when we listen, we focus on the meaning of the entire message—not the number of words it contains. However, we can count the number of spoken words because we are aware of words as separate entities. This word awareness is not readily apparent to young children. In print there are spaces between words, but in speech there are no pauses to separate one word from another. We speak in one continuous speech stream. Have you ever heard someone speaking an unfamiliar foreign language? Can you tell how many words they are saying? Probably not, because speakers do not separate words with pauses, and your ignorance of that language prevented you from distinguishing individual units of meaning. Children gradually learn to attend to individual words as they develop oral vocabulary and as they interact with print. "As children become aware of the one-by-oneness of words in print, they begin to notice and isolate words in speech" (Adams, 1990, p. 52).

A *syllable* is a speech sound that you can produce in isolation. For example, in the word *hotel* there are two syllables, and you can say each one separately: *ho* and *tel*. Awareness of syllable sounds predicts future reading success (Adams, 1990). How can you identify a syllable if you are not aware of its existence? It is much like expecting people to identify the rules of a game that they have never heard of.

Phonological Awareness

Language consists of units of sound called *phones*. Some units, like a syllable, contain several phones; some units contain only one. Phones are represented in print by letters and letter patterns. However, just as words are not separated in the speech stream, neither are phones. Many cannot even be spoken in isolation. For example, pronounce the sound represented by the letter *b*. I would guess that you said *buh*. But that is attaching the sound of the short vowel *u* to the sound of *b*. Remove *uh* and pronounce *b* without it. What did you get? Just a puff of air. Children must learn to distinguish phones as separate units if they are to match letters and sounds within syllables and words. Distinguishing phones is more difficult than becoming aware of words as separate units.

Goswami (2000) lists three types of phonological structures that are important for the development of reading: the *syllable*, the *onset–rime*, and the *phoneme*. The syllable is a unit that includes a vowel sound. Two sound units within a syllable make up an onset–rime: the sound that precedes the vowel (in *crash*, *cr* is the onset), and the vowel and the sounds that follow it (in *crash*, *ash* is the rime). A phoneme is the smallest unit of sound and is represented by a single letter. *Phonological awareness* and *phonemic awareness* are terms that are used interchangeably. However, phonological awareness is the larger category of which phonemic awareness, the awareness that words can be divided into individual sounds, is one component. I use *phonological awareness* throughout this chapter.

Phonological awareness is not the ability to hear the sounds, but the ability to perceive their separateness. It is difficult for literate adults to conceptualize phonological awareness. If I ask you how many sounds are in the word *hotel*, probably you will mentally compare the spelling of the word with the sounds and arrive at an answer. But phonological awareness is actually separate from print awareness. It is the awareness of separate sounds in words—even those words that you cannot read, write, or spell.

Let me use an analogy to describe phonological awareness. Pretend that I am sitting at a piano and you cannot see my fingers on the keys. If I play one chord and then another chord, you would be able to say whether they are alike or different. That is auditory discrimination. But could you tell me how many notes I played in each chord? If I played a short segment composed of multiple chords, could you tell me how many I played? Unless you were trained in music, I doubt that you could. Being able to say how many notes or sounds in a chord or how many chords in a line of music is analogous to phonological awareness—that is, being able to distinguish and differentiate the sounds in a spoken word.

Much research has demonstrated that a child's ability to identify and manipulate sounds is highly related to later achievement in reading and spelling (Ehri et al., 2001; National Institute of Child Health and Human Development, 2000; Ball & Blachman, 1991; Byrne & Fielding-Barnsley, 1991; Stanovich, 1988). In fact, next to alphabet knowledge, phonological awareness is the second best predictor of reading success! How is this determined? Researchers first measure phonological awareness in preschoolers. They then correlate these preschool scores with later achievement scores in reading and spelling. Preschoolers with high levels of phonological awareness demonstrate higher reading achievement at the end of first grade and into second grade. Juel (1988) followed a group of children from first grade through fourth grade and determined that poor phonological awareness was the best predictor of poor reading achievement in first grade. Moreover, a low level of phonological awareness in first grade was very predictive of reading problems in fourth grade.

What kind of tasks measure phonological awareness? *Segmentation* tests determine whether a child can break a syllable into phonemes. Children are asked to listen to a spoken one-syllable word and then tap out the number of phonemes they hear. For example, if presented with *cat*, they should tap three times. *Manipulation* tests ask a child to manipulate phonemes by saying a word without a certain phoneme. For example, the child is asked to say *cat* without the *c*. In *blending* tests, the examiner presents the child with phoneme segments (*s . . . a . . . t*) and asks the child to blend these into a word (*sat*). Some tests present three or four spoken words, and the child is asked to determine which one is different. The difference may be based on the beginnings or ends of the words. For example, if the words are *cat, cut, sat,* and *cot,* the odd word is *sat* because it represents a different beginning sound. If the words are *jump, lump, damp,* and *dark,* the odd word is *dark* as representative of a different ending sound.

Teachers and coaches should identify children who lack phonological awareness and who may therefore experience difficulty in learning to read and spell. The teachers or coaches can then provide instructional support. Research suggests that phonological awareness can be trained, with subsequent gains in reading and spelling (National Institute of Child Health and Human Development, 2000; Bradley & Bryant, 1983; Lundberg, Frost, & Peterson, 1988; Ball & Blachman, 1991).

What Children Need to Know about Print

In order to learn to read and write, children must develop basic concepts about how print works. The most important concept is the awareness that print stands for meaning. Those little black squiggles on the page represent spoken language. They hold information, but they are different from pictures. Another important concept is the understanding that print comes in many forms and can be found in many places (such as billboards, television screens, books, road signs, and soup cans). The form or size of the letters or words, and the places where they may be found, do not change their meaning. The meaning of *stop* remains the same, whether it is printed on an octagonal red sign, in a book, or on a warning label. Children need to learn that print can be produced by anyone, including themselves. How do children develop these concepts? "Such development does not occur in a vacuum. It depends on growing up in an environment where print is important. It depends on interactions with print that are a source of social and intellectual pleasure for the individual children and the people who surround them" (Adams, 1990, p. 61).

Children must also learn the conventions of print. Books have a beginning and an end. Print goes in a certain direction. In English, we begin at the top of the message or page and move to the bottom. We begin reading on the left side and move to the right side. Print is made up of words, and words have spaces between them. Words are made up of letters, and there are no spaces between the letters.

Children must learn to identify the letters of the alphabet. This is not as easy as it sounds. The alphabet is probably the first thing in a young child's life that changes with direction. A chair is a chair no matter what direction it is facing. It is a chair whether it is upside-down, right-side-up, or lying on its side. Mother is Mother, whether she is standing up, lying down, or standing on her head. This is called *object constancy*. But consider the alphabet. If you reverse the direction of the letter *b*, you have the letter *d*. The letter *n*, turned upside-down, becomes the letter *u*. Letters are also very abstract; that is, they do not resemble a concrete object in any way. There are very small differences between two letters. The only difference between the letter *c* and the letter *o* is the closed loop. The letter *b* and the letter *h* look similar. Only the horizontal crosspiece distinguishes the letter *l* from the letter *t*.

Research indicates that the ability to identify and name alphabet letters is a powerful predictor of later success in literacy (Adams, 1990). Many children who have lived in a print-rich environment enter school already knowing the names of the letters. They can sing the alphabet song and discriminate among written letters. This is an important first step to learning the letters' sounds and learning to read words. Unfortunately, some children enter school with little understanding of the purpose of print or the conventions of print, including the letters of the alphabet.

First Stages of Reading Words

What do beginning readers look like? What strategies do they use to identify words and construct meaning from text? Children progress through different stages as they learn about print and develop their ability to recognize words (Ehri, 1991; Gough & Juel, 1991; Spear-Swerling & Sternberg, 1996).

Let's consider 4-year-old Zachary, who climbs into his grandmother's lap and announces, "I'm going to read you a story." He settles himself comfortably and opens *The Three Little Pigs*. "It's about these pigs, and they are going to leave their mother. It says so right here." Zachary points to the words. "And this is the word *pig*. I can tell because it has a tail on the end just like a pig." He carefully turns the page. "One pig made a house. He used straw. The middle pig made a stick house." Zachary points to the print and carefully turns another page. "The last pig made a house of bricks, and then this mean old wolf came. Here's a picture of the wolf." Zachary turns the page and continues. "The wolf said he was going to huff and puff and blow down the straw house. And he did! See how it all came down!" Zachary continues in this fashion until he finishes the book. "I'm a good reader, aren't I, Grandma?" Zachary's proud grandmother assures him that he is.

Now Zachary is obviously telling the story to his grandmother and using the pictures as guides. The words he uses are not an exact match for the words on the page. Is Zachary really reading? Not in the sense that you are reading this book right now. But Zachary has grasped a key concept. He knows that print stands for meaning, for something that he can say (Adams, 1990). And he knows that he can't just say anything as he "reads" a book. What he says must match what is on the page, and Zachary matches his words to the pictures of the pigs, their houses, and the wolf.

Zachary is in the first stage of reading words, called the *logographic* stage (Ehri, 1991) or the stage of *visual cue reading* (Spear-Swerling & Sternberg, 1996). In this stage, children identify words by using visual cues. They do not try to match letters and sounds. They can identify the word *McDonald's*, but only in the presence of the familiar logo, the golden arches. Zachary is confident that he can recognize the word *pig* because it has a tail at the end. Chances are that Zachary will identify any word ending in *y* as *pig*. (In a similar fashion, a youngster once confided to me that he could always recognize *dog* because the dog was barking. Its mouth was open in the middle of the word! Of course, he confidently pronounced *got* and *from* as *dog* and was quite proud of himself for doing so.) Still, Zachary has made a fine beginning.

Cynthia, a first grader, selects *Mrs. Wishy Washy* by Joy Cowley (1999) to read. She first looks at the picture and then points to each word with her finger. " 'Oh, lovely mud,' said the cow," Cynthia reads. She looks at the next page and goes on, "And she jumped in it." Cynthia turns the page, looks at the picture, and continues. " 'Oh, lovely mud,' said the pig, and she jumped in it. No! She rolled in it." Like Zachary, Cynthia uses the pictures to help her recognize the words and comprehend the story. Seeing the pig rolling as opposed to jumping, she changes *jumped* to *rolled*; unlike Zachary, however, she basically reads the words as they are on the page. Later, when Cynthia goes through a set of word cards, she attempts to use letters and sounds as opposed to visual cues, but identifies *down* as *day* and *out* as *over*. Cynthia is in the *alphabetic* stage (Ehri, 1991) or the stage of *phonetic cue recoding* (Spear-Swerling & Sternberg, 1996).

Children in this stage try to match letters and sounds, but they depend heavily on context and pictures to help them pronounce words and understand what they read. Cynthia reads *jumped* in the context of *Mrs. Wishy Washy*, but misses it on the word card. She correctly identifies *mud* during her reading of the story, but calls it *man* on the word card. Readers in this stage focus on the beginning and the ends of words and tend to ignore vowels. Gradually, however, children begin to pay attention to vowels and to note sound and spelling patterns in words. They move into later stages of reading development. They are no longer beginning readers. They become more confident and proficient in identifying words. They develop strategies for remembering and understanding what they read. I discuss the later stages of reading development in Chapters 7, 8, and 9.

Early Literacy and the CCSS

The Reading Standards: Foundational Skills begin with the kindergarten level and focus on basic knowledge of letter–sound correspondences. In order to acquire this basic knowledge, students must have the prerequisite skills discussed in this chapter. They must have adequate levels of oral language proficiency. They must be phonologically aware of words, syllables, and sounds. They must have print awareness, realizing that print stands for meaning and that what people say can be written down for others to read. Finally, they must know the letters of the alphabet and recognize that letters stand for sounds. When these early literacy skills converge, students have the necessary tools to pronounce unfamiliar words. So, when you are working on developing and strengthening these skills, you are actually building a strong foundation for the Standards. To put it another way, if a child does not develop the early literacy skills described in this chapter, there is little chance that he or she will be able to meet the Standards in grade-level text.

Early Literacy and RTI

It just make good sense for those who design RTI assessment and instruction for young children to determine the extent to which they have developed the early literacy skills that are so critical to reading development. Dorn and Henderson (2010) include emergent language and literacy as one of nine components that make up their RTI interventions. The emergent language and literacy intervention "emphasizes six essential elements for learning to read: oral language fluency, early concepts about print, phonemic awareness, vocabulary development, attention to print, and talking about literacy" (pp. 101–102). In a similar fashion, Scanlon and Anderson (2010) describe RTI in kindergarten as focused on assessment of phonological awareness and several measures of early literacy skill.

Assessment of the phonological structure of language is still important for older students who have severe reading problems, Their problems may well be associated with underdeveloped phonological awareness (Brady, 1997; Ebro, Borstrum, & Peterson, 1998). However, phonological awareness is only one part of the big picture we call reading, and RTI teachers and curriculum directors should not mistake the part for the whole. Phonological awareness assessments as well as methods of instruction do not resemble real reading tasks. RTI assessment and instruction should also focus on other components of reading such as phonics, fluency, vocabulary, and comprehension. It is critical that students be involved in real reading and "teacher read-alouds coupled with student discussion are just as important as phonological activities in developing reading proficiency" (Caldwell & Leslie, 2013, pp. 62–63).

Guidelines for Early Literacy Assessment

Any teacher or coach who works with young children should be aware of those skills that are so important to the development of literacy: oral language development, phonological awareness, print awareness, alphabet knowledge, and early reading strategies. The teacher or coach cannot assume that all are in place when a child enters school, but must carefully assess the child's awareness and knowledge of each. "The ability to read does not emerge spontaneously, but through regular and active engagement with print. For a child who is well prepared to learn to read, the beginning of formal reading should not be a abrupt step, but a further step on a journey well under way" (Adams, 1990, p. 71). For the child who is not well prepared, sensitive and timely assessment by a teacher or coach may provide the first steps in his or her journey to literacy.

Recognition of the importance of early literacy assessment has dramatically increased over the years, and many different assessment instruments are now available. In fact, one could say that early literacy assessment has become a thriving business. Early literacy assessment methods can take one of two forms: published instruments or informal assessment activities that teachers or coaches can use in the classroom. Most examples of both types are individually administered. Some published instruments only focus on early literacy, but a number are complete assessment batteries that also address word identification, phonics, fluency, vocabulary knowledge, and comprehension. Some are limited to preschool or kindergarten through second or third grade, while others extend up through sixth grade and higher. Published instruments can be *norm-referenced* or *criterion-referenced*. Norm-referenced tests have scoring guidelines based on the scores of a large pilot sample or norm group. In criterion-referenced measures, the author of the test sets a criterion or cutoff score for determining student proficiency. Some instruments provide online scoring analysis and recording options that extend to the school or district.

It is not the purpose of this book to recommend a specific early literacy assessment instrument or activity to a teacher or coach. Schools vary widely, and an instrument or activity may fit the curriculum and purposes of one school but be quite unsuitable for another. Teachers and coaches are seldom involved in the selection of a schoolwide early literacy assessment; however, it is important that they understand all the components of a chosen instrument. Whether you are involved in the selection process or are examining and preparing to use an already chosen instrument, there are some guidelines to follow.

• *First, know exactly what the instrument assesses.* The first step of the assessment process that I discussed in Chapters 1 and 2 is: identify what to assess. Some instruments base their scoring process on the administration of all subtests; others allow for choice on the part of the teacher. Appendix 6.1 lists questions that should be asked about early literacy assessments.

• *Do not confuse the assessment instrument with the reading process.* Many early literacy assessments do not look like real reading. Recall what you did in Chapter 1 when you read the account of Taffy and Diane. That was real reading. You identified words, chunked them into meaning units, built visual images, made inferences and predictions, asked questions, found answers, and generally enjoyed yourself! Asking children to name letters or initial sounds in a timed format is not real reading. The same goes for asking children to say how many sounds are in a word. Although such assessments may provide hints to a teacher or coach that skills crucial to the reading process have not yet been mastered, letter naming and sound differentiation and counting do not represent the real reading process.

Is it possible that a child may fail such an assessment and still be able to read text and comprehend its contents? Possibly. What this means is that any assessment that does not look like real reading should always be evaluated in comparison to an assessment that more closely approximates what readers do when they read. No child should be referred for intervention, grouped for instruction, or held back from promotion on the basis of such assessments without the addition of an assessment that more closely parallels real reading. Such an assessment could involve taking a running record (which I discuss in detail later in this chapter) or using the IRI process (described in Chapter 5).

• *Do not teach to the format of the test.* If a child cannot point to pictures representing the initial sounds in words, the temptation exists to use this format for future instruction. However, remember that the assessment format stands for a bigger picture: making sense of print. If a child can point to the picture that begins with the sound of *p*, for example, this suggests the ability to discriminate initial sounds. For children who cannot do this, teach sound discrimination by using a variety of activities and resist the temptation to mimic the format of the test. If instruction consistently parallels test format, you run the very real danger that a child will learn to perform in a single picture format and not learn to discriminate sounds in different contexts. Unfortunately, the importance of raising scores can lead to assessments that "define what is taught and the outcomes that are measured so that progress may not be much more than what was tested and taught. In other words, students may be performing better on tests . . . but not in terms of larger goals for literacy: expanded use of various literacies to serve a range of purposes" (Tierney & Thome, 2006, p. 520).

• *Carefully examine an assessment before making a selection or before administering it.* Do not depend totally upon publisher-provided text. Publishers and test makers obviously believe in their product and want to sell it. To do this, they present it in the most positive light possible. Move beyond the publishers' information. Do a web search for any articles that may offer positive or negative information on your proposed choice. Check out websites for the experiences of educators who have already used the assessment. If possible, contact them by e-mail and ask them their opinions after using the instrument. Would they order it again? What problems did they meet in administering and scoring? Does the assessment provide appropriate and needed information?

• *As much as is possible, keep early literacy assessment consistent throughout the school.* Given the importance of early literacy development, all teachers or coaches who work with young children should assess their developing competence in oral language, phonological awareness, alphabet knowledge, print awareness, and early letter–sound matching. Such assessment is more meaningful if it is consistent throughout the early grades. It is less effective if teachers or coaches all "do their own thing." Preschool, kindergarten, and primary teachers should agree on the assessment or activity to be used, as well as when and how often it should be administered. And this guideline leads to the next one.

• *Involve all teachers and coaches in choosing early literacy assessment methods.* Unfortunately, this is not often the case. Early literacy assessments are often chosen by individuals in the central office and distributed to teachers as a "done deal." In most cases, assessment of early literacy falls on the shoulders of classroom teachers or coaches. Therefore, it is only fair that teachers and coaches have input into the selection process. Teachers and coaches should have the opportunity to discuss and examine different instruments and activities, to consider the match of these with their curriculum and instruction, to evaluate the complexity of the administration process, and to estimate the amount of training that they will need. Such collaborative circumstances will elicit their active support of whatever decision is made.

• We have all heard warnings about buying a new car during the first year it is manufactured and before "all the bugs are out." The same holds true for published assessment instruments. No matter how careful a test author may be, there are always unforeseen things that appear when the instrument is administered to real, live students. As a test author myself, I can attest that a lot of revision occurs during the pilot-testing process. Passages must be adjusted, questions need rewriting, and scoring directions require clarification. It makes good sense to avoid such issues by choosing an instrument that has been pilot-tested, has been revised, or is in a second (or subsequent) edition.

• *Choose a published assessment that provides information about validity and reliability.* A valid test measures what it claims to measure, and a reliable test is scored the same way by all examiners. I am not going into detail here about validity and reliability, but there are different ways in which they can be determined.

Manuals that accompany tests should clearly explain how validity and reliability were established. For example, does the instrument adequately predict later reading achievement? Are scores on the instrument significantly correlated or related to other measures of the same component? Did a test–retest study or interrater agreement establish the reliability of the scoring system? Such data contribute to the credibility of the instrument as an assessment of early literacy.

• *Tape-record first administrations.* No matter how well trained and confident you may be, if you are a novice test examiner, it is wise to tape-record your first efforts. Distractions can occur during the testing process that affect what you hear and what you record as an answer. It might be different if testing always occurred in a quiet room free of distractions, but this seldom happens. Much testing takes place in a busy classroom while other students are involved in a variety of activities, and it is easy to miss what a student says. Sometimes you may be unsure of exactly how to record or score an answer, and occasionally, when you return to the testing protocol, you may find it difficult even to read your notes! I know that this has happened to me many times. It just helps to have the audiotape to fall back on, and it increases the accuracy and reliability of your scoring. Eventually you will no longer need the tape as a crutch, but it is comforting to have in the early stages of administering a new instrument.

• *Examine both individual results and group results.* When an assessment is given to all the students in a class, teachers and coaches tend to focus on individual students who performed poorly. They reflect less frequently on group performance and how to adjust classroom instruction accordingly (Schmoker, 2006). We must continue to identify those students who need additional help, but we also need to consider the needs of the larger group. Many of the published early literacy assessment instruments have a variety of subtests, and charting group performance can offer clear directions for adjusting classroom instruction. If you administer an informal assessment activity, record your findings and consider how your students performed as a group.

• *Use the instrument to chart student progress.* One of the purposes of assessment is to document student progress. Administer your chosen instrument or activity several times throughout the year, and use it to chart the progress of individuals and the class as a whole. Some might argue that this will take too much time away from instruction. However, I hope I have made the case that assessment and instruction are two sides of the same coin. How can a teacher or coach individualize or differentiate instruction without knowing the needs of the students? In a sense, it would be like driving without ever checking the gas gauge: It might work for a while, but you could eventually encounter big trouble. Assessment guides a teacher or coach in choosing appropriate good reader behaviors for instructional focus. It does not detract from instruction; it actually enhances it!

• *Share and discuss assessment implementation and results with peers.* One of the most unfortunate aspects of our educational system is the isolation of teachers and coaches within the same school and grade level. Rarely do they have the time to talk with each other, share what works for them, and gain new ideas of how to improve instruction. Administrators should provide time for teachers and coaches to discuss the early literacy assessment. Whether teachers or coaches are using a published instrument or an informal classroom assessment activity, they should have the opportunity to compare scoring, discuss concerns and problems with the implementation of the instrument, and talk about what the scores mean with regard to daily instruction. And this leads to the final and most important guideline!

• *Tie assessment results to instruction.* Again, I have made what I hope is a strong case for the shared nature of assessment and instruction. The final step in the assessment process is that of decision making. If a teacher or coach only makes a decision about the performance of a student or group of students, the assessment cycle is incomplete. The teacher or coach must also decide how instruction should be continued or modified. This makes a lot of sense, but unfortunately it does not always happen. I have worked with schools and districts where assessments were administered, scored, and reported, but no link to instruction was visible. When I specifically asked what the assessment results meant for instruction, some teachers seemed genuinely puzzled. They tended to accept the assessment as required by administrators but, once it was finished, thought it did not have an impact on daily activities. This is not solely the fault of the teachers. As mentioned previously, they need time to examine assessment results, especially if instruction must be modified. Teachers and coaches need time to interact with their peers and to learn from each other. Schmoker (2006) suggests that much professional development provided by schools and districts is meaningless in that it provides no opportunity for teachers or coaches to translate learning into actual classroom lessons or units. Perhaps a more effective form of professional development would be having teachers and coaches pool their knowledge and work in teams to evaluate assessment results and change classroom practices accordingly.

Informal Classroom Assessments of Early Literacy Development

While published assessment batteries provide much information about a student's early literacy skills, there are many informal classroom assessment activities that a teacher or coach can employ.

Language Development

Many published early literacy tests contain subtests that assess developing language competence. In addition, there are extensive measures for assessing oral language that can identify a child's level of development and his or her language strengths and needs. These tests measure a variety of skills (such as the length of a child's utterance, the use of different language conventions, the clarity of articulation, and the depth of the child's concept base). Such comprehensive measures are administered and scored by trained individuals. It is not the role of the teacher or coach to do so.

Many schools and districts assess oral language prior to school entrance, and a teacher or coach should know whether such an assessment has taken place. If not, the teacher or coach has a very important function: to identify any child whose language development may be questionable and to refer that child for more in-depth assessment. As a teacher or coach, how do you make this call without special training? If you carefully listen to all the students in your class or group over a period of several weeks, you will soon notice language differences. Children whose language is not as developed as their peers just do not sound right. You do not need extensive checklists to figure this out. Just listen to children and engage them in dialogue. If you are unsure about a specific child, ask a more experienced teacher or coach to listen with you. Like many teachers and coaches, you may be afraid of making a wrong identification—that is, sending a child for more assessment, only to find out that no problem exists. Because of the importance of oral language, however, it is better to refer for assessment when none is needed than not to refer when assessment is actually warranted.

Phonological Awareness

A teacher or coach can use the Assessment Test (Adams, Foorman, Lundberg, & Beeler, 1998) to evaluate individual students or to evaluate an entire group of students. The test is part of a book that provides a phonemic awareness curriculum based on language games and sound activities. The Assessment Test is a paper-and-pencil group test that allows a teacher or coach to evaluate individual phonological awareness and suggest an appropriate placement level for classroom activities. It is made up of six subtests: Detecting Rhymes, Counting Syllables, Matching Initial Sounds, Counting Phonemes, Comparing Word Lengths, and Representing Phonemes with Letters. The authors recommend that it be administered to no more than 15 first graders at one time or six kindergartners at one time. They also suggest that two teachers work together to administer the test to ensure that children follow directions and pay attention.

Dividing phonological awareness into separate categories suggests areas for classroom instructional emphasis. By adding together the scores of each child on a specific subtest and dividing this total by the number of children who took the test, a teacher or coach can arrive at a class average for that subtest. The authors suggest that a score of less than 4 indicates a need for instructional support in that particular area of phonological awareness.

A teacher or coach can both develop and assess phonological awareness for individuals or groups of students using a variety of language games and sound activities (Yopp, 1992; Yopp & Yopp, 2000). The Yopp–Singer Test of Phonemic Segmentation (Yopp, 1995/1999) is a very user-friendly instrument that is easy for a teacher or coach to administer and score. It is made up of 22 words that represent combinations of two and three sounds, and a child's score is the number of correctly segmented words based on sounds, not letters. The test is a free and quick measure of phonemic awareness and can be downloaded from numerous web sources. Although the above references are relatively "old," they still represent effective suggestions and activities for assessing and fostering phonological awareness and they are relatively easy to administer and implement.

Concepts of Print

You can learn about a child's developing print awareness simply by asking the child questions and by observing his or her behaviors. You can also evaluate this skill by sharing a book with a student. Choose a simple book with one or two lines per page. Tell the child, "We are going to read this book." Note the child's reaction to this instruction. Does he or she exhibit interest and enthusiasm? Ask the child to pick it up. Does the child hold it right-side-up? Does the child hold it so the front of the book is facing him or her? Ask the child to point to the title and the author. Open the book and ask the child to point to "what we will be reading." The child should point to print, not pictures. Ask the child to point to "where we begin" and "where we will go next." Does the child point to the beginning of the first line and move from right to left? Does the child return to the second line? Ask the child to point to a word. Read the text on the first page, moving your hand under the lines so the child can see. After reading, pronounce one of the words and ask the child to point to it. Ask the child to point to a letter. Can the child identify any letters by name? Can the child identify a sentence by noting beginning capitalization and ending punctuation? Use the accompanying Print Awareness Checklist to keep track of the child's performance.

Assessing print awareness works best with individual children. It does not take long. However, it can also be done with a very small group. The nice thing about assessing print concepts in the fashion described here is that it represents a very natural and authentic literacy situation: an adult and a child interacting

Print Awareness Checklist

____ Regards print with enthusiasm

____ Holds book right way up

____ Identifies front of book

____ Points to title

____ Points to author

____ Points to print, not pictures

____ Recognizes top–bottom direction

____ Recognizes left–right direction

____ Can point to a word

____ Can point to two words

____ Can match spoken word with printed word

____ Recognizes an upper-case letter

____ Recognizes a lower-case letter

____ Can identify letters by name

____ Can identify a sentence

together about print and enjoying the process. Assessing print concepts lets a teacher or coach know the specific type of instructional support that is needed to move a child on his or her journey toward literacy.

Alphabet Knowledge

Assessing alphabet knowledge involves three components: Can the child recognize individual letters? Can the child differentiate between upper- and lower-case letters? And can the child write these letters? Alphabet knowledge, like phonological awareness, is a sensitive predictor of early reading achievement (Adams, 1990).

As a teacher or coach, you do not need a formal test to assess alphabet knowledge. Simply type the alphabet letters in lower case at the top of a page and in upper case at the bottom. Mix the letters up (do not type them as *a, b, c,* etc.). Ask your student to identify the lower-case letters first; they tend to be more common and therefore more familiar. Then ask the student to identify the upper-case letters. Finally, say a letter and ask your student to write it. You can record answers on a duplicate of the student's sheet. You can also use this sheet to determine whether the student knows the sound that is represented by a letter. Point to the letter and ask the student what sound it makes. What about letters that can stand for more than one sound, like the vowels and the consonants *c* and *g*? Don't worry about whether the student knows all the sounds. Knowledge of one sound is enough to indicate the student's understanding that alphabet letters represent sounds.

Early Efforts in Word Identification: Running Records

When children begin reading text, it is important for teachers and coaches to evaluate individual progress. Is a child becoming more skilled in identifying words and gradually moving from success in very easy selections to success in increasingly difficult ones? A *running record* allows a teacher or coach to assess a child's performance in any selection. The teacher or coach counts the number of word identification errors that a child makes and uses this count to determine whether the text was easy, difficult, or appropriate for the child.

It can also be very helpful to attempt to get inside a child's head to determine what strategies he or she uses in attempting to identify words. Is the child using meaning cues, as Zachary does in the earlier example? Is the child trying to match letters and sounds, as Cynthia does? Is he or she predicting from the sentence structure? What behaviors indicate that the child is progressing as a reader? Does the young reader hesitate before words or repeat words, perhaps stalling for time as he or she attempts to figure out the next word? Does the young reader skip unknown words, ask for help, or attempt to identify the word on his or her own? Does the child self-correct errors? A teacher or coach can employ the running record process to find answers to these questions.

A *running record* is a way to record what an individual child does while reading orally. The primary purpose of a running record is to determine whether a specific text is easy, difficult, or appropriate for a child. This is probably not something that you as a beginning teacher or coach will do immediately. First, you should become confident in recording word identification errors and in determining whether the text is easy or difficult for a child. Later, when you feel comfortable with the basic elements of a running record, you can move to analyzing the child's strategies for identifying words.

A running record is very similar to the IRI process (discussed in Chapter 5). Both are used with a single child, and both involve the recording of oral reading performance. However, there are differences. In the IRI process, the teacher or coach records oral reading errors on a duplicate copy of the text that is being read by the child. In a running record, the teacher or coach records oral reading performance on a blank sheet of paper. In the IRI process, only errors or deviations from the text are marked. In a running record, the teacher or coach places a checkmark on the paper for each word read correctly.

The IRI process employs miscue analysis to determine what strategies the student uses in attempting to identify words. This involves rewriting the miscues on a separate sheet of paper and examining each one according to several categories. (Miscue analysis is explained in Chapter 7.) When using a running record, the teacher or coach records possible word identification strategies on the original record sheet. Both the IRI process and the running record code the child's errors as to type and use the number of errors to arrive at some evaluation of the difficulty level of the text for the student.

Because a running record does not demand that a teacher or coach duplicate the text that will be read by the student, it is, in a sense, a more flexible process. The teacher or coach can decide to use a running record on the spur of the moment, because no advance preparation is required. However, unless the teacher or coach records oral reading performance in an orderly and uniform way, later interpretation of the running record can be difficult.

Working with a running record is not easy. Like the IRI process, it requires practice and takes time to examine and score. Scoring can involve determining the difficulty level of the text for a child, or it can be more complex and include an analysis of word identification strategies. As a beginning teacher or coach, you will probably find that a running record is most helpful in determining which book a child can read with comfort and success. If this is the only use that you make of a running record, it is a very helpful one. Don't feel guilty about not engaging in more detailed strategy analysis. Chances are that you will not have the time. However, it is a good idea for you to be aware of the scope and power of the running record, even if you do not use it to its full extent.

Coding Oral Reading Performance in a Running Record

As the child reads, record what he or she says. Transcribe each separate line that the child reads as a separate line on the blank record sheet. Once the child is finished, return to the coding sheet and make additional notations. These notations are indicated below as "Later analysis."

You may choose to mark only those words that are correctly identified, as opposed to identifying, coding, and analyzing errors. The process of identifying and coding errors is much more time-consuming and complex. Marking only the correctly identified words will be sufficient to determine how difficult the text is for the child. Identifying, coding, and analyzing errors may represent too great an expenditure of time for you as a busy teacher or coach. However, I illustrate in

Appendix 6.2 how it is done, so that you can understand the power of a running record. Ideally, when you become adept at recording correctly identified words, you can move on to a more detailed analysis.

- *Words read correctly.* Mark words read correctly with a check.

Text:	Who do I see on the log?
Student:	Who do I see on the log?
Running record:	✓ ✓ ✓ ✓ ✓ ✓

- *Omissions.* Mark omitted words with a dash. After the running record is completed, return to the record and write in the omitted word.

Text:	Oh! I bet it is a frog.
Student:	I bet it is a frog.
Running record:	— ✓ ✓ ✓ ✓ ✓
Later analysis:	$\frac{}{oh}$ ✓ ✓ ✓ ✓ ✓

- *Substitutions.* If a student substitutes words, write in the substitution and later fill in the text word.

Text:	Who do I see on the plant?
Student:	What do I see on the plant?
Running record:	*what* ✓ ✓ ✓ ✓ ✓
Later analysis:	$\frac{what}{who}$ ✓ ✓ ✓ ✓ ✓

- *Insertions.* If a student adds a word, write in the addition. Later on, when you return to the record, simply place a dash under the word to indicate that there was no matching word.

Text:	Oh! I bet it is an ant.
Student:	Oh! I bet it is a big ant.
Running record:	✓ ✓ ✓ ✓ ✓ ✓ *big* ✓
Later analysis:	✓ ✓ ✓ ✓ ✓ ✓ $\underline{big}$ ✓

- *Self-corrections.* When readers self-correct, write the original word and follow it with an SC. Later, indicate the text word.

Text:	Who do I see on the rug?
Student:	Who do I see on the rag rug?
Running record:	✓ ✓ ✓ ✓ ✓ ✓ *rag SC*
Later analysis:	✓ ✓ ✓ ✓ ✓ ✓ $\frac{rag}{rug}$ *SC*

• *Repetitions.* When readers repeat a word or several words, mark each word with an R. If they repeat an entire line, draw a line and mark the line R. If they repeat a word or words twice, indicate that this happened with a 2.

Text:	Oh! I bet it is a bug.
Student:	Oh! Oh! I bet it is is is a bug bug.
	Oh! I bet it is a bug.
Running record:	✓R ✓ ✓ ✓ ✓ R² ✓ ✓ ✓R
	R

• *Attempts.* Children often attempt several different pronunciations before they settle on the one that satisfies them. Coding their attempts can often indicate what strategies they are using. Record each attempt and draw a vertical line between each one.

Text:	Who do I see in the truck?
Student:	Who do I see in the to/ter/trick/truck?
Running record:	✓ ✓ ✓ ✓ ✓ ✓ to/ter/trick ✓
Later analysis:	✓ ✓ ✓ ✓ ✓ ✓ to/ter/trick ✓
	truck

• *Try again.* Sometimes a child becomes hopelessly confused and makes so many errors that he or she either stops reading or asks for help. Feel free to ask the child, "Why don't you try that again?" Code the new effort, but mark that line with a bracket; then you can compare the second reading to the first one.

Text:	And who is dancing that happy jig?
Student:	And what who is decing the silly happen decking I don't know that word
	And who is decing that happen happy jug jig?
Running record:	✓ what SC ✓ decing the silly happen decking
	[✓ ✓ ✓ decing ✓ happen SC jug SC]
Later analysis:	[✓ ✓ ✓ decing ✓ happen SC jug SC]
	dancing happy jig

Let's try another example and see how you do. We will take it line by line. Record Amanda's performance in the space provided. Then check my recording and my explanation of what I did.*

Text:	It was a warm spring day.
Student:	It was a super day.

---

*The selection read by Amanda, "A Trip" (which is also the selection read by Jamaela in Appendix 6.2), is from Leslie, L., & Caldwell, J. S. (2006). *Qualitative Reading Inventory 4* (pp. 133–137). Boston: Pearson. Copyright 2006 by Pearson. Adapted by permission.

Your running record:

My running record: ✓ ✓ ✓ – <u>super</u>   ✓
                                        spring

Explanation: Amanda omitted *warm*, so I indicated this with
                      a dash. She substituted *super* for *spring*, so I wrote
                      super and later filled in the missed word below the
                      substitution.

Text: The children were going on a trip.
Student: The children were gone on a trip.
Your running record:

My running record: ✓ ✓ ✓ <u>gone</u>   ✓ ✓ ✓
                                  going

Explanation: Amanda substituted *gone* for *going*, so I wrote in the
                      substitution and later indicated the original word.

Text: The trip was to a farm.
Student: The trip was to the a farm.
Your running record:

My running record: ✓ ✓ ✓ ✓ <u>the</u> SC
                                        a

Explanation: Amanda substituted *the* for *a* but corrected it. I
                      recorded *the* as a substitution, and marked it SC to
                      indicate that she corrected it.

Text: The children wanted to see many animals.
Student: The children were to see many animals there.
Your running record:

My running record: ✓ ✓ <u>were</u>   ✓ ✓ ✓ <u>there</u>
                              wanted   –

Explanation: Amanda substituted *were* for *wanted*, so I wrote
                      in *were*. She inserted *there*, so I wrote in *there*, but
                      indicated with a dash that it was an insertion.

Text: They wanted to write down all they saw.
Student: They wanted to write down to write down all they
                      saw.

Your running record:

My running record: ✓ ✓ ✓ ✓ ✓ R R R ✓ ✓ ✓
Explanation: Amanda repeated *to write down*, so I indicated this with an R for each repeated word.

Text: They were going to make a book for their class.
Student: They were going to make a book for their class.
Your running record:

My running record: ✓ ✓ ✓ ✓ ✓ ✓ ✓ ✓
Explanation: Amanda made no errors. I recorded each word that she correctly pronounced with a check.

Text: On the way to the farm the bus broke down.
Student: On their way to the farm the bug broke down.
Your running record:

My running record: ✓ $\frac{their}{the}$ ✓ ✓ ✓ ✓ $\frac{bug}{bus}$ ✓ ✓

Explanation: Amanda substituted *their* for *the* and *bug* for *bus*. I wrote in the substitutions and later indicated the original words.

Text: The children thought their trip was over.
Student: The children threw their trip their trip was over.
Your running record:

My running record: ✓ ✓ $\frac{threw}{thought}$ ✓ ✓ R R ✓ ✓

Explanation: Amanda substituted *threw* for *thought*, so I wrote in *threw*. She repeated *their trip*, and I indicated this with an R for each word repeated.

Text: Then a man stopped his car.
Student: Then a man his car.
Your running record:

My running record: ✓ ✓ ✓ $\frac{\text{—}}{stopped}$ ✓ ✓

Explanation:	Amanda omitted *stopped*. I indicated this with a dash and later wrote in the omitted word.

Text:	He helped to fix the bus.
Student:	He hoped helped to fix to fix the bus.
Your running record:	

My running record: ✓ *hoped* SC ✓ ✓ R R ✓ ✓
                        helped

Explanation:	Amanda substituted *hoped* for *helped*, but she then corrected her error. I wrote down the original substitution and indicated that it was corrected by SC. Amanda also repeated *to fix*, and I indicated this with R for each repeated word.

Text:	The bus started again.
Student:	The bus started up again.
Your running record:	

My running record: ✓ ✓ ✓ *up* ✓
                            ‒

Explanation:	Amanda inserted *up*, and I wrote down her insertion. Later I placed a dash under it to indicate that there was no matching word.

Text:	The children said, "Yea!"
Student:	The children said, "Yea!"
Your running record:	

My running record: ✓ ✓ ✓ ✓

Explanation:	Amanda made no errors. Each word that she correctly pronounced was indicated with a check.

Text:	The children got to the farm.
Student:	The children thought got to the farm to the farm.
Your running record:	

My running record: ✓ ✓ *thought* SC ✓ ✓ ✓ ✓R R R
                         ‒

Explanation:	Amanda substituted *thought*, but corrected her error.

I wrote down the substitution, but indicated the self-correction with SC. She repeated *to the farm*. I indicated the repetition of each word with an R.

Text: They saw a pig.
Student: They saw pigs.
Your running record:

My running record: ✓ ✓ _a pigs_
                             —   pig
Explanation: Amanda omitted *a*, and I indicated this with a dash. She substituted *pigs* for *pig*, and I wrote in the substitution.

Text: They saw a hen and cows.
Student: They saw a hen and they saw cows.
Your running record:

My running record: ✓ ✓ ✓ ✓ ✓ _they saw_ ✓
                                  —   —
Explanation: Amanda inserted *they saw*, and I wrote in each inserted word. Later I indicated with a dash that there was no matching word in the text.

Text: They liked petting the kittens.
Student: They liked po/pit/putting/petting the kittens.
Your running record:

My running record: ✓ ✓ _po/pit/putting_ SC ✓ ✓
                              petting
Explanation: Amanda attempted several pronunciations of *petting*. I recorded each attempt and indicated with SC that she eventually arrived at the correct pronunciation. Later I indicated the word that she was attempting to pronounce.

Text: They learned about milking cows.
Student: They leaned about making cows about milking cows.
Your running record:
My running record: ✓ _leaned_ ✓ _making_ ✓ R ✓ R
                          learned   milking

Explanation:	Amanda substituted *leaned* for *learned*. She substituted *making* for *milking*. Then she repeated the entire phrase *about milking cows* and self-corrected her original mispronunciation of *milking*. I indicated her later self-correction with a check as opposed to an SC, because she made the correction during a repetition as opposed to immediately after the original substitution.
Text:	They liked the trip to the farm.
Student:	They liked going on the trip to the farm.
Your running record:	

My running record: ✓ ✓ <u>going on</u> ✓ ✓ ✓ ✓
                          —   —

Explanation:	Amanda inserted *going on* before *the trip to the farm*. I wrote in these two words and later indicated with dashes that there were no matching words in the text.
Text:	They wanted to go again.
Student:	The they wanted to go there again.
Your running record:	
My running record:	<u>The SC</u> ✓ ✓ ✓ <u>there</u> ✓ They —
Explanation:	Amanda substituted *the* for *they*. I wrote in the substitution, but indicated her immediate correction with an SC. She inserted *there*. I wrote this in and indicated with a dash the lack of matching text.

Computing Error Rate and Accuracy Rate

Once you have listened to the child read and you have taken a running record, the next step is to analyze the child's performance. What does the number of errors tell you? It provides a rough estimate of the difficulty level of the text for an individual child. Johnston (1997) offers the following guidelines. A rate of 1 error in 20 words, or a 5% error rate, suggests that the text is easy. An error rate greater than 1 in 10 words, or 10%, indicates that the text is hard. Anything between 1 in 20 (5%) and 1 in 10 (10%) suggests an appropriate level of difficulty for the child.

Amanda read a total of 119 words. If we count all errors (even those that were self-corrected), and if we do not count repetitions, she made a total of 24 errors. To figure out her error rate, divide the number of errors, 24, by the total number

> ## GUIDELINES FOR ERROR RATES AND
> ## ACCURACY RATES IN RUNNING RECORDS
>
> *Easy text*:
>   5% or lower error rate
>   95% accuracy rate
>
> *Appropriate text*:
>   Between 6% and 9% error rate
>   Between 91% and 94% accuracy rate
>
> *Difficult text*:
>   10% or higher error rate
>   90% or lower accuracy rate

of words, 119. The answer is .20. Multiply .20 by 100 to get rid of the decimal, and you have a 20% error rate. Subtract 20% from 100% to get the accuracy rate, which is 80%. According to the guidelines just described, the text that Amanda read was too difficult for her.

Let's try another computation of error and accuracy rates. Claudia made 13 errors in a 76-word text. Figure out Claudia's error rate and accuracy rate, and then check with my scoring.

The number of errors, 13, divided by the total number of words, 76, is .17. If .17 is multiplied by 100, we have an error rate of 17%. If 17% is subtracted from 100%, we have an accuracy rate of 83%. According to the guidelines above, the text that Claudia read was too difficult for her.

These error and accuracy rates roughly correspond to the IRI process levels of independent, instructional, and frustration levels of reading. An error rate of 5% or less, or an accuracy rate of 95% or above, indicates an independent reading level. An error rate of 6–9%, or an accuracy rate of 91–94%, indicates an

> ## FORMULA FOR COMPUTING ERROR RATES
> ## AND ACCURACY RATES
>
> Number of errors divided by total number of words multiplied by 100 equals error rate.
>
> Answer subtracted from 100 equals accuracy rate.

instructional level (or what Johnston, 1997, calls a *learning level*). An error rate of 10% or above, or an accuracy level of 90% or below, indicates a frustration level. The difference is that the IRI process levels are attached to a numerical grade level and interpreted in terms of the grade level of the selection that was read. The running record levels are attached to a specific book.

Counting Errors

What do you count as an error? Is repetition or self-correction an error? If the error does not alter the meaning of the text, should it be counted? These are the same questions that plague teachers and coaches who use the IRI process. Make your decision as to what constitutes an error and stay with it. I recommend that you employ the same system for the IRI process and for running records. It is easy to get confused if you use different guidelines for the two processes. I have always employed the following guidelines.

- Count all errors, even those that were self-corrected. Many people disagree with me about self-corrections, but I believe that the initial error indicates lack of automatic decoding and should be counted. When you decide whether the text was easy, appropriate, or difficult, you can note the number of self-corrections as one indication that a child is moving toward word identification accuracy.

- Do not count repetitions.

- Count all substitutions, insertions, and omissions even if they do not distort meaning. Again, people disagree with this method, but I find the process of determining whether meaning is or is not altered too time-consuming. As I mentioned in Chapter 3, the difference between errors that distort meaning and those that do not seldom results in a level change.

- If a child encounters the same word in the text and mispronounces it each time, count it as an error each time it is mispronounced.

- If a line is omitted, count each word as an error.

Interpretation of Coding

If you wish to probe further into a child's strategies for identifying words, you can analyze his or her errors. Most teachers and coaches are too busy to do this on a regular basis. I include the procedure to give you an idea of the power of the running record process, but I do not suggest that you attempt this analysis until you are very comfortable with recording errors and with computing error and accuracy rates.

There are basically three sources of information that readers can draw on when faced with an unfamiliar word. These are discussed again in Chapter 7 in relation to miscue analysis. First, a reader can use semantics or meaning to identify a word. For example, in the sentence *I fed peanuts to the big elephant*, *peanuts* and *big* might act as powerful meaning clues to the identification of *elephant*. Second, a reader can use syntax or the structure of the language to identify a word. In the sentence *The little cat hid under the bed*, *hid* and *bed* could act as structure clues to *under*. Finally, the reader can use the visual information provided by letters and can attempt to match letters and sounds.

Once the running record is completed, you can examine each deviation from the test to determine which information source the child is using. You can mark each error as M (meaning), S (structure), or V (visual). Sometimes you will be unable to decide which source was used; in that case, mark any that seem probable.

Text:	Once there was a mouse.
	He lived in a wall of an old house.
	Each night the mouse went to the kitchen.
	He wanted to find something to eat.
Student:	Once there went was a mouse.
	He lives in a wall of an old house.
	Each night the mouse went to the kitten.
	He wants to find simming to eat.
Running record:	✓ ✓ went SC ✓ ✓
	✓ lives ✓ ✓ ✓ ✓ ✓ ✓
	✓ ✓ ✓ ✓ ✓ ✓ ✓ kitten
	✓ wants ✓ ✓ simming ✓ ✓
Later analysis:	✓ ✓ went SC ✓ ✓ M ✓
	was
	✓ lives ✓ ✓ ✓ ✓ ✓ ✓ ✓ S ✓
	lived
	✓ ✓ ✓ ✓ ✓ ✓ kitten M ✓
	kitchen
	✓ wants ✓ ✓ simming ✓ ✓ S ✓ ✓
	wanted something

The substitution of *went* for *was* could be marked as both a meaning cue and a visual cue. The child might have predicted a story action (meaning), and both words began with the same letter (visual). Of course, the error was self-corrected, so the child paid attention to letters and sounds—visual cues. The substitution of *lives* for *lived* could involve both visual and structure cues. The child paid attention to the initial letters (visual), but substituted present for past tense (structure).

The present tense is a structure often used in beginning stories, so we can hypothesize that the child may have been drawing upon this convention. The substitution of *kitten* for *kitchen* involves both meaning and visual cues. Both words begin with the same three letters (visual), but in a story about a mouse, the substitution of *kitten* could be taken as a meaning cue. The substitution of *wants* for *wanted* follows the pattern of *lives* for *lived*. The substitution of *simming* for *something* represents attention to a visual source—the beginning letter and the ending. Because it represents a nonword, we cannot say that meaning was involved.

Beginning readers tend to depend on meaning for word identification. As they become more knowledgeable about letter–sound matching, they begin to emphasize the visual source. You want a child to emphasize meaning, because reading is, after all, a process of making meaning. But you also want the child to use the visual system to identify words. Good readers identify unfamiliar words by matching letters and sounds, and it is important that young readers learn how to do this. Running records can demonstrate changes over time in the strategies used by young readers.

Which should you as a teacher or coach use: a running record or the IRI process? It is up to you unless your school or district mandates one or the other. Is one more time-consuming than the other? I do not think so. Both require practice before you feel comfortable and confident in using the process. Both can involve a simple counting of errors or a more detailed analysis of oral reading patterns.

The IRI process culminates in the determination of a general independent, instructional, or frustration level. It is based on the assumption that a child who experiences success in a specific passage will probably experience success in passages of similar difficulty. The running record indicates that a particular book is easy, hard, or appropriate. Both methods allow you to evaluate the appropriateness of any text for a particular child. Both can be used with any text, although the IRI process requires more advance notice in order to duplicate the examiner copy. The running record may be more appropriate for shorter and simpler text, and the IRI process may be easier for longer and more complex selections.

Summary

• The development of literacy begins with the development of oral language. Oral language is necessary for literacy development, but it is not sufficient. The amount and quality of preschool literacy experiences, especially reading aloud to children, have a profound effect on literacy development.

• Children need to acquire an awareness of words and syllables as separate units. They also need to develop an awareness of sounds as separate units in a word. A child's ability to identify and manipulate sounds is highly related to his or her later reading and spelling achievement.

• Children must develop basic concepts about how print works, and they must learn the conventions of print. Children must also learn to identify the letters of the alphabet. Alphabet knowledge is a powerful predictor of later reading achievement.

• Beginning readers first identify words by using visual cues. Later they begin to match letters and sounds. Early readers rely on context and pictures to help them identify words and understand text.

• The Reading Standards: Foundational Skills begin with the kindergarten level. Early literacy skills often develop prior to kindergarten. As important prerequisites to reading development, they should be assessed and fostered in RTI assessment and instruction.

• Teachers and tutors may use a variety of published instruments to assess early language skills such as language development, phonological awareness, concepts of print, and alphabet knowledge.

• The following guidelines will assist teachers and coaches in choosing and/or understanding early literacy assessments: Do not confuse the assessment instrument with the reading process. Do not teach to the format of the test. Carefully research an assessment before making a selection. Keep early literacy assessment consistent throughout the school. Involve all teachers and coaches in choosing early literacy assessment methods. Choose an assessment that has been pilot-tested or revised. Choose a published assessment that provides information about validity and reliability. Tape-record first administrations. Examine both individual results and group results. Use the instrument to chart student progress. Share and discuss assessment implementation and results with peers. Tie assessment results to instruction.

• Teachers and coaches can informally assess phonological awareness with the individually administered Yopp–Singer Test of Phonemic Segmentation.

• Teachers or coaches may informally assess language development by listening to the student and print awareness while talking to a child about a book. They can informally assess alphabet knowledge: recognition of individual letters, differentiation of upper- and lower-case letters, and ability to write the letters.

• A running record can be used to determine whether a selection is easy, difficult, or appropriate for a child. A running record can also be used to identify word identification strategies.

• The IRI process and a running record are very similar.

Activities for Developing Understanding

• Download and administer the Yopp–Singer Test of Phonemic Segmentation. Score the child's performance and make a judgment regarding the child's level of phonemic awareness.

• Use the Print Awareness Checklist provided in this chapter to assess a child's developing understanding in this area.

• Make a letter template and use it to assess a child's recognition of uppercase and lower-case letters. Assess the child's ability to write these letters.

• Listen to a child read a short piece of text. Tape-record this reading so you can refer to the tape. Take a running record as the child reads. Then listen to the tape and refine your running record.

• Use the running record to compute the child's accuracy.

• Use Appendix 6.2 for further practice in coding an IRI process and a running record.

Questions to Ask
about Early Literacy Assessments

There are many published instruments that focus on early literacy as well as many suggestions for such assessment in teacher manuals. Older instruments are often updated to new editions and new instruments are designed and published every year. In addition, a variety of informal assessment measures are free for downloading on the web. Published instruments change quickly, and a list of assessments prepared at one time can easily become outdated. A search using the following terms will call up more instruments than you may wish to consider: early language screening/assessment; developmental reading assessment; early reading assessment; assessment of basic reading skills; phonemic awareness screening/test; phonological awareness screening/test.

It is not the purpose of this book to recommend a specific instrument. A teacher or coach may be part of a group that is selecting an instrument for school or district use or choosing an instrument for personal use in his or her classroom. In any case, it is important to ask certain questions about any early literacy instrument and use the answers to direct your choice.

• Is the instrument a formal or informal instrument? Formal instruments are generally standardized. Informal instruments are seldom standardized but may have been piloted (see Chapter 3). Your purpose in selecting the instrument should dictate whether you want a standardized instrument or not. Standardized instruments may be more appropriate for an entire district as opposed to single or several classrooms. If you are comfortable selecting an informal instrument, one that has been piloted, that is, tried out and revised as a result of piloting, is probably a better choice.

• Is the instrument specifically focused on early literacy skills or does it span the entire reading process, that is, does it include measures of phonics, fluency, vocabulary, and comprehension? If it includes more than early literacy, is this congruent with your specific purpose? In other words, would you be purchasing something that you will not use in its entirety?

• How much time will it take to administer the instrument? How much time will it take to score? Of course this depends on how many children you intend to test: an entire class or only those who seem to be experiencing difficulty. Time is precious and while lengthy instruments may be more appealing, administration to an entire class may not be reasonable.

• How much time will it take for teachers and coaches to learn how to administer and score the instrument? This probably involves only a ball-park figure on your part and may depend on previous experience. Publishers' materials often focus on ease of administration but seldom the time it takes for a teacher or coach to prepare him- or herself for the process. The number of pages in the manual that addresses administration and scoring is a very rough estimate of its complexity.

• What do you get from the instrument besides the test and directions for administering it? For example, if it is a standardized measure, do you report raw scores to the publisher for conversion into standardized measures, or is this something you have to do based on conversion sheets that come with the instrument? Does the instrument come with downloaded score sheets and you are expected to run off copies or does the instrument provide printed score sheets at a reasonable cost?

• What specific early literacy skills does the text assess? Are these in alignment with your curriculum? Or, if as often happens, the content of the assessment directs the curriculum, are these skills that you feel comfortable with? Does the instrument offer suggestions for curricular adaptations?

• What is the cost of the instrument? Expense is always an issue. The instrument may be relatively inexpensive as is the previously mentioned Assessment Test (Adams, Foorman, Lundberg, & Beeler, 1998), or it may represent a considerable outlay in district funds.

Practice in Coding an IRI Process and a Running Record

The following exercise provides more practice in recording and counting oral reading performance. Jamael orally read a first-grade selection entitled "A Trip" (the same selection read by Amanda in the earlier example). Using the transcript of Jamael's reading, record his performance according to the guidelines of the IRI process. Then record his performance as a running record. Afterward, check my recording and compare your results. This exercise points out the similarities between the IRI process and the running record.

Jamael's Reading

It was a warm summer day. The children were gone on a trip. The trip was to a farm. The children went to see many aminals animals. They wasn't to write all they was. They were gone to make a book for their kalass. On the way to the farm the bus broke down. The children thogut their trip was over. Then a man stops his car. He here helped to fox fix the bus. The bus started again. He the children said, "Yes!" The children got to the farm. They saw pigs. They saw a hen and cows. They liked pigs petting the kittens. They liked about making cows. They liked the trip to the farm. They went to go again.

Your Recording

IRI process	Running record

It was a warm spring day.

The children were going on a trip.

The trip was to a farm.

The children wanted to see many animals.

They wanted to write down all they saw.

They were going to make a book for their class.

On the way to the farm the bus broke down.

The children thought their trip was over.

Then a man stopped his car.

He helped to fix the bus.

The bus started again.

The children said, "Yea!"

The children got to the farm.

They saw a pig.

They saw a hen and cows.

They liked petting the kittens.

They learned about milking cows.

They liked the trip to the farm.

They wanted to go again. (119 words)

Number of all errors:	Number of all errors:
Accuracy level:	Error rate:
Level:	Text difficulty:

My Recording

IRI process	Running record

IRI process

It was a warm *summer* spring day.

The children were *gone* going on a trip.

The trip was to a farm.

The children *went* wanted to see many *aminals C* animals.

They *wasn't* wanted to write (down) all they *was* saw.

They were *gone* going to make a book for their *kalass* class.

On the way to the farm the bus broke down.

The children *thogut* thought their trip was over.

Then a man *stops* stopped his car.

He helped to *here C* fix *fox C* the bus.

The bus started again.

The children said, *He C* "Yea!" *Yes*

The children got to the farm.

They saw (a) *pigs* pig.

They saw a hen and cows.

They liked petting *pigs C* the kittens.

They *liked* learned about milking *making* cows.

They liked the trip to the farm.

They *went* wanted to go again. (119 words)

Number of all errors: *21*

Accuracy level:
   119 − 21 = 98 ÷ 119 = 82%

Level: *Frustration*

Running record

✓ ✓ ✓ ✓ *summer*/*spring* ✓

✓ ✓ ✓ *gone*/*going* ✓ ✓ ✓

✓ ✓ ✓ ✓ ✓ ✓

✓ ✓ *went*/*wanted* ✓ ✓ ✓ *aminals SC*/*animals*

✓ *wasn't*/*wanted* ✓ ✓ —/*down* ✓ ✓ *was*/*saw*

✓ ✓ *gone*/*going* ✓ ✓ ✓ ✓ ✓ *kaylass*/*class*

✓ ✓ ✓ ✓ ✓ ✓ ✓ ✓ ✓

✓ ✓ *thogut*/*thought* ✓ ✓ ✓ ✓

✓ ✓ ✓ *stops*/*stopped* ✓ ✓

✓ *here SC*/*helped* ✓ *fox SC*/*fix* ✓ ✓

✓ ✓ ✓ ✓

he SC/*the* ✓ ✓ *yes*/*yea*

✓ ✓ ✓ ✓ ✓

✓ ✓ —/*a* *pigs*/*pig*

✓ ✓ ✓ ✓ ✓

✓ ✓ *pigs SC*/*petting* ✓ ✓

✓ *liked*/*learned* ✓ *making*/*milking* ✓

✓ ✓ ✓ ✓ ✓ ✓

✓ *went*/*wanted* ✓ ✓ ✓

Number of all errors: *21*

Error rate:
   21 ÷ 119 = .18 × 100 = 18%

Text difficulty: *Hard*

CHAPTER 7

Word Identification

How Can We Assess a Student's Word Identification Ability?

The Role of Word Identification in the Reading Process

Good readers pronounce words both accurately and automatically. But this is just the beginning. If reading were only saying words, it would be a very dull process. However, readers also construct meaning—and when they do, wonderful things happen! Readers attach meaning to words, phrases, sentences, and paragraphs. Readers create visual images, become emotionally involved with the characters, and tie the events in the text to their own lives. Readers predict what will happen next and identify what is important. Readers may argue with the author and accept or reject the author's views. And these are only a few of the activities that go under the general heading of "comprehension." But comprehension cannot take place if readers are unable to identify the words they read both accurately and automatically.

Word identification has often been confused with the reading process as a whole. Even today, there are people with an oversimplified view of the reading process: They believe that teaching students to pronounce words is all that is needed. This is untrue. Word identification is a necessary element in reading, but it is not sufficient. Reading is a process of constructing meaning. Word identification is the key that opens the door to the exciting world of comprehension. Without comprehension, what would be the purpose of reading?

I once worked with a second grader whose parents were graduate students at a large university. Aushabell's native language was extremely phonetic; that is, there was an almost exact and perfect match between the letters of her language and its sounds. Using her skill in letter–sound matching, Aushabell was able to identify English words with amazing accuracy. She read a short story to me with very few oral reading errors. However, she had no idea what she read. Although she could say the words, she was not able to attach meaning to them. As a result, Aushabell comprehended little, if anything. Unfortunately, Aushabell's teacher confused saying words with the reading process as a whole and informed her parents that Aushabell was an excellent reader!

Strategies for Identifying Words

How does a reader identify or pronounce a word? Ehri (1997) suggests that there are basically four ways. The most common way for good readers is to identify words from memory. Most of the words that you and I encounter are very familiar to us (words such as *and, mother, club, with,* etc.). We pronounce them immediately, without any analysis and without consciously matching letters and sounds. We call these words *sight words.* Instant recognition of a large store of sight words allows us to read quickly and fluently. We do not have to stop and try to figure out each word. And because we do not have to pay attention to word identification, we can focus on comprehension.

What strategies do we use when we meet an unfamiliar word, one we have never before seen in print? In the following sentence, there is a word you have probably never seen before:

Mary's sudden *tergiversation* surprised all her friends and especially her family.

Were you able to pronounce *tergiversation*? I am sure you were. What strategy did you use? Did you match individual sounds to single letters beginning with *t*, moving on to *e*, and continuing until each letter and its accompanying sound were identified? Then did you blend all the individual letter sounds to arrive at the correct pronunciation? This is the second strategy that readers can use. Ehri (1997) calls it *decoding* or *word attack*. However, it does not always work, especially with multisyllabic words or long words.

Did you attempt to predict the pronunciation of *tergiversation* from the context of the sentence? Perhaps you read the sentence and then returned to *tergiversation*. Did the sentence help you with pronunciation? I doubt it. All you know is that the *tergiversation* surprised people, but there were no clues to help you with its pronunciation. Predicting from context is yet another strategy for identifying words, but, again, it does not always work. Using context for word pronunciation is very typical of beginning readers. They can pronounce *elephant* when a picture accompanies the text, but are unsuccessful if *elephant* is printed on a word card.

So how did you pronounce *tergiversation*? You probably broke the word into familiar chunks and matched your pronunciation to words you already knew as sight words. Perhaps you knew *ter* because of its similarity to *her* or because you knew *termite*. You had no problem with *give*; it was a sight word for you. And, of course, if you knew *conversation* (and I'm sure you did), the rest was easy. In other words, you quickly analyzed the word by using analogies to known words. Let's try another word:

twisdorsercleck

See how fast you did this? What known words (called *analogues*) did you use? *Twine* for *tw*? *Horse* for *dorse*? *Heck* for *cleck*? Each reader chooses different analogues. Sometimes the analogue is a syllable, and sometimes it is a whole word. How would you pronounce *souquet* and *fongue*? Did you use *bouquet* or *tongue* (Ehri, 1997)? Using analogues to pronounce unfamiliar words is not a foolproof process. Sometimes it results in inaccurate pronunciation because the wrong analogue was chosen. Consider *disland* (Ehri, 1997). Did you use *is* and *land*, or did you pronounce the word using the analogue *island*? But, for the most part, analyzing unfamiliar words by analogy to known words and word parts works extremely well, especially for long words. It may not result in an exact and complete pronunciation, but it usually gives you enough clues to arrive at an approximate one. If you have heard the word before, that is probably all you need.

For example, suppose you have never seen the word *hotel* in print, but you certainly know what a hotel is. Your eyes meet *hotel*. Now you probably pause and mentally try out two possible pronunciations, *hot el* and *ho tel*. The second matches the word you have heard, so you choose *ho tel* and read on. The process is so efficient that you are hardly aware of your actions. However, success in analyzing by analogy is based on two things: a large store of sight words to use as analogues and a large listening vocabulary. A *listening vocabulary* consists of all the words you have heard; when you use analogues to arrive at an approximate pronunciation, you match that pronunciation with a word in your listening vocabulary. Teachers and coaches need to be aware of the importance of sight vocabulary and listening vocabulary in word identification.

Were you a bit troubled with *tergiversation*? I imagine you are fairly confident that you pronounced it accurately, but you were probably not able to match it to a known word in your head. Therefore, you were not totally certain of your pronunciation accuracy, and you certainly were confused about the meaning. Just saying words is not enough. Remember Aushabell? A reader must know the meanings of the words. If you could not attach meaning to *tergiversation*, the wonderful comprehension process was hampered. However, if you know that a tergiversation is a desertion of a cause (usually a religious or political one), then things change. Read the sentence again. Now what predictions about Mary and her friends and family can you make?

The Role of Context in Word Identification

One of the strategies that younger readers use is to predict word pronunciation from the context of the story or picture. According to some popular theories, all good readers do this. Such theories propose that good readers are skilled in identifying words because they rely heavily on context to predict word pronunciation. A substantial body of research, however, suggests exactly the opposite: As readers become more skilled, they no longer need or use context to recognize words (Stanovich, 1991, 1993–1994, 2000).

Good readers rarely use context to identify words because they have a large sight vocabulary and have mastered the letter–sound system of their language. In fact, the ability to identify words accurately and quickly *out of context* is a characteristic of good readers (Perfetti, 1985, 1988; Stanovich, 1980, 1991). Their word recognition is too rapid and automatic for context usage to play a meaningful part. This is true for both familiar and unfamiliar words. Instead, context is a "mechanism in the comprehension process" (Stanovich, 1993–1994, p. 282). For example, readers use context to assign meanings to new and unknown words, as you no doubt attempted to do with *tergiversation*. Poor readers who have not developed a large sight vocabulary and who have not mastered the letter–sound patterns of their language often overuse context (Perfetti, 1985; Stanovich, 1986). However, context clues do not always work well for them. In order to use context to recognize a word, a reader needs to identify most of the other words accurately. Students with reading problems often cannot recognize enough words to do this (Adams, 1990; Pflaum, Walberg, Karegianes, & Rassher, 1980). In addition, their word analysis skills are so poor that they ignore the sense of what they are reading to focus on laboriously matching individual letters and sounds.

It is important for teachers and coaches to understand the role of context in word identification in order to choose appropriate evidence for assessing word identification skill. For example, a student's reading of a story with pictures may suggest effective word identification. However, that same student's reading of a text without pictures may offer a very different view. Some people question asking students to read word lists or word cards because these are not authentic measures. However, comparing performance on a word list with word identification performance while reading a story may indicate the extent to which a student relies on context. Good readers recognize words accurately and automatically, and they do not use context to do this once they have moved through the initial stages of reading development.

Later Stages of Reading Words

Children tend to move through stages as they learn to identify words. In Chapter 6, I described the first two stages of learning to read words: the stages of visual cue recoding and phonetic cue recoding (Ehri, 1991; Gough & Juel, 1991; Spear-Swerling & Sternberg, 1996). Remember Zachary, who uses the pictures to tell the story and who recognizes the word *pig* because it has a tail at the end? Remember Cynthia, who attempts to match consonant letters and sounds, but depends heavily on context and pictures to pronounce words? Ideally, just as Zachary will move into Cynthia's stage of phonetic cue recoding, so too will Cynthia move on and become more competent and confident in reading words.

José, a second grader, chooses a book about turtles to read to his parents. When he meets an unfamiliar word, he knows that the letters and sounds are the clues to word pronunciation. He no longer depends on pictures, he recognizes that not any word will do. The word must fit the meaning of the passage. José has begun to notice word patterns and to use them as analogues. He divides an unfamiliar word between the initial consonant(s) (called the *onset*) and the vowel pattern (referred to as the *rime*). Gough and Juel (1991) estimate that this is the stage when word pronunciation becomes almost effortless. A child who knows *cake* probably also will know *flake, make, bake, fake*, and so on, even if he or she has never seen these words in print before. José is in the stage of *controlled word reading* (Spear-Swerling & Sternberg, 1996)—a very typical stage for second graders. However, his reading is slow and often laborious, and José needs to move into the next stage, where most words are recognized automatically.

Eight-year-old LaKendra's favorite pastime is reading. She eagerly participates in the activities of her school's book club and enjoys regular trips to the library. Each night, LaKendra reads a story to her little brother and then reads to herself before bedtime. However, LaKendra is less enthusiastic about reading science and social studies textbooks. Although she can successfully pronounce most of the words, she does not remember a lot of what she reads. "They're hard books," she complains to her mother, "and I have to read them over and over." LaKendra, like many second and third graders, is in the stage of *sight word reading* (Ehri, 1991) or *automatic word recognition* (Spear-Swerling & Sternberg, 1996). Children in this stage can recognize many words automatically without "sounding out." LaKendra has learned how to identify unfamiliar words. Now she needs to learn strategies for more advanced comprehension, such as identifying important information, summarizing content, and synthesizing information, all reading behaviors addressed by the CCSS.

It is important to realize that these stages are not discrete stages. In other words, a child does not approach all words in the same way. The child may use sound–letter matching for the majority of unfamiliar words, have a store of automatically recognized sight words, and still rely on visual cues for other words. In order to understand this process, think about how you read. Spear-Swerling and Sternberg (1996) would say that you are in the stage of *proficient adult reading*, in which pronunciation of words is seldom an issue. What do you do when you meet a word you have never seen in print before? You revert to letter–sound matching and sound it out! Even though the stages are not discrete, they provide a useful benchmark for describing good reader behaviors, and for choosing activities to move a reader to the next highest stage.

Word Identification and the CCSS

The CCSS address word identification in The Reading Standards: Foundational Skills K–5. Students are expected to "know and apply grade-level phonics and word analysis skills in decoding words " (CCSSI, 2010, p. 16). At each level, the Standards list specific behaviors, that is, what students should know and do as part of the word identification process at their grade level. These behaviors are basically the same as lists of word identification skills that are present in basal readers or in published assessments of word identification.

Word Identification and RTI

Assessment and instruction in word identification has always been a strong focus of RTI efforts. Early intervention for younger children clearly indicated a need for this as did efforts centered on older students (Scanlon & Anderson, 2010; Dorn & Henderson, 2010; Gelzheiser, Scanlon, & Hallgren-Flynn, 2010). There is no reason to believe that this requirement will change in the future. As mentioned previously, word identification is the key to opening the door to comprehension.

Purposes of Word Identification Assessment

This chapter focuses on the ability of a reader to pronounce a word accurately by using letter and sound patterns. A teacher or coach needs to know three things about word identification assessment in order to plan future lessons and group students effectively. First, the teacher or coach needs to know whether a student can accurately pronounce words at an appropriate grade level. Second, the teacher or coach needs to know what strategies the student uses to accomplish this, as well as any areas of weakness. Does the student predict from context, as is typical of readers in the early stages of reading development? Does the student match letters and sounds? Does the student note word patterns and recognize words by analogy? Third, the teacher or coach must be able to recognize a student's progress in word identification. Appendix 7.1 lists questions that you can ask about word identification assessments.

Assessing Word Identification Levels

A teacher or coach can assess word identification levels in several ways: listening to students orally read grade-level passages, asking students to read leveled word lists, and administering published instruments that focus on word identification.

Listening to Students Orally Read Grade-Level Passages

In Chapter 5, the IRI process was described. The teacher or coach chooses a graded passage from a published IRI or from a classroom text. If the teacher or coach uses an IRI passage, it could take two forms. It could be a passage at a student's suspected instructional level or a passage that is appropriate for the student's chronological grade level. The student reads the passage orally, and the teacher or coach marks all oral reading errors. The teacher or coach then counts these errors and, based on the number of words in the passage, determines a percentage score for word identification accuracy. An accuracy score of 98–100% represents an independent level, and a score of 90–97% signals an instructional level (if all errors are counted, as opposed to only counting those that change meaning). A score below 90% represents a frustration level—evidence that the student does not yet adequately recognize words at the grade level represented by the passage. This process offers an effective way to provide evidence about a student's ability to recognize words accurately.

It admittedly takes time to use the IRI process to collect evidence about a student's word identification ability. Many teachers and coaches tend to avoid it because of difficulty in scheduling time to work with an individual child.

However, the IRI process has been successfully used for many years (Johnson, Kress, & Pikulski, 1987). The sensitivity of this measure more than makes up for the inconvenience of scheduling an individual session and arranging activities to occupy the other students in the class or group.

I strongly suggest that the word identification progress of every student in grades 1–3 be assessed at least three times during the year, via the IRI process or with some other instrument. Why? Because the IRI process most closely approximates a real reading context. It tells the teacher or coach whether the student is identifying words at an appropriate grade level. It signals whether there is any problem in this area that needs special attention. If administered at the beginning, middle, and end of the year, the assessment provides evidence of student growth in word identification.

Listening to Students Read Graded Word Lists

Let's admit from the very beginning that reading word lists is not an authentic measure. Authentic measures parallel the actual reading process. Asking a student to read a passage and retell what he or she remembers is an authentic measure. But nobody ever curled up with a good list of words! However, word lists have their place in assessing a student's word identification ability. In the first place, a graded word list is highly predictive of a student's ability to identify words in a passage at a similar grade level (Leslie & Caldwell, 2011). Therefore, a graded word list can provide a quick estimate of grade level with regard to word identification. Of course, using a graded word list says absolutely nothing about a student's ability to construct meaning.

How are graded word lists constructed? Some words in our language are very frequent; that is, they occur over and over. Words like *the*, *of*, and *to* occur much more frequently than words like *system*, *public*, and *water*. There are lists of words arranged from most frequent to least frequent (Zeno, Ivens, Millard, & Duvvuri, 1995). The more frequent words are obviously found in selections at the lower grade levels. *And*, *the*, and *be*, for example, can be found in most preprimer texts. As words become more infrequent, they are assigned higher grade levels.

Where can a teacher or coach obtain a graded word list? Most published IRIs include graded word lists in their array of assessment options. Such IRIs also offer guidelines for determining independent, instructional, and frustration levels for word list performance. For example, the Qualitative Reading Inventory 5 (Leslie & Caldwell, 2011) uses the following scoring system for graded lists of 20 words. A score of 90–100% (18–20 correct words) represents an independent level. A score of 70–85% (14–17 correct words) indicates an instructional level. Any score below 70% (14 correct words) suggests a frustration level. Also, many published assessment batteries contain graded lists of words.

A teacher or coach could construct a list of words taken from selections appropriate for a specific grade level, but I would not suggest this approach. First, it can be a very time-consuming process. Second, the teacher or coach would need a rationale for choosing each word. And, finally, unless some pilot testing of the list was done, there would be no certainty that the list would represent a valid predictive measure of a student's ability to identify other words at that grade level. Teachers and coaches do not have time for this task. If you intend to use a graded word list, use one that has been either pilot-tested or shown through extensive use to be a valid predictor. This means that the best choice of a word list is one associated with a published IRI or a pilot-tested assessment battery.

Using word lists can also help a teacher or coach determine a student's reliance upon context. It is very natural for students in the stages of visual cue recoding and phonetic cue recoding to depend on context for word identification. However, it is important that they move beyond this stage as quickly as possible. It has been demonstrated over and over that good readers are able to identify words without any supportive context. If a student is more successful pronouncing words in a passage than identifying the same words on a list, this ability may indicate reliance upon context. A teacher or coach can choose words that a student has pronounced when supported by context, present them to the student in a list format, and compare the two performances.

Of course, having students read word lists can be as time-consuming as engaging in the IRI process. If a choice between the two is necessary, asking students to read authentic text is always preferable to using a word list.

Perhaps of more importance than a graded word list is the student's ability to accurately and quickly read words presented during instruction, such as vocabulary words drawn from a story or textbook chapter. The teacher or coach can place these words on word cards and ask students to read through the pile. For some time, word cards were frowned upon as lacking authenticity. However, it has been my experience that many students enjoy manipulating word cards and testing their ability to read them. They enjoy placing them into separate piles: known words, unknown words, and almost known words. Teachers and coaches can construct a simple checklist to record individual progress.

Assessing Student Strengths and Needs in Word Identification

Good readers identify words by analogy to known sight words. They tend to break words and syllables into onsets (the beginning consonant or consonants) and rimes (the vowel pattern). They match the onsets and rimes to those in known words, as you did with *tergiversation* and *twisdorsercleck*. When they arrive at a possible pronunciation, they match this to a word in their listening vocabulary. Good readers focus on meaning as they do this. While they pay attention to correct pronunciation, they are primarily concerned with the sense of what they read. How can a teacher or coach assess what students do when they meet an unfamiliar word? In other words, how can we ascertain that a student is paying attention to letters and sounds, to meaning or to both?

A process called *miscue analysis* can suggest what a student is paying attention to during the reading process. Using word sorts and nonsense words can suggest the extent to which a student is focusing on letter–sound matching and, in particular, on letter patterns. Asking students how they identify words can also reveal the presence or absence of effective strategies for identifying words.

Miscue Analysis

Oral reading errors are often called *miscues* —a term coined by Goodman (1969), who felt that students made errors because they paid attention to the wrong cues. In other words, they were miscued. A reader, influenced by *semantic* or *meaning* cues, might read *My friends gave me birthday presents* as *My friends gave me birthday gifts.* One could infer that the substitution of *gifts* for *presents* was due to semantic information, specifically the word *birthday.* A reader might be misled by syntactic cues referring to the grammar structure of our language. The student who reads *He dug up the plant* as *He digged up the plant* is probably paying attention to the grammar of the language. Another cue system identified by Goodman is the *graphophonic* cue system, which focuses attention on letters (*graphemes*) and sounds (*phonemes*). The student who reads *house* as *hoose* may be focusing on this cue system.

Goodman devised an extensive system, called *miscue analysis*, for analyzing reader miscues and attempting to identify the cue systems that were overused or underused. Many variations of miscue analysis exist today, and most published IRIs include some form of miscue analysis as an assessment option.

Engaging in miscue analysis can help a teacher or coach identify good reader word identification strategies. A good reader focuses both on letter–sound patterns and on meaning. Although good readers do not use context to help them pronounce words, they are very conscious that the words they pronounce must make sense in the context of the selection. I remember glancing at a newspaper headline and reading *Mayor blasts urban police.* Intrigued as to what the police department was doing to incur the mayor's wrath, I read on. I quickly discovered that the word I read as *police* was actually *policies*! I misread a word, but as a good reader, I paid attention to meaning and corrected my error.

Miscue analysis takes time—something that few teachers or coaches have enough of. I am not suggesting that teachers or coaches engage in miscue analysis, but it is important for them to know what it is and what it can reveal. In most schools and districts, reading specialists or diagnosticians use miscue analysis as an assessment tool. However, teachers or coaches should know enough about the process to understand the results of such an analysis if it is applied to one of their students.

Miscue analysis helps to determine whether a reader is paying attention to letters and sounds, to meaning, or (ideally) to both. Of course, enough miscues to base the analysis upon are needed. Making judgments on the basis of 5 miscues is poor practice. A minimum number would be 10 to 12.

Some forms of miscue analysis record word omissions and word insertions as well as word substitutions and mispronunciations. In order to simplify the miscue analysis process, even for a reading specialist (who is also very busy!), it is better to record and analyze just word substitutions (such as *said* for *shouted*) and mispronunciations (such as *orcheds* for *orchards*). The purpose of miscue analysis is to answer two questions. First, is the student paying attention to letter–sound matching? Second, is the student maintaining a focus on meaning? Insertions and omissions do not really say anything about letter–sound matching, but real word substitutions and mispronunciations do. The teacher or coach records the miscues on a worksheet (such as the one provided on page 165) using the following guidelines.

Miscue analysis is basically a way to analyze the strategies that a student uses to identify words by looking for patterns to the errors made during oral reading. Begin miscue analysis by writing the text word in the first column of the worksheet followed by the student's miscue in the second column. The student's miscue may be a real word or a mispronunciation that does make any sense such as *piloneer* for *pioneer*. Does the miscue show that the student is using letter and sound cues? For example, do the miscue and text word begin with the same letter or consonant pattern (*ball* for *bead*; *this* for *that*)?

Do they share a common vowel pattern or phonogram (*did* for *hid*; *fail* for *pail*)? Are they similar with regard to final letters or letter patterns (*fits* for *sits*; *sick* for *trick*; *tops* for *pops)* or do they share a common word ending (*going* for *running* or *jumped* for *hopped*)? If the miscue is similar to the actual word in the beginning, middle, or ending letters and sounds, place a check in the third column, *Similar Letter–Sound Pattern*.

Some miscue analysis systems differentiate between miscues in the beginning, middle, and end of a word. I do not recommend this approach. First, it takes a lot of time, and time is a precious commodity for a teacher or coach. Second, it is not as straightforward as one might think. It is relatively easy to determine the beginning, middle, and end of the following miscues: *run* for *fun*, *hot* for *hat*, and *jump* for *junk*. However, it is much less clear-cut when faced with miscues like *inspiration* for *expression* or *communicated* for *continued*. Finally, pilot data for The Qualitative Reading Inventory 5 (Leslie & Caldwell, 2011) suggested no significant differences between miscues made at the beginning, middle, and end of a word. A miscue, wherever it is placed, suggests some difficulty with letter–sound matching.

Did the miscue change meaning? If so, place a check in Column 4 under "Changed Meaning." Was it corrected? If the student corrects a miscue that distorted meaning, you can infer that he or she is paying attention to the sense of the passage. Place a check in Column 5.

Was the miscue acceptable, that is, it did not change text meaning? Indicate this by placing a check in Column 6. Was it corrected? If the student corrects an acceptable miscue, he or she may be paying more attention to letter–sound patterns than to meaning. Place a check in the final column.

Once the miscues are recorded and evaluated as to letter–sound matching and meaning, how do you determine strategies used by the reader? You look at the pattern of checkmarks across the columns. How many miscues involved similar sounds (Column 3)? This suggests the reader was trying to match letters and sounds even if not always successfully. How many miscues changed meaning (Column 4)? Changes in meaning suggest more attention to pronunciation than to the sense of the text. How many meaning change miscues were corrected (Column 5)? Correction of something that does not make sense suggests attention to meaning. How many miscues did not change meaning (Column 6)? Substitution of synonyms or similar grammatical structures suggests a focus on the sense of the passage. How many of these were corrected (Column 7)? Correcting miscues

---

MISCUE PATTERNS

Attention to letter–sound matching:

   The miscue is similar in the beginning sound.

   The miscue is similar in the middle sound

   The miscue is similar in the ending sound.

   The miscue did not change meaning but was corrected.

Attention to meaning:

   The miscue did not change meaning.

   The miscue changed meaning but was corrected.

Attention to both letter–sound matching and meaning:

   A miscue that represents any combination of the above.

Miscue Analysis Worksheet

Student Name _____

Date _____

Selection _____

1. Text Word	2. Miscue	3. Similar Letter–Sound Pattern	4. Changed Meaning	5. Corrected	6. Did Not Change Meaning	7. Corrected
1.						
2.						
3.						
4.						
5.						
6.						
7.						
8.						
9.						
10.						
11.						
12.						
13.						
14.						
15.						
16.						
17.						
18.						
19.						
20.						
21.						
22.						
23.						
24.						
25.						

that do not change meaning may indicate a focus on letters and sounds. You are not looking for percentages but for patterns. A good reader will pay attention to both meaning and letter–sound patterns.

Do you remember Jamael, whose reading about a class trip is presented at the end of Chapter 6 as Appendix 6.2? You have been given the option there to score Jamael's reading by using the IRI process guidelines or a running record. Here, Jamael's substitutions and mispronunciations have been recorded on a Miscue Analysis Worksheet on page 169. The following are the reasons for how the miscues were coded.

- *spring/summer*: Both began with the sound of *s*, so I marked the error and the text word as having similar letter–sound patterns and checked Column 3 (Similar Letter–Sound Pattern). Did *summer* represent a change in meaning? Obviously spring and summer are separate seasons but because they both involve warm weather, I did not mark the miscue as representing a major meaning change. I marked it in Column 6 (Did Not Change Meaning). You might disagree and choose to describe it differently. Miscue analysis is not an exact science. Some miscues clearly represent meaning change and others are more ambiguous. Just be as consistent as you can. Jamael did not correct the miscue so no further markings on the Miscue Analysis Worksheet were necessary.

- *going/gone*: The miscue and the text word began with the same sound, so I checked Column 3 (Similar Letter–Sound Pattern). The miscue did not change meaning, so I checked Column 6 (Did Not Change Meaning). No further markings on the Miscue Analysis Worksheet were necessary.

- *wanted/went*: Both were similar in the beginning, so I checked Column 3 (Similar Letter–Sound Pattern). I checked Column 4 (Changed Meaning) because I believe there is a semantic difference between *went* and *wanted* — between going somewhere and wanting something.

- *animals/aminals*: The substitution and the text word were similar in the beginning and ending sounds, so I checked Column 3 (Similar Letter–Sound Pattern). "Aminals" is not a word, so I checked Column 4 (Changed Meaning). I marked Column 5 (Corrected) because he self-corrected an error that distorted meaning.

- *wanted/wasn't*: I checked Column 3 (Similar Letter–Sound Pattern) and Column 4 (Changes Meaning).

- *was/saw*: The error was similar to the text word in the medial position (Column 3) and it changed meaning (Column 4).

- *going/gone*: This error is identical to the one made earlier by Jamael. The error is similar to the text word in the beginning sound, so I marked this in Column 1. I marked it as changing meaning unlike his previous substitution of *gone* for *going*. I felt there was a subtle shift in meaning between *gone on a trip* and *gone to make a book*. You may disagree. This happens with miscue analysis; two individuals can score the same miscue slightly differently. Don't worry about this issue. You are looking for patterns, and one miscue will not destroy a pattern.

- *class/kalass*: Jamael substituted a nonword for *class*, but it was similar with regard to beginning and ending sounds (Column 3). Because it was meaningless, it changed meaning (Column 4).

- *thought/thogut*: Again, Jamael substituted a nonword that was similar to the text word in beginning and ending sounds (Column 3). No meaning was retained, so I marked it as changing meaning (Column 4).

- *stopped/stops*: This miscue involved a change in tense. It was similar to the text word in the beginning (Column 3) and it did not really change meaning (Column 6).

- *helped/here*: The miscue was similar in the beginning (Column 3), it changed meaning (Column 4), and Jamael corrected it (Column 5).

- *fix/fox*: The miscue was similar in both beginning and ending sounds (Column 3), it changed meaning (Column 4), and Jamael corrected it (Column 5).

- *the/he*: The miscue retained the same ending as the text word (Column 3), it changed meaning (Column 4), and Jamael corrected it (Column 5).

- *yea/yes*: Both were similar in beginning sounds (Column 3), and I did not believe that meaning was changed by the substitution (Column 6).

- *pig/pigs*: The miscue and the text were similar in the beginning and medial sounds (Column 3). Because Jamael omitted *a* before *pig*, the substitution of *pigs* did not change meaning (Column 6).

- *petting/pigs*: The substitution of *petting* for *pigs* was similar in the beginning sound to the text word (Column 3), but it changed meaning (Column 4). Jamael corrected it (Column 5).

- *learned/liked*: The substitution was similar to the text word in the beginning and ending sounds (Column 3). However, it changed meaning (Column 4).

- *milking/making*: The same coding was applied to this substitution. It was similar in beginning and ending sounds to the text word, but it changed meaning.

- *wanted/went*: Again, the miscues was similar in sound and letters (Column 3), but it changed meaning (Column 4).

What patterns do you see? All of Jamael's 19 miscues were similar in letter–sound patterns. For Jamael, this is clearly the prevailing strategy. Fourteen of these changed meaning, but only 5 were corrected. While Jamael has some awareness that what he reads should make sense, he is primarily focused on matching letters and sounds and does not seem to be bothered by pronunciations that do not make sense.

What do such patterns as this mean for instruction? Assessment should always inform instruction. As a reader who focuses primarily on letter–sound matching, Jamael may need to pay more attention to meaning. But what about the opposite pattern? Is it possible to overemphasize meaning? Yes, meaning *as a word identification strategy* can be overemphasized. Such a strategy may work very effectively in text on familiar topics and in text with supportive context. But it tends to break down when the reader faces more complex selections containing unfamiliar words and concepts. When a reader encounters a new word, letter–sound matching provides the first clue. Remember your strategies with *tergiversation* and *twisdorsercleck*! A reader who avoids matching letters and sounds, or is unable to do so quickly and effectively, will soon encounter difficulties in higher-level text.

Appendix 7.2 provides additional practice using miscue analysis.

Word Sorts

As I have mentioned previously, it is difficult to separate assessment and instruction. Very often, the instructional activity that a teacher or coach employs is also the evidence that he or she collects. Engaging in word sorts is a perfect example of this blend of assessment and instruction. The teacher or coach writes words on separate cards, and the student separates these words into categories. The words can be placed on a SMART board or some other display format, and the students form different categories on paper. Depending on the words that are included in the sort, the teacher or coach can then evaluate the student's understanding of basic principles of letter–sound matching. Word sorts can shed light on a student's recognition of consonant sounds; they can also indicate whether the student can differentiate rime or vowel patterns.

Word sorts are of two kinds: *closed* sorts and *open* sorts. In a closed sort, you, the teacher or coach, provide the categories. In an open sort, the students devise the categories themselves and sort accordingly. When you first begin using word sorts, it is less confusing for both you and the students if you provide the categories. Later, when the students have experience with word sorts, you can move into open sorts.

Consider the following words: *hat, nut, top, hate, rat, bite, rate, bit, cute,* and *rope.* What categories could you give? You could ask students to sort these words

Miscue Analysis Worksheet

Student Name: *Jamael*

Date _____

Selection: *Class Trip* _____

1. Text Word	2. Miscue	3. Similar Letter–Sound Pattern	4. Changed Meaning	5. Corrected	6. Did Not Change Meaning	7. Corrected
1. spring	summer	✓			✓	
2. going	gone	✓			✓	
3. wanted	went	✓	✓			
4. animals	aminals	✓	✓	✓		
5. wanted	wasn't	✓	✓			
6. saw	was	✓	✓			
7. going	gone	✓	✓			
8. class	kalass	✓	✓			
9. thought	thogut	✓	✓			
10. stopped	stops	✓			✓	
11. helped	here	✓	✓	✓		
12. fix	fox	✓	✓	✓		
13. the	he	✓	✓	✓		
14. yea	yes	✓			✓	
15. pig	pigs	✓			✓	
16. petting	pigs	✓	✓	✓		
17. learned	liked	✓	✓			
18. milking	making	✓	✓			
19. wanted	went	✓	✓			
20.						
21.						
22.						
23.						
24.						
25.						

according to the initial consonant in order to determine whether they recognize the difference between the letters. The resulting sort might look like this.

hat	*nut*	*top*	*rat*	*bite*	*cute*
hate			*rate*	*bit*	
			rope		

You could also assess their recognition of short and long vowel patterns by asking them to separate them into words in which the vowel says its own name (long vowels) and words in which the vowel makes a different sound (short vowels).

hat	*hate*
nut	*bite*
top	*cute*
rat	*rate*
bit	*rope*

There are some guidelines for choosing words for a word sort. First, choose words to illustrate what you are teaching. If you are emphasizing rhyming word families or *phonograms* (like *-at*, *-an*, and *-ap*), make words containing these phonograms the focus of your word sort. If you are calling your students' attention to consonant–vowel–consonant patterns that do not rhyme (like *lap*, *lip*, and *stop*), choose words to illustrate these. As you use a word sort to teach a word identification concept, you simultaneously assess your students' skill. You can also form sorts based on common phonograms such as *-ay*, *-unk*, and *-ow*. Fry (1998) compiled a list of 38 very common phonograms.

You do not want too many words in a single sort—from 10 to 12 is an adequate number. The sort should involve only two or three categories. More than three can be somewhat confusing for the students as well as for you (since you need to keep track of what is going on!). Santa and Hoien (1999) suggest a nice sequence for sorting beginning with single vowels in similar rimes and progressing to vowel patterns with varied rimes. Bear, Invernizzi, Templeton, and Johnston (2011) also offer suggestions for sorting words.

Nonsense Words

What are nonsense words? Often called *pseudowords*, they are pronounceable combinations of letters, such as *pleck* and *glomb*. They do not stand for meaning. *Tergiversation* is a real word with a meaning that can be found in the dictionary. In contrast, *twisdorsercleck* is a pseudoword—a nonsense word that I have made up. Individuals who regard the use of word cards as nonauthentic will probably be even more opposed to nonsense words. However, nonsense words do have a place in assessing students' ability to engage in letter–sound matching. They can be quite effective in pointing out which letter and sound elements the students know and which ones they do not know.

Consider the following scenario. A teacher or coach asks a student to read a list of real words. The student is successful with some words. Does this mean that the student is adept at letter–sound matching? Possibly not. These words may be sight words that the student is pronouncing from memory. In other words, the student's successful pronunciation may not be the result of matching letters and sounds.

Nonsense words allow a teacher or coach to present a student with word units the student has never seen before. In order to pronounce a nonsense word, the student must apply letter–sound matching. There is just no other way. Some published assessment instruments use nonsense words; however, it is easy for the teacher or coach to construct nonsense words that parallel instruction. Suppose a teacher or coach has been focusing instruction on the following vowel patterns: -eat, -ight, and -ock. The teacher or coach could construct a short list like the following: *pight, dreat, trock, weat, cright, brock, keat, gight,* and *vock*. Asking a student to read these words can provide a brief assessment of which vowel patterns and which consonant and consonant blends are known or unknown.

Doesn't the use of nonsense words confuse the student? Doesn't it ask the student to do something that is alien to the reading process—that is, to making meaning? These concerns can be alleviated by carefully explaining that you are asking the student to read "pretend" words—words that do not really exist. Explain that you just want to see whether he or she can pronounce these words. Most students accept this explanation quite readily and even enjoy the process. They often delight in making up meanings to fit certain pseudowords. I remember one little fellow who, after successfully pronouncing *blash*, announced that if *blash* were a word, it would probably mean a splash of black mud!

Asking Students How They Identify Words

Asking a student what he or she does when faced with an unknown word can often provide valuable insights into the student's word identification strategies. Some students find it very difficult to talk about how they attempt to pronounce a word, and this problem can suggest a need to bring such strategies to a more conscious level. Other students are very aware of their strategies and of their success or lack of effectiveness.

Toby was a second grader who was not doing well in reading. I asked Toby this question: "What do you do when you come to a word that you can't pronounce?"

Toby promptly replied, "I ask my teacher." "But what if your teacher is busy?" I asked. Toby thought for a minute and responded, "I would wait for her or ask Megan, who knows all the words." Probing a bit deeper, I asked Toby to pretend that he was all by himself reading and he came to an unfamiliar word. What would he do? Toby replied, "I would put the book down and wait till someone came." Clearly, Toby had no strategies for pronouncing words. He was totally dependent on adults or peers to help him out.

When I asked Twinda what she would do if faced with an unfamiliar word, she stated, "Sound it out." "How do you sound the word out?" I asked her. Twinda was clearly puzzled, and it was evident that she had never considered the matter. Finally she responded, "I don't know how I do it. I just do." When I asked her whether sounding out worked for her, she admitted, "Not really. Most of the time, I have to ask someone."

Contrast Toby's and Twinda's strategies with that of Alton, a third grader. Alton first said he would sound out the unknown word, but he then expanded upon this strategy. "I would take each letter and try to give it a sound, and then try to kinda run the sounds together to make a word. Sometimes this works and sometimes it doesn't." Alton had a measure of strategy awareness, and he had grasped the basics of letter–sound matching. However, his strategy of matching individual letters and sounds might be unworkable when he encountered longer words.

Consider Damon, who also said he sounded out words. When I asked him how he did this, he offered the following explanation. "I look for parts in words that I know, like maybe letters and maybe a bunch of letters. Like in this one [pointing to *celebrate*], I know *rate* and I know *cell*. [He then pointed to *boundaries*.] I wasn't sure of *boundaries* right away, but I knew *bound*, and I tried the last part in a couple of different ways and then I got it." Damon's strategy was certainly more advanced than any of the other children's. He was clearly focusing on larger units than single letters; he was aware of his mental processes; and he was not relying on others for word identification. Sometimes the simplest form of assessment is to ask the students what they do or how they do it!

Assessing Student Progress in Word Identification

A teacher or coach can assess individual progress in word identification by using the IRI process and graded word lists to compare performance on the same passage or list at different points in time.

At the beginning of the school year, Nancy asked each of her first graders to read a preprimer word list. Many were only able to read one or two words. She repeated this procedure each month and recorded individual scores. When a student reached an independent level on the preprimer list, Nancy moved to the primer list. In this way, she maintained an ongoing record of each student's progress throughout the year.

Jeremy employed the same technique with his second graders, but he asked each student to orally read a passage as opposed to a word list. One he had determined a student's highest instructional level for word identification, he asked that student to read the same passage approximately 6 weeks later. If the student scored at an independent level for word identification, Jeremy moved to the next highest passage. Each time Jeremy asked a student to read the same or a higher passage, he compared it to previous readings in order to note progress.

Documenting progress can be rewarding for the teacher or coach, and it can also be very motivating for the student. Lack of progress can be disturbing and frustrating to the teacher or coach, but it can also signal the need for changes in instruction. Perhaps the teacher or coach needs to provide additional instructional support for a student or to reexamine how students are grouped for instruction. It is important to remember that assessment that does not influence instruction is questionable at best.

Summary

- Word identification is a necessary part of the reading process, but it is not sufficient. Reading is constructing meaning. Word identification is the key to comprehension, but skill in identifying words does not ensure comprehension.

- There are basically four ways to identify words. One way is to pronounce the word from memory; words that are identified in this way are called *sight words*. Words can also be identified by matching individual letters and sounds, or by predicting the pronunciation from context. Finally, good readers identify unknown words by analogy to known words.

- Younger and beginning readers use context as an aid to word identification, but they soon move beyond this. Good readers rarely use context to identify words because they have large sight vocabularies. Poor readers often overuse context as a word identification aid.

- A teacher or coach can assess word identification levels by listening to students orally read grade-level passages and by asking students to read graded word lists.

- The teacher or coach can assess strengths and weaknesses in word identification by using miscue analysis. The teacher or coach evaluates word substitutions and mispronunciations to determine whether a student is paying attention to letter–sound matching, to meaning, or to both.

- Word sorts allow the teacher or coach to examine how well the student understands principles of letter–sound matching.

- Using nonsense words as an assessment tool can indicate how well the student can analyze completely unfamiliar words.

- Asking a student how he or she pronounces unfamiliar words can reveal which strategies the student uses or does not use.

- A student's progress in word identification can be indicated by comparing oral reading performance on the same graded passage and by comparing performance on the same graded word list.

Activities for Developing Understanding

- Here is a list of words that you may not have seen in print before. Attempt to pronounce them. What analogues did you use? Compare your analogues with those of a peer.

contumacious
dreadnaught
mephitic
exacerbate
misogynist

- Here are three of these words placed within the context of sentences. Notice how the context helps you with word meaning, not pronunciation. What do you think these words mean?

April was such a *contumacious* child that her parents had extreme difficulty finding a babysitter.
He wrapped his *dreadnaught* tightly around him and stepped into the raging blizzard.
Jon's yard was so *mephitic* that his neighbors chipped in to buy him a pooper-scooper.

- Choose a short selection with pictures and type it on a plain sheet of paper. Contrast a student's word identification in the text with pictures and without pictures.

- Using a published IRI, contrast a student's word identification performance on a graded word list with performance on the passages.

• Fill out a Miscue Analysis Worksheet and analyze a student's focus on letter–sound matching and on meaning. (Appendix 7.2 provides practice with this task.)

• Construct a word sort to illustrate components of letter–sound matching. Ask students to sort according to the categories you chose and evaluate their performance.

• Construct nonsense words for the following phonograms: *-ash*, *-ump*, *-ore*, *-ame*, and *-unk*. Administer these words to a student and evaluate his or her performance.

Questions to Ask
about Word Identification Assessments

Many word identification assessments are part of extensive test batteries that assess early literacy, phonological awareness, phonics knowledge, fluency, and comprehension. Others focus strictly on phonics. Basal readers also contain suggestions for word identification assessment. If you are looking for something beyond your classroom text, a web search of "phonics tests/assessments" or "word identification tests/assessments" will call up a variety of instruments. It is also a good idea to search the websites of publishers who focus on education materials.

- Is the instrument a standardized or informal measure? Standardized instruments may be more appropriate for a district; informal measures may better suit a classroom.

- If the instrument is informal in nature, to what extent was it piloted prior to publication? Instruments that were piloted are more valid than those that were just written and published without ever being administered.

- How much time will it take to administer and score? Do you intend to administer it to your entire class or only to those students who seem to be experiencing difficulty? Do you plan to administer it only once or do you intend to use the instrument for progress checks? If it is time-consuming, your best intentions for progress checking may never occur.

- What word identification skills are covered? Some assessments focus on a few important ones, those that are applicable to a large number of words. These would include consonant sounds (single consonants, digraphs, and blends) and vowel sounds (long, short, and digraphs). Others focus on all possible phonics combinations. Do the skills included in the assessment match your curriculum? Do they extend beyond your curriculum, and is this a good or problematic thing?

- Does the assessment cover recognition and use of phonograms or word families such as *ack, eep, ide, ock,* and *ure*? Does it address reading by analogy? These are strategies that are used effectively by able readers. For example, they decode *publisher* by analogy to known words such as *club, dish,* and *her*. It is important to asses the extent to which young readers recognize and use decoding by analogy because it is a critical strategy for decoding in upper-level text.

- Does the assessment focus on decoding words in a list format as opposed to words in text? While the text can help a reader to recognize an unfamiliar word, recognition of words without a supportive context is important. It is what good readers do.

• What is the source of the test words? Some assessments use nonsense words as a "pure" measure of phonics knowledge; others use real words. Some individuals take issue with nonsense words, which can influence your choice of a specific instrument. If the test words are real words, how are they divided into lower- and higher-level words?

• To what extent do the questions match the CCSS? I suspect that most word recognition assessments focus on consonants and vowels in regularly spelled words as well as in common irregular combinations. However, the Foundational Standards address prefixes, suffixes (including those derived from Latin), multisyllabic words, and irregularly spelled words that are less common. Does the assessment address these parts of speech in any way? If not, you will have to provide an additional assessment focus beyond any published assessment that you might purchase in order to assess and develop the dictates of the Standards.

Changes

In Chapter 5, I described Billy's reading of a second-grade selection. Billy's substitutions and mispronunciations (not his insertions and omissions) have been recorded on a Miscue Analysis Worksheet. Code Billy's errors and determine what strategy he used. Is he focusing on letter–sound patterns, meaning, or both. Afterward, compare your coding to mine and to my reasons for coding Billy's errors as I did.

Your Coding of Billy

Student Name *Billy*

Date

Selection *The Family's First Trip*

1. Text Word	2. Miscue	3. Similar Letter–Sound Pattern	4. Changed Meaning	5. Corrected	6. Did Not Change Meaning	7. Corrected
1. Atlantic	Atlantica					
2. aunt	auntie					
3. unlike	uncle					
4. had	was					
5. decide	dakide					
6. what	that					
7. decided	discovered					
8. realized	really					
9. wouldn't	would					
10. decided	deeded					
11. favorite	favored					
12. country	court					
13. brought	bought					
14. long	along					
15. that	the					
16. pajamas	pananas					
17. embarrassed	embraced					
18. went	want					
19. quickly	quick					
20. begged	began					
21. luckily	lucky					
22. remembered	reminded					
23. their	they					
24. heated	hetten					
25. they	there					

My Coding of Billy

Student Name *Billy*

Date

Selection *The Family's First Trip*

1. Text Word	2. Miscue	3. Similar Letter–Sound Pattern	4. Changed Meaning	5. Corrected	6. Did Not Change Meaning	7. Corrected
1. Atlantic	Atlantica	✓	✓			
2. aunt	auntie	✓			✓	
3. unlike	uncle	✓	✓			
4. had	was		✓	✓		
5. decide	dakide	✓	✓			
6. what	that	✓	✓			
7. decided	discovered	✓	✓			
8. realized	really	✓	✓			
9. wouldn't	would	✓	✓			
10. decided	deeded	✓	✓			
11. favorite	favored	✓			✓	
12. country	court	✓	✓			
13. brought	bought	✓	✓	✓		
14. long	along	✓	✓			
15. that	the	✓	✓			
16. pajamas	pananas	✓	✓			
17. embarrassed	embraced	✓	✓			
18. went	want	✓	✓	✓		
19. quickly	quick	✓			✓	
20. begged	began	✓	✓			
21. luckily	lucky	✓			✓	
22. remembered	reminded	✓	✓			
23. their	they	✓	✓	✓		
24. heated	hetten	✓	✓			
25. they	there	✓	✓	✓		

My Reasons for Coding

- *Atlantic/Atlantica*: Both the text word and Billy's error contain identical letters and sounds except for the final letter. I marked it as similar in letter–sound patterns (Column 3). I also marked Column 4 because it changed meaning; there is no such word as "Atlantica."

- *aunt/auntie*: Except for the last syllable, the two words contain identical letters and sounds, so I marked Column 3. I also marked Column 6 because there is little if any difference in meaning between *aunt* and *auntie*. One could hypothesize that Billy may call his own aunt "auntie" and carried this over to his reading of the passage.

- *unlike/uncle*: Both words are similar in the initial syllable, so I marked Column 3. However, the miscue obviously changed meaning, so I marked Column 4 as well. Billy may have assumed that a reference to an aunt would be logically followed by one to an uncle. However, he did not correct this assumption when it proved false.

- *had/was*: This miscue changed meaning (Column 4), and Billy corrected it (Column 5).

- *decide/dakide*: This miscue contained a similar letter–sound pattern (Column 3) and, as a nonword, it changed meaning (Column 4).

- *what/that*: I checked Column 4 because the text word and the miscue were identical except for the initial letter. Billy did not correct it, even though it made little sense (Column 4).

- *decided/discovered:* The miscue and the text word were similar in the initial and final position (Column 3) and it was not corrected (Column 4).

- *realized/really*: Because of similarity in the initial and medial position, I checked Column 3. It was not corrected (Column 4).

- *wouldn't/would*: I checked Columns 3 and 4. There is no exact way of determining why a reader does not correct a miscue. However, in this case, one could hypothesize that Billy said "would use his eyes" because it made some sense in a sentence that followed three preceding sentences that dealt with reading. We do use our eyes when we read. However, he did not correct his error; chances are he may not even have noticed the subtle shift in meaning.

- *decided/deeded:* Again I checked columns 3 and 4. This was Billy's second attempt at pronouncing *decided*. As we have mentioned previously, readers match pronunciations with words they already know, that is, words that are present in their meaning vocabulary. *Decided* may not be a word that Billy knows so he is comfortable with his pronunciation attempt.

- *favorite/favored:* The test word and the miscue were identical except for the final letter–sound pattern (Column 3). I do not believe the miscue involved a change in meaning so I checked Column 6.

- *country/court*: The miscue was similar to the text word and it changed meaning (Columns 3 and 4). At this point it is becoming evident that Billy seldom corrects errors, even though they change meaning in substantial ways. It is difficult to know why but one could hypothesize that, as a second grader, his attention is primarily directed at word pronunciation not word meaning.

- *brought/bought*: I checked Columns 3, 4, and 5. This is one of the few meaning-change words that Billy corrected.

- *long/along:* The words were similar in letters and sounds (Column 3) but changed meaning (Column 4). Although it makes sense to say that "he brought along pants," this contradicts the text meaning that "he brought long pants."

- *that/the*: The words are similar in the initial position (Column 3) but the miscue changes meaning as there is no word to follow "the." Billy was probably predicting that the text would say where the tee shirt would be worn, but he failed to correct his assumption when he encountered a period ending the sentence.

- *pajamas/pananas*: This miscue illustrates Billy's strong focus on letter–sound patterns; the text word and the miscue are identical except for one letter (Column 3). However the miscue changes meaning; there is no such thing as a *pananas* (Column 4).

- *embarrassed/embraced*: Billy made a valiant effort at identifying this word. His attempt matched the text word in the beginning and ending positions (Column 3). However, it made no sense in the context of the passage (Column 4).

- *went/want.* The text word and miscue are similar in the initial and final position (Column 3), they represent a change in meaning (Column 4), and Billy corrected his error (Column 6).

- *quickly/quick:* I checked Columns 3 and 6. The words were similar in letters and sound, but I did not feel that they represented a change in meaning.

- *begged/began:* Like so many of Billy's miscues, this miscue was similar in letter and sound pattern (Column 3) but changed meaning (Column 4).

- *luckily/lucky*: I checked Column 3 and Column 6. I did not feel that the deletion of the -ly ending represented a major meaning change.

- *remembered/reminded*: Here we have another miscue that is similar in letter and sound patterns (Column 3) but considerably changes meaning (Column 4).

- *their/they*: I checked Columns 3, 4, and 5. The miscue was similar in the initial letter/sound position, it changed meaning, and it was corrected.

- *heated/hetten*: I checked Columns 3 and 4. The words were similar in letter and sound patterns, but a nonword always distorts text meaning.

- *there/they*. I checked Columns 3, 4, and 5. The miscue was similar in sound pattern and changed meaning but was corrected.

What does miscue analysis tell us about Billy? Billy was assessed in the fall of his second-grade year, and his miscues suggest a strong classroom focus on decoding. All of his miscues except one showed careful attention to letter–sound matching. Billy clearly knows that letters and sounds are the key to pronouncing unfamiliar words. Nine of his miscues represented words of more than two syllables. These errors suggest a need for an instructional focus on multisyllable words.

While Billy needs to retain his attention to letter–sound patterns, he must also pay more attention to the meaning of the text. Billy should ask himself if what he reads makes any sense. Billy seldom corrected his errors. Perhaps he felt his pronunciations were correct and it represented a word he did not know. Perhaps he just wanted to complete the task and not pause for additional attention to words. His ability to explain the gist of the passage suggests he was paying some attention to meaning and was aware that reading should make sense.

CHAPTER 8

Reading Fluency

How Can We Assess Reading Fluency?

The Role of Fluency in the Reading Process

Fluent readers read orally with speed, accuracy, and proper expression or intonation. Fluent readers identify words accurately. Moreover, they do this automatically and instantaneously, without pausing to analyze letters and sounds. As noted in Chapter 7, words that are recognized immediately and without analysis are called *sight words*. Good readers have large sight word vocabularies that include most of the words they meet. These are words they have seen before. When they first encountered them, good readers may have analyzed the words by matching letters and sounds; now, however, having met them over and over again, they can identify them from memory. Even if good readers come across an unfamiliar word, they are so skilled at matching letters and sounds that they hardly pause. (Remember how quickly you pronounced *tergiversation*?)

Because good readers do not have to think about word identification and can read at an appropriate rate of speed, they can direct their attention to meaning. This focus on meaning, in turn, allows them to read with proper intonation. Intonation involves reading at a rhythm that approximates natural speech (i.e., quickly, but not so fast that meaning is lost), paying attention to punctuation signals, and using the rise and fall of the voice to make the text sound meaningful, often referred to as *prosody*. The fluent reader is a smooth and expressive reader and is enjoyable to listen to. Have you ever listened to taped books? These represent wonderful examples of oral reading fluency.

The ultimate aim of reading is comprehension, and there is a complex relationship between fluency and comprehension. Fluency can result from comprehension as well as contribute to it. Adequate fluency can contribute to comprehension and lack of fluency can limit it (Kuhn, Schwanenflugel, & Meisinger, 2010). There are significant relationships between fluency and comprehension scores on standardized tests (Fuchs, Fuchs, Hosp, & Jenkins, 2001). This relationship weakens, however, in grades 4 and above when other factors such as vocabulary knowledge play a greater part (Stahl & Hiebert, 2005).

Achieving fluency is one of the stages that students approach in their journey toward good reading. Ehri (1991) refers to this stage as *sight-word reading*, and Spear-Swerling and Sternberg (1996) call it the stage of *automatic word recognition*. Kame'enui and Simmons (2001) suggest that oral reading fluency represents the automatic use of those early literacy skills that I have previously discussed in Chapter 6 (phonological awareness, alphabet understanding, and sound–symbol matching) and can be used to predict proficiency in later reading skills.

In contrast to good readers, many students with reading problems lack fluency. They do not have adequate sight-word vocabularies and are forced to analyze almost every word. Unfortunately, they often lack effective strategies for matching letters and sounds as well, so word identification becomes a laborious process. Because poor readers direct most of their attention to identifying words, they have few resources left for interpreting meaning. Their oral reading is slow and halting. They pause often and repeat words. Because they do not comprehend what they are reading, their voices lack expression, and they ignore punctuation signals. After reading, they have little comprehension of the meaning of the passage.

There are three requirements for developing and maintaining reading fluency. First, a reader must have a large store of sight words. Second, the reader needs efficient strategies for analyzing new and unfamiliar words. Third, the reader must focus on meaning. The interaction of these three elements forms the basis of reading fluency.

How does fluency develop? It seems simplistic to say this, but you learn to read fluently by reading. The National Institute of Child Health and Human

Development (2000) has recognized that reading practice is a critical contributor to fluency. In other words, the more you read, the more your sight-word vocabulary grows. You meet some new words and efficiently analyze them by matching letters and sounds. As you meet them again and again, their identification becomes fixed in your memory, and your sight-word vocabulary expands. This is certainly an argument for providing students with many opportunities to read. Unfortunately, many students who are experiencing reading difficulties tend to avoid reading. As a result, they do not develop large sight-word vocabularies. In turn, reading becomes more difficult, and a vicious cycle develops (Stanovich, 1986).

Students need models of fluent oral reading in the home and in the classroom. In too many classrooms, students of similar ability are grouped together for oral reading. This practice ensures that fluent readers listen to fluent readers. On the other hand, nonfluent readers, who are in most need of fluent reading models, are forced to listen to their peers stumble and hesitate their way through the text.

Students need to be aware of the importance of fluency. Many think that the most important aspect of oral reading is accuracy, and they therefore emphasize avoiding pronunciation errors. Teachers and coaches should encourage students to focus on expression and on making the oral reading meaningful and enjoyable for their audience.

Fluency may be best fostered if a student reads independent- or instructional-level text and text that is on familiar topics (Allington, 2001). Frustration-level text contains too many unfamiliar words and concepts to allow for fluency development. Perhaps an analogy will clarify this. Do you consider yourself a fluent driver—that is, a skilled driver who steers, brakes, and accelerates almost automatically in a variety of situations? I imagine you do. Think back to when you first learned to drive. Where did you practice? You probably began in a large parking lot and on relatively familiar and traffic-free roads in the country or a suburb. As you gained confidence and competence, you moved to city streets with more traffic and more signals to attend to. As you became more fluent in this arena, you ventured onto the expressway, possibly during the midmorning or early afternoon. Finally you tackled rush-hour traffic. Now think what would have happened if you had begun your driving practice on the expressway during rush hour! This may help you to understand why it is difficult to develop fluency in a frustrating and anxiety-fraught situations.

Let's carry the analogy a bit farther. Your present ability to drive on an expressway is very different from your first attempts to do so. The environment has not changed but your driving skill has. You are more confident. You can listen to the radio or a CD while you drive. You can engage in meaningful conversation. You are aware of the scenery, such as it is. You can even enjoy a cup of coffee as you drive. These were things you could not do during your first attempts to navigate the expressway. But you learned through repeated experiences. In much the same way, we need to move students from fluency in independent- and/or instructional-level text to fluency in grade-level text according to the dictates of the Standards. This text may well represent a frustration level for some students, and like your expressway experiences, it will take practice to achieve fluency.

Fluency and the CCSS

The CCSS address fluency under the Reading Standards: Foundational Skills K–5 (CCSSI, 2010, pp. 16–17). "These foundational skills are not an end in and of themselves; rather they are necessary and important components of an effective comprehensive reading program" (p. 15). Kindergarten students are expected to "read emergent-reader texts with purpose and understanding" (p. 16); first through fifth graders are expected to read "with sufficient accuracy and fluency to support comprehension" (pp. 16–17). This involves reading on-level text with purpose, understanding, accuracy, appropriate rate and expression and confirming or self-correcting word recognition and understanding. Rereading may be necessary in order to achieve these goals. The focus of the Standards on purpose and understanding clearly places fluency as a determinant of comprehension. To put it another way, fluency is the servant of comprehension. Comprehension cannot develop without some fluency but fluency in the absence of comprehension is meaningless.

We must realize that all reading cannot be fluent. Can you think of some examples of nonfluent reading? Perhaps an income tax form or a mortgage agreement come to mind or a specific textbook in a college class. I well remember several statistics textbooks. I could hardly call myself fluent as I struggled through each chapter. Of course there were words that I pronounced quickly and accurately, others that I managed with brief hesitance, and still others that stopped me cold! I still remember meeting *homoscedasticity* !

The Standards emphasize the ability to read grade-level text as preparation for college and career readiness. Students at each level should meet "challenging texts that elicit close reading and re-reading" (Coleman & Pimentel, 2011, p. 4). Close reading is not fluent reading. Close reading, as explained in Chapter 10, involves reading, pausing, rereading, questioning, putting forth possible interpretations of text meaning, and refining these often several times. While close reading may become more fluent with repeated reading, fluency does not necessarily foster close reading. Fluency develops to the extent that close reading is successful.

In Chapter 10, I discuss reading to and with students of all ages in order to foster comprehension of difficult text. One by-product of teacher read-alouds may be the development of fluency. Teacher read-alouds provide a wonderful model of fluent reading. Students see a word and hear its correct pronunciation at the same time and they are exposed to effective phrasing and intonation.

Fluency and RTI

As mentioned previously, early designs for RTI focused on the younger struggling reader, and fluency played a major role in the choice of assessment, the design of instruction, and the determination of growth (Dorn & Henderson, 2010; Scanlon & Anderson, 2010; Taylor, Pearson, Peterson, & Rodriguez, 2010). A focus on fluency continued when RTI moved to the adolescent level (Gelzheiser et al., 2010). Paris (2010) described the attractiveness of fluency assessments and cautions that they may be misused because they are "quick and quantitative" and thus relatively easy to measure (p. 104). Appendix 8.1 lists questions that you should ask about fluency assessments.

Purposes of Fluency Assessment

A teacher or coach needs to know at what level a student demonstrates fluency and in what kind of text. A student may be at an instructional level for word identification and comprehension, but may still lack fluency. The IRI process uses accuracy in word identification as one measure of determining reading level. However, accuracy is only one component of fluency; the other two components, as noted above, are speed and intonation. A student may be accurate but slow or accurate but expressionless. The teacher or coach needs to determine whether word identification accuracy at any level is tied to lack of speed and intonation. Because a student may read quickly but with little expression, speed and intonation may need to be assessed separately. Finally, the teacher or coach must note student progress in fluency.

Assessing Fluency Levels

A teacher or coach can assess a student's general level of reading fluency simply by listening to the student read orally. It is easy to recognize lack of fluency. Non-fluent reading can be *choppy, monotonous,* and/or *hasty.* In choppy reading, the student hesitates often and repeats words and phrases. It almost sounds as if the student is reading a list of unconnected words. In monotonous reading, there is little variation in the student's tone of voice. This lack of expression suggests that the student is paying little attention to meaning. In hasty reading, the student races through the text, ignoring sentence breaks and punctuation. Finishing the reading as quickly as possible seems to be the hasty reader's goal. Most nonfluent readers demonstrate a combination of these three patterns. They are very easy to recognize!

To assess fluency, simply ask the student to read aloud a selection and use your judgment to decide whether the student demonstrates acceptable fluency. If you use independent- or instructional-level text, do not assume that a fluency level obtained at those levels will transfer to frustration-level text. You may wish, in accord with the CCSS, to assess fluency in grade-level text. However, there is still an issue of fluency transfer. Recognize that fluency in reading a narrative may not transfer to fluency in reading a social studies or science selection. (Think about your reading of the sports page as opposed to an insurance policy or directions for filling out income tax forms!)

When can you find time to assess fluency? If you are using the IRI process to determine reading level, make the observation of fluency a part of your procedure. You can also assess fluency during self-selected silent reading time. For pleasure reading, students tend to choose books that they can read fairly easily. This provides an opportunity to assess fluency at independent or instructional reading levels. As you move around, ask individual students to read short segments of their books aloud, and make notes on their performance. When students are involved in independent or group work during content classes, you can use this opportunity to assess fluency in grade-level material.

Assessing Components of Fluency

Various means of assessing the first component of fluency, accuracy, have been described in previous chapters. The IRI process, the running record, and miscue analysis can all be applied to a student's oral reading to determine the student's accuracy level. For that reason, accuracy is not discussed further here. My emphasis is on assessing the other two components of fluency: speed or reading rate and intonation.

Determining Reading Rate

Reading rate indicates reading speed. It is one factor in fluency, but it is not the whole picture. Reading rate suggests automaticity of word identification. However, it says nothing about accuracy or intonation. Reading rate is measured in *words per minute* (WPM). As the student reads (either orally or silently), the teacher or coach times how long this takes. A stopwatch is the most accurate measure of reading time, but a watch with a second hand will also suffice. If you are measuring silent reading rate, you need to ask the student to look up the minute he or she has finished reading so you can note the time. Multiply the numbers of words in the passage by 60, and divide this by the number of seconds it took to read the passage. This results in a WPM score. For example, Sandie read a 288-word passage in 2 minutes and 40 seconds, for a total of 160 seconds. The number of words in the passage, 288, multiplied by 60, equals 17,280. This product, divided by Sandie's 160 seconds, equals 108 WPM. Both oral and silent reading rate can be measured in this way.

Another way to measure fluency is to compute *correct words per minute* (CWPM), or WPM minus the number of errors or miscues made. Kame'enui and Simmons (2001) suggest that this method is a more sensitive measure of fluency, in that it measures both speed and accuracy, while WPM only measures speed. So, if Sandie read at 108 WPM but made six errors or miscues, her CWPM would be 102.

Once you have a WPM or a CWPM score, what does it mean? As a teacher or coach, you must realize that reading rate is extremely variable. Reading rate varies according to the passage read. More difficult and unfamiliar passages tend to be read more slowly than narratives. Rate also varies according to readers' purposes. Think about how your rate varies when you read a textbook or an editorial versus an adventure novel or some other form of escapist reading. Readers' interests can affect reading rate as well. Reading rate also varies within a single selection, with some sentences being read more slowly than others (Flurkey, 2006). Moreover, reading rate varies across individuals; students at the same instructional level often display very different reading rates. Carver (1990) suggests that some readers are just naturally faster than others, and a faster reading rate may be related to individual cognitive processing speed.

Silent reading is generally faster than oral reading. Huey (1908/1968) suggested a century ago that good readers read one and a half to two times faster silently than they do orally. This just makes good sense. In oral reading, people have to pronounce the words. In silent reading, they do not, and good readers can process words much faster than they can say them.

Because of this natural variability in reading rates, a teacher or coach should never compare the reading rates of two individual students. In addition, 1-minute tests of reading rates should be regarded with some degree of suspicion. If a teacher or coach uses such a brief measure, it should be accompanied by other and longer samples of rates before any decision is made regarding a student's performance. But what about choosing a specific reading rate as a goal for students at a certain grade level? Various assessment instruments, such as published IRIs, contain general guidelines for grade-level reading rates. These can be used to set a general goal for rate improvement, as long as the teacher or coach keeps in mind the variability of reading rate across individuals, different types of text, and different reading purposes. To put it simply, a teacher or coach should never interpret grade-level rate guidelines as absolute goals.

Once you have a measure of rate for a grade-level passage, do not assume that this rate will carry over to other passages at that same grade level. It may or it may not. A student may read an expository passage more slowly than a narrative passage. If a student is interested in the topic of the selection, the student may read more quickly. It is best to compare the reading rate of an individual student in oral and silent reading of passages that are as similar as possible. This is most important at the end of second grade or the beginning of third grade when students normally make the transition to efficient silent reading strategies. A student whose oral and silent reading rates are the same may not be actually reading silently, but may be mentally pronouncing each word—something that good readers do not do.

Reading rate is perhaps most valuable in identifying students who are extremely slow readers at their independent or instructional levels. Several things can cause such slow reading. The student may be mentally analyzing each word in the absence of an adequate sight-word vocabulary. Or the student may be overly deliberate; slow reading can signal an undue focus on word identification accuracy.

Should teachers or coaches be concerned about slow reading? What about a student who reads slowly but understands what he or she is reading? Should this worry a teacher or coach? I think it should. Think about the result of slow reading. A slow reader takes much longer to read assignments than his or her peers, which affects homework as well as class activities. If the teacher or coach asks students to read something in class, the slow reader seldom finishes and is generally aware that classmates have all completed the selection, while he or she may be only halfway through it. This easily leads to frustration. It is natural to avoid a frustrating situation, so the slow reader avoids reading whenever possible. Then what happens? Because fluency is fostered by reading, and because the slow reader chooses not to read, the problem not only continues but probably worsens. For these reasons, teachers and coaches must evaluate reading speed even if understanding is in place.

If reading rate is so variable, how do we interpret it? A colleague and I examined the oral and silent reading rates of normal readers reading at their instructional level. We found a steady rise in oral and silent reading rate as reading level increased and a drop in silent reading rate in upper middle school and high school passages, due no doubt to the increased difficulty of the passages. The accompanying chart summarizes our findings (Leslie & Caldwell, 2011). It is important to understand that these rates simply suggest typical reading rates and should only be used as rough estimates or general guidelines of acceptable reading speed.

Reading Rates

Level	Leslie & Caldwell (2006) (oral WPM)	Leslie & Caldwell (2006) (oral CWPM)	Leslie & Caldwell (2006) (silent WPM)
Preprimer (with pictures)	23–59	13–55	
Preprimer (without pictures)	22–64	11–59	
Primer	28–66	10–52	
First	37–77	20–68	
Second	43–89	19–77	
Third	51–97	32–86	
Fourth	55–105	27–87	
Fifth	61–133	30–114	73–175
Sixth			91–235
Upper middle school (narrative)			119–233
Upper middle school (expository)			105–189
High school			65–334

Curriculum–Based Measurement

In curriculum-based measurement (CBM), students read aloud from grade-appropriate passages for 1 minute while a teacher or coach records the number of words read correctly (Fuchs, 1992; Fuchs & Fuchs, 1999). This assessment occurs frequently throughout the year using passages of equivalent difficulty. The purpose is to evaluate the extent to which students are successful in reading their classroom text. Thus a fifth grader reading on a third-grade level would read fifth-grade selections. This differs from the use of an IRI, which establishes student fluency in independent- or instructional-level materials. CBM is more in accord with the grade-level focus of the CCSS. It functions as a screening device to identify students who are performing below the level of their classmates, and, if administered frequently, it can be used to graph and document progress throughout the year (Davidson & Myhre, 2000). Hasbrouck and Tindal (1992, 2005, 2006) list typical CBM-derived CWPM scores for second through fifth grades. For example, in third grade, low-performing readers reading grade-level text progressed from 65 CWPM to 87 CWPM at the end of the year. Average readers progressed from 79 to 114 CWPM, and high-performing students improved from 107 to 142

CWPM. However, it is important to insert a word of caution. CBM assessment does not address comprehension, and it is possible that a student may increase his or her reading level without an accompanying raise in comprehension.

Timed Administration of Word Lists

A student's ability to identify single words automatically can be assessed through timed administration of a word list. Does the student identify each word immediately, or does the student pause? A pause may indicate that a word is not a sight word, but a word the student must analyze in order to identify.

Take a graded word list and ask the student to pronounce the words. If the student correctly pronounces a word within 1 second, mark it A to indicate automatic identification. How can you time 1 second? Simply say to yourself "one thousand." If the student pronounces the word before you have finished, it is probably within 1 second. If the student takes longer, mark the word as C if correctly identified. Of course, mark all incorrect responses. Count the total number of correct words. Compare this number to the number of words that were identified automatically. If a student's total number of correct words is greater than the number of words recognized automatically, the student may lack a sight-word vocabulary appropriate to that grade level.

Donika read a list of second-grade words from a published IRI and scored at an instructional level for the total number of words that she recognized correctly. Of the 17 correct words, only 3 were identified automatically, which suggested that Donika was primarily analyzing words in instructional-level text. When Donika read a second-grade selection, her oral reading was very accurate, but her reading rate was only 35 WPM. It was not surprising that she remembered very little of what she read. All of Donika's energies were taken up with analyzing words, and she did this quite efficiently. However, she needed to develop and expand her sight-word vocabulary.

A different picture emerged with Jeffrey. His performance on a word list from a published IRI placed him at an instructional level for preprimer text. Jeffrey identified 14 words correctly, and all of them were identified automatically. However, he was not able to analyze words such as *make, place, write,* and *other.* Jeffrey either knew the word or he didn't. If he didn't, he had no word analysis skills to help him with unfamiliar words. Unlike Donika, Jeffrey needed help with word analysis.

Remember that use of a word list is a "quick and dirty" way of estimating automaticity. Listening to a student read orally offers a far richer opportunity for fluency assessment. Also, fluency in reading a word list is not related to reading comprehension as strongly as oral passage reading is (Fuchs et al., 2001).

Intonation Checklist

____ Read at a rhythm resembling natural speech (quickly, but not too fast to be understood).

____ Read smoothly without hesitations and repetitions.

____ Used vocal expression.

____ Noted punctuation signals.

____ Grouped words into meaningful phrases.

Assessing Intonation

Good readers are accurate and automatic in their identification of words. Marking oral reading errors (as described in other chapters) indicates reading accuracy; determining reading rate and the timed administration of word lists suggest reading speed. But what about the third component of fluency, intonation? Good oral readers are expressive. Their performance pleases and delights their audience. Teachers and coaches can use a simple checklist (such as the one provided above) to assess intonation whenever students read orally during classroom instruction. Using a simple coding system such as "Yes," "No," and "Sometimes" on this checklist may be more informative than simply checking off the items.

Assessing Student Progress in Fluency

A teacher or coach can and should assess a student's fluency at different points in time. One of the key purposes of CBM is continual assessment of CWPM across a school year. The teacher or coach can also compare reading rates before and after oral reading practice or after several months of instruction. Some students enjoy recording their reading rate and watching it increase as they become more fluent. Administering a simple checklist of intonation behaviors (as described above) at different points may be the most effective means of assessing this component of fluency over time.

Given the importance of fluency, it is a good idea to schedule regular oral reading practice. Asking students to engage in repeated reading of a selection has been found to increase fluency (Rasinski, 1986; Stahl, Heubach, & Cramond, 1997). Students can practice part of a selection alone or with peers. They can tape their first reading and their last reading to note progress. They can use a checklist to evaluate their own and their peers' intonation during oral reading. In fact, they can use the same checklist to evaluate their intonation as the teacher or coach uses. This checklist provides a wonderful opportunity to assess the progress of each student. It is a time when instruction and assessment truly merge.

Should a teacher or coach group students according to their fluency? Probably not. First, it would be very difficult to do, given the variability among readers' fluency in different kinds of text. Second, students profit from the modeling of their more fluent peers, as noted earlier. Consider what often happens when students of similar reading ability are grouped together for oral reading practice. The good readers and the more fluent ones listen to peers who are as skilled as they are. On the other hand, the poorer readers are subjected to repeated examples of slow, halting, choppy, or inexpressive reading. It makes more sense to group students of mixed fluency levels. If the practice activity is motivating enough, students will learn from each other and eagerly work together to improve their performance.

There are various instructional activities for practicing oral reading and for assessing student progress in developing fluency (Caldwell & Leslie, 2013; Johns & Berglund, 2006). Because students enjoy performing, teachers or coaches can foster repeated reading by assigning character and narrator roles to stories and having the students practice for the final performance. Or they can put on actual plays. Class choral reading can also promote fluency development. Older students can practice reading stories in order to read to younger students. All of these activities provide teachers or coaches with opportunities to evaluate their students' developing fluency.

Summary

- Fluency involves accuracy, speed, and intonation. Fluency allows the reader to pay attention to meaning.

- There is a complex relationship between fluency and comprehension. Fluency can result from comprehension as well as contribute to it.

- There are three requirements for developing and maintaining fluency. First, a reader must have a large store of sight words. Second, the reader needs efficient strategies for analyzing new and unfamiliar words. Third, the reader must focus on meaning.

• Fluency develops through reading, through models of fluent reading in the home and classroom, and through the kind of reading that students do.

• The CCSS address fluency under the Reading Standards: Foundational Skills K–5 (CCSSI, 2010, pp. 16–17). The focus of the Standards on purpose and understanding clearly places fluency as a determinant of comprehension.

• Close reading, as required by the Standards, is not fluent reading. While close reading may become more fluent with repeated reading, fluency does not necessarily foster close reading. Fluency develops to the extent that close reading is successful.

• Early designs for RTI focused on the younger struggling reader, and fluency played a major role in the choice of assessment, the design of instruction, and the determination of growth. A focus on fluency continued when RTI moved to the adolescent level.

• A teacher or coach can assess general fluency level by listening to students read orally in instructional-level text. Do not assume that fluency level in instructional-level text is the same as level of fluency in grade level text.

• The teacher or coach can assess accuracy by recording oral reading errors (as described in other chapters). The teacher or coach can assess intonation by using a checklist.

• The teacher or coach can assess speed by determining reading rate and by timed administration of graded word lists. Reading rate is measured as WPM or as CWPM. Reading rate varies across individuals and texts; it also varies according to readers' purposes. Compare a student's reading rate in oral and silent reading or at different points in time. Do not assume that reading rate on one graded passage will be the same as on other passages at that grade level. Do not compare the rates of different students.

• Oral reading practice should be regularly scheduled in the classroom or coaching session, and used as an opportunity for assessment.

Activities for Developing Understanding

• Choose an unfamiliar and difficult selection. Read it orally and tape-record your reading. Then practice the selection by repeatedly reading it. Tape yourself a second time. Listen to the two tapes. What differences do you note?

• Listen to several students read orally and tape-record their reading. Listen to the tapes and determine accuracy and speed. Use a checklist to assess intonation.

• Time someone silently reading a difficult selection, such as a newspaper editorial. Then time the person reading an easy selection, such as a movie review. Determine the reading rate in each selection. What differences do you notice?

• Ask a student to read a graded word list and tape-record his or her performance. When you listen to the tape, differentiate between words that are identified automatically and those that were analyzed.

• Compare the fluency of a struggling reader in instructional-level text and grade-level text. What differences do you notice besides reading rate?

Questions to Ask about Fluency Assessments

Fluency assessments are seldom stand-alones; that is, they are generally part of test batteries that assess a variety of skills and can be located by such search terms as "reading diagnostic assessments," "reading skill indicators," and "literacy screenings." All informal reading inventories include fluency assessment. Whether you are searching for a fluency assessment or reviewing one that is part of a test battery, ask the following questions.

• Is fluency defined by standardized scores based on a norm group, or is it defined more informally in reference to a list of typical reading rates at different grade levels? The list of fluency levels may be more helpful to a teacher or coach who can use it to evaluate a variety of fluency measurements. A standardized score can only apply to the fluency measurement on which it is based, that is, specific passage length and/or directions for administration.

• What is the source of the fluency rates? Do they derive from narrative text, expository text, or both? Fluency while reading a narrative and fluency while reading an expository passage are two very different entities. At lower grade levels, it may be sufficient to assess fluency only in narrative text. At upper grade levels, however, assessing fluency in both narrative and expository text is desirable.

• What is the length of the fluency passage? Some fluency measures can be as short as 3 minutes. Others can involve a relatively lengthy text. While short passages are less time-consuming to administer and score, longer passages may be more reflective of what students are asked to read in the classroom.

• Does the assessment only focus on speed or does it also offer suggestions for assessing intonation or expression? A student who reads text slowly but with attention to intonation may well comprehend the material and lack of appropriate rate is the result of text difficulty.

• Does the instrument offer suggestions for measuring progress in fluency? Is progress measured by repeated reading of the same text or reading of different texts at presumably the same level? Texts at the same level can so differ in content and style that lack of progress may be due to the text, not a student's improved fluency.

• You cannot expect that fluency measures will be specifically related to the CCSS. The Standards require close and careful reading and rereading. Close reading is seldom fluent. Grade-level reading as required by Standard 10 may involve fluency for some texts but not for all. For that reason, it is perhaps best to use lack of fluency as an indicator of uncertain word identification and/or conceptually difficult text. This suggests a focus on words and concepts, not reading speed.

CHAPTER 9

Vocabulary Knowledge

How Can We Assess Comprehension of Words?

How We Learn Words

Few would argue that understanding word meanings is a critical and essential component of comprehension. Many studies have demonstrated that vocabulary knowledge strongly predicts comprehension (Nagy, 2010; Pearson, Hiebert, & Kamil, 2007; Stahl & Nagy, 2006; RAND Reading Study Group, 2002). Vocabulary learning occurs in a variety of ways. We learn new words by listening to parents, friends, and television commentators, to name but a few. We learn new words by engaging in conversation. At times, we may ask a speaker to explain the meaning of a particular word; however, in most situations, the context of the conversation provides enough clarification. We also learn new words by reading. Some time ago I was deeply engrossed in a novel and met the word *solecism*. The character had committed a serious solecism. I gathered from the context that this was not a good thing, but the exact nature of what the character did escaped me and the text did not offer any explicit clues as to what had happened. I was interested enough to put the book down and seek out a dictionary, where I learned that a *solecism* is an error or mistake, specifically a breach of good manners or a social blunder. I suppose if I had not used the dictionary I would have eventually learned this through multiple encounters with the word. Nagy (2010) describes word learning as a gradual process and "a matter of many small steps" (p. 83). However, learning new words through reading is only possible if you read. Unfortunately, that route is closed to students who do little reading.

We learn and remember new words by connecting their meanings to what we already know, particularly if the new word represents a known concept. *Solecism*, for example, fits well with what I already knew about acceptable manners and what I had personally experienced. I could recall various examples of solecisms both on my part and on the part of others. What else do I know about *solecism* besides its meaning? I know how it fits into the syntax of our language, that is, its position in a sentence. We can say "It was an unforgivable solecism" or "His solecism made people angry." *Solecism*, as a noun, can act as the subject or object of a sentence; it cannot act as a verb. *Solecism* became a permanent part of my mental lexicon or dictionary.

How are our mental dictionaries organized? In other words, when I determined the meaning of *solecism*, what did I do with it? I certainly did not store it in my mental dictionary alphabetically! I stored it with similar or related words or concepts such as *mistake* and *faux pas*. I stored it with related experiences involving ignorance of word meaning and/or the need for or use of a dictionary. And when I meet that word again, I may well recall these other items as well. In fact, while writing this segment on *solecism*, I recalled two other experiences involving unknown words: an embarrassing mispronunciation of *idiot* in third grade and an even more problematic mispronunciation of *banal* during a college literature class. What is so fascinating is that we store and organize our mental dictionary unconsciously; it just happens.

What does it mean to know a word? For any word, we can know a little about it or a lot (Beck, McKeown, & Kucan, 2002). We may have absolutely no idea what it means, or we may have a general sense that it represents something positive or negative. We may recognize the word if it is surrounded by a supportive context but not be able to recall and use it in our own speech or writing. We may have a rich and extensive knowledge of the word that allows us to employ it in a figurative or connotative sense or our knowledge may be literal and limiting. We may understand how a word can fit into a variety of contexts. You might expect to find *solecism* in a literature text as I did or perhaps in a social studies text or news magazine that describes the unfortunate effects of solecisms committed by political leaders. I doubt we would find *solecism* in a science text, but we would certainly encounter *organelle* and *mitochrondria* in a chapter on cell organization. Are these unfamiliar words for you? If so, and because you know little or nothing about their meaning, you cannot connect them to related items in your mental dictionary. Many students meet such unfamiliar words on a regular basis and they resort to memorization of definitions in order to pass a chapter test. Unfortunately, such memorization seldom lasts.

Vocabulary Assessment and the CCSS

Standard 4 of the College and Career Readiness Anchor Standards for Reading states that "students should be able to: interpret words and phrases as they are used in the text, including determining technical, connotative and figurative meanings, and analyze how specific word choices shape meaning or tone" (CCSSI, 2010, p. 10). The Reading Standards for Literature and Informational Text specify that vocabulary learning involves much more than matching a word to a definition. It involves the following activities: identifying words that suggest feelings or that appeal to the senses; distinguishing literal and nonliteral language; explaining figurative language such as similes, metaphors, and connotations; recognizing the impact of an author's word choice on meaning and tone; understanding multiple meanings; and determining the meaning of general academic and domain-specific words. While the above expectations vary somewhat with regard to the level of a text and whether it is literary or informational in nature, there is one variable that crosses all grade levels. Students must define, understand, and/or expand word meaning as the word is used in the text.

According to the CCSS, vocabulary learning and vocabulary assessment center on the words in the text. Vocabulary lists and vocabulary exercises that are separate from the text no longer have a place in our classrooms. The words that are focused on, studied, and ultimately tested are the words that are present in the text. They may be identified as important in the teacher's manual or they may be words recognized as problematic for students or essential to content by the teacher, but they are words that are critical to understanding of what the text says. In addition, the text augments the reader's interpretation of the word. By connecting the word to the framework and perspective of the text, the reader expands his or her understanding of its meaning.

Does this mean that students should not use dictionaries and glossaries? No. Text does not always provide a handy definition of a word. Just as I was faced with confusion regarding *solecism*, so will readers often have to resort to the dictionary or glossary to identify word meaning. However, most words have multiple meanings and choosing the correct one involves using the context of the passage. For example, consider the word *respond*. As a relatively familiar word, it means to reply when someone speaks to you or asks you to do something. However, consider this sentence:

Cells sense and respond to changes in their environment.

Obviously, in this context, *respond* does not mean reply or talk back. Given the content of the surrounding paragraph, *respond* means react, adapt, or change. Most words have multiple meanings and choosing the correct meaning involves using the context of the passage.

A text can provide four different types of context to aid the reader in determining the meanings of words (Baumann, Ware, & Edwards, 2007; Baumann et al., 2002). One form of context is an actual definition of a word as in the following two sentences:

The United States has five regions. A region is an area that shares certain characteristics such as climate.

Sometimes, a text will define a word by a following phrase, as in

Erosion, a process that transfers soil and sediment to a different location, and changes earth's surface.

Morphological context includes meaning clues within the word itself such as prefixes, suffixes, and roots. Endings such as *-s* suggest a noun, as in *areas*; *-ed* suggests a verb, as in *altered*; *-ic* suggests an adjective, such as *athletic* or *artistic*. Morphological context, in particular, is a powerful meaning clue. The meaning of many multisyllabic words can be determined through attention to prefixes, suffixes, and word roots (Nunes & Bryant, 2011; Carlisle, 2010; Nagy, 2010). This may be especially helpful for older students inasmuch as the number of morphologically complex words tends to increase in higher-level text.

Syntactic context includes meaning clues derived from placement of the word in a sentence that signals a specific part of speech. For example, sentence placement following a modifier suggests a noun; placement following a noun suggests a verb; placement before a noun suggests an adjective. Semantic context includes four components: synonyms, antonyms, examples, and general words or statements that offer clues to meaning.

Focusing on context represents an activity that closely supports the intent of Standard 4. Teachers and coaches should teach students how to identify and use different forms of context as an aid to determining word meaning, and context should be a natural part of discussion. It is important for teachers and coaches to regularly assess students' ability in this regard.

Vocabulary Assessment and RTI

Vocabulary assessment and instruction in RTI at the primary levels generally include a focus on oral language development and recognition of high-frequency words. However, Scanlon and Anderson (2010) and Anderson (2010) used interactive read-alouds and repeated encounters with words in multiple contexts to develop word meaning. Some adolescent RTI programs also address strategies for learning and remembering word meaning (Gelzheiser et al., 2010; Goetze, Scanlon, & Ehren, 2010). While a focus on vocabulary development in RTI seems to take a back seat to word identification and fluency components, this imbalance may change as RTI programs adapt to the demands of the Standards.

Selecting Words to Assess

The first and possibly the most important step in vocabulary assessment is your choice of words to instruct and ultimately to assess. As mentioned above, often the choice is made for us by the teacher's manual or our own knowledge of the students. However, at times, we are faced with having to decide which specific words to emphasize. What guidelines should we follow?

The first and foremost guideline is an obvious one. The chosen words must come from the text in accordance with the dictates of the CCSS.

Second, select words that are important. They should be words that the reader needs to know in order to arrive at a rich understanding of the text (Harmon, Hedrick, Soares, & Gress, 2007). They should be useful words, that is, words that are frequent enough that the reader will probably meet them again and again. But how can a teacher or coach select words when faced with numerous possibilities for choice? Several guidelines may be of help.

Hirsch compiled a list of terms that he felt students should know as part of their cultural literacy and selected key items for each grade level (Hirsch, 1987; Hirsch, Kett, & Trefil, 1993). Marzano, Kendall, and Gaddy (1999) selected words from state benchmarks and standards and compiled word lists based on grade level and content areas. You may find such lists helpful in selecting words for instructional emphases. Beck et al. (2013) describe three tiers of words. The first tier is composed of familiar words. These seldom require instructional attention because they are very familiar and students already know them. At a fourth-grade level such words might include *change, water, dangerous,* and *journey.* The second tier of words includes high-frequency and useful words that occur often in multiple contexts, such as *constant, diminish,* and *reinforce.* These may represent words that the student has never seen before but they stand for familiar concepts. The third tier of words are words specific to different content areas such as *nucleus*, *evaporates*, and *nullification*. Stahl and Nagy (2006) state that learning third-tier words generally represents learning unfamiliar words for unfamiliar concepts, a difficult endeavor at best. Third-tier words also involve learning new meanings for familiar words such as *envelope* as the outer covering of a virus and *plates* as pieces in the earth's crust. You should select words for instructional emphasis from the second and third tiers.

In a similar fashion, Greenwood and Flanagan (2007) recommend grouping words into four levels. The first level includes words that are essential to a reader's understanding of the passage. For example, *nullification* is a critical term if one is to understand the actions of Andrew Jackson with regard to an unpopular tariff. The second level includes new words for known concepts (*electorate* for *voters*) and new words for new concepts (*terrigenous* for describing sediment that originates on land). Level-3 words are words that can be addressed during or after reading because of students' apparent misunderstanding. Level-4 words are not important to teach because their meaning can be easily inferred from the text.

Coxhead (2000) analyzed 3.5 million words from college texts and identified "frequently occurring words and those which occur in many different kinds of texts" (p. 215). Five hundred and seventy word families occurred at least 100 times across all content areas. A word family is a stem such as *legis* and related affixed forms: *legislated, legislates, legislating, legislation, legislative, legislator, legislators*, and *legislature*. Coxhead's Academic Word List can provide a handy reference for a teacher who is trying to decide which of several possible words to emphasize. An examination of social studies and science teacher manuals across grades four through high school revealed the inclusion of many words from this list at all levels.

Assessing Word Knowledge

How will you know if a student knows a word? According to Stahl (1986) and Stahl and Fairbanks (1986), there are three levels of word knowledge: association, comprehension, and generation. *Association* means that a student can associate a word with other words; however, it does not necessarily follow that the student knows its meaning. For example, a student can associate *terrigenous* with *sediment* without having any idea of what the word means. *Comprehension* means that the student knows a common meaning for a word. The student knows *features* as facial features or perhaps as features in a magazine or newspaper but does not understand features as topographies or landscapes. *Generation* means that the student can provide or use a word in a new context, for example, *pursuing* learning as opposed to *pursuing* a fugitive. Appendix 9.1 provides questions that a teacher or coach can ask about any vocabulary assessment.

In a similar manner, Beck et al. (2013) suggests that knowing a word can range from simple to complex. Providing a simple association for *pursue* (*pursue* and *thief*) is probably easier than offering a full explanation (*pursue means to seek someone persistently, carry something out, or continue with something*). A general explanation (*pursue means to hang in there*) may be easier than giving a specific example (*the student pursued learning beyond a bachelor's degree*). This in turn may be less complex than offering a synonym (*tail, hound, continue, strive for*) or a full definition (*to follow in order to overtake or to continue with a plan of action*). This suggests that the difficulty of the assessment may depend on what we ask students to do with a word. It may also depend on the nature of our instruction. If we ask students to provide explanations during instruction but require them to provide examples during assessment, this disconnect may affect their ability to provide a correct answer.

In the past (and, I suspect, even now), our assessment of students' vocabulary knowledge left much to be desired. A typical method was some form of paper-and-pencil vocabulary test. Students chose a word's definition from four possible choices or matched a column of words to a second column of definitions. I imagine that many students received acceptable grades because they were lucky guessers, not because they had a profound understanding of word meanings.

A second common method of assessing vocabulary knowledge was to ask a student to use a word in a sentence. If the student used the word correctly, it was assumed that he or she understood it. This was probably true for students who demonstrated correct usage, but what about those students who offered an incorrect, incomplete, or ambiguous usage? Did this mean that they did not understand the word? Perhaps they knew the meaning, but failed to construct a sentence that adequately demonstrated their understanding. I remember assigning the word *extrovert* as part of a vocabulary exercise. One student wrote, "I extroverted down the hall on my birthday." The student obviously had some sense of the word's meaning, but did not understand that *extrovert* was a noun rather than a verb. And then there were the students who knew how to play the vocabulary game and offered correct but ambiguous sentences, such as "I saw an extrovert" or "There goes an extrovert!" What did they understand about the meaning of *extrovert* beyond recognizing it as a noun? Perhaps these students' performance was a function of disliking the sentence construction task as opposed to knowing the word meanings. I cannot recall any students who approached the sentence-writing assignment with enthusiasm. Most picked up their pencils with glum resignation, and some with downright antipathy.

Assessing word knowledge can be divided into two general categories: selected response and constructed response. *Selected response* takes the form of multiple-choice questions and is probably the most common form of vocabulary assessment. The student reads a word in isolation or context and then selects the correct meaning from three or four choices. Standardized vocabulary tests primarily take the form of selected response. How do such tests select words? They primarily choose words according to their frequency of usage at different levels and in different disciplines (Zeno et al., 1995), and chosen words may or may not be present in your classroom texts. I consider selected response as a very general index of vocabulary knowledge. In real life, we do not meet lists of words, nor do we select word meaning from four choices. We meet words in the context of a passage and use that context to determine meaning. Assessing comprehension through passage reading is more natural or authentic. Besides, even if a student can define test words at a certain level, this does not mean that the student can put it all together and comprehend a lengthy passage containing such words. Also, what about all the words that the student will meet during storybook or textbook reading that are not on the list?

Constructed response vocabulary items fall into several general categories. You can ask students to provide a synonym, antonym, or definition for a word. Students can compare the word to other words or categorize it in some way. They can extend the word by providing examples or nonexamples. The final category is usage; the student uses or applies the word to a new context.

Selected response questions are relatively easy to construct and to score. Constructed response items are not. However, constructed response offers more in terms of what a teacher or coach can learn about a student's word knowledge. In Chapter 4, I discussed how a rubric can make assessment easier and more reliable. If you assess vocabulary through constructed response questions, the following rubric may be of help (Caldwell, 2008).

3	2	1	0
Comprehension of word meaning is clearly evident.	Comprehension of word meaning is evident but some vagueness is present.	Comprehension of word meaning is vague and lacks specificity.	There is no indication that word meaning is understood.

Some teacher manuals provide helpful suggestions for vocabulary assessment; others simply indicate words that are important for students to know. One social studies manual listed six to eight words along with page numbers where the word could be found. The student was instructed to write a sentence describing what the word means in the context of the passage. This activity matches well with Standard 4 that asks the reader to interpret a word as it is used in the text. The above rubric would be of help in evaluating such a constructed response activity.

A vocabulary application activity that reveals whether students understand a word is to ask them to put a word in their own lives. That is, instead of composing a dull sentence using the word, they must describe how the word could fit into their world. Students can relate a word to their life orally or in writing. Does the word describe someone in their family, neighborhood, or favorite television program? Does the word depict an event, an action, or an emotion that they have experienced or observed in others? What are the circumstances surrounding this word? While this can be effective in literature and social studies text, it would not be suitable for discipline-specific words such as *prokaryotes*. Can you imagine asking students to put *organelles* in their lives?

Vocabulary words are also parts of speech. They are nouns, verbs, adjectives, and adverbs. Only in a word list do parts of speech stand alone. In sentences, nouns join with verbs and adjectives. Adverbs join with verbs. So ask students to match each vocabulary word with another part of speech. If the vocabulary word is a noun, match it to a verb. What would this noun do? In order to make a reasonable match, the student has to understand the word's meaning. What does a *submersible* do? It collects underwater data. What do *organelles* do? They capture and release energy in a cell. If the word is a verb, students tell who or what would perform this action, and/or why they would do so. What noun would match with *projected* or *contend*? Andrew Jackson *projected* himself as a common man. The two political parties *contended* for victory. If the word is an adjective, whom or what would it describe? What nouns could be joined with the adjectives *fundamental* or *precise*? A belief in state's rights was *fundamental* for the southern states. *Precise* measurements are important in scientific research. At times, word matches will come from the student's own lives. At other times, they can and should be drawn from the text. In accordance with the CCSS, asking students to return to the text to locate matches is effective for both instruction and assessment.

Another application activity is to have students sort a group of words on the basis of their meaning. Chapter 7 talked about word sorts as a way of assessing knowledge of letter–sound patterns. The activity of meaning sorts can develop vocabulary knowledge as well as reveal it. Students can work individually or in pairs to sort the words. You can also use sorting as a whole-class or large-group activity. Simply state a category, such as "something you can buy," and ask individuals to identify a word/s that matches the category and provide a rationale for the match.

This is an effective activity for reviewing vocabulary words that were part of past units of instructions. Forgeting takes place all too quickly and review activities keep word meanings fresh in the students' mind. As a teacher or coach, you can provide the categories for sorting or can allow students to choose their own categories. The categories for meaning sorts must be rather general in order to allow students to realistically group words that have very different meanings. Of course, the key to an effective meaning sort is a student's reason why a word fits a

CATEGORIES FOR MEANING SORTS

- Words that stand for something you can touch, see, hear, taste, or smell.
- Words that stand for something you can buy, sell, own, trade, learn, or make.
- Words that stand for something that is in your house, book bag, kitchen, bedroom, classroom., etc.
- Words that stand for something you can do or be.
- Words that stand for something you saw someone do on TV, in the movies, in your neighborhood, etc.
- Words that stand for something an animal, plant, or machine can be or do.
- Words that can describe a person, an animal, a plant, a food, a sport, etc.
- Words that stand for something that is helpful, necessary, unnecessary, harmful, etc.
- Words that make you feel happy, sad, angry, resentful, etc.

certain category. You can assess a student's understanding of words by observing his or her participation in a meaning sort. You can also ask the student to sort several words in writing and provide reasons for the chosen grouping.

Vocabulary application activities like these stimulate student discussion about word meanings. They help students expand their word knowledge. They also offer a teacher or coach opportunities to assess their understanding of vocabulary words. If the activity is oral, the teacher or coach must take care to record student behavior on the kind of checklist described in Chapter 2. Such a checklist may be quite simple and involve only two categories: *Applies word correctly* and *Does not apply word correctly.* If the vocabulary application activity is written, the teacher or coach will need a simple rubric to assess the effectiveness and accuracy of the student's vocabulary application. If the teacher or coach has a page in his or her grade book that is labeled for the good reader behavior of learning and refining word meanings and/or Standard 4, student performance on this behavior can be recorded and evaluated over each grading period.

Your interest as a teacher or coach is in the *process* of learning new words and expanding the meanings of old ones based on how they are used in the text. The process is the focus of assessment, not the meanings of individual words. Word knowledge is very personal. Students may understand a word in one context and not in another. They may remember a word because they are interested in a specific topic. They may forget a word because the topic bores them. It is unrealistic to expect that all students at a certain grade level should know the meanings of the same body of words. Learning word meanings and expanding upon them go on throughout life. Teaching students to apply word meanings fosters the development of this good reader behavior and/or Standard 4. Assessing their ability to apply word meanings indicates that the process is in place, even if some words are still unknown.

General Guidelines for Assessing Word Comprehension

Share with your students the words that will be included on the assessment. Knowing this information in advance focuses their attention and directs them to more meaningful studying. By doing this, you ensure that students study what you want them to study. Do you remember studying for a test and discovering that most of what you studied was not even on the test? Did you feel cheated in some way? I did. If I had known more precisely what the instructor considered as important, I would have focused on this subject area and probably learned more than by trying to master and remember everything. Assessment should not be a guessing game. It should be a precise measure of what the instructor considered to be the most important or relevant content.

Tell your students how you will test their vocabulary knowledge. Will they be asked to provide synonyms? Will they be asked to offer definitions or examples? Giving students these specifics ensures that they will study exactly what you want them to study. Also, as mentioned previously, a focus on definitions will not necessarily transfer to the ability to provide an example or synonym.

Make your assessment a parallel to class activities. If you focus on categorizing words in class, make this the format of the assessment. In this way you ensure that poor performance is probably not due to lack of understanding of the activity itself.

Consider an open-book format, especially for new and unfamiliar content. Select words that you feel are important for students to know. Ask them to use the text to determine their meaning. This assignment represents a match to Standard 4. Having students define a word based on the text itself is not as easy as it sounds. Much content text is concept-dense and locating the explicit definition of a word is not always easy. In fact, definitions are rarely present in the text. What is available are four types of context clues that we discussed previously. Instruct students in how to infer word meaning based on context clues and model the process for them (Flynt & Brozo, 2008).

Actively involve students in discussion of prefixes, suffixes, and roots (Baumann et al., 2007). These meaning clues take on increased importance as students move into disciplinary text.

Summary

• We learn words through listening, engaging in conversation, and reading. We remember new words by connecting their meanings to what we already know and we store it in our mental dictionaries with similar or related concepts.

• We can know a little or a lot about an individual word. Our understanding may be general or specific. It may be limited or expansive. We may only have a literal understanding of its meaning, or we may be able to use the word in speech or writing and understand how it fits into a variety of contexts.

• Standard 4 of the College and Career Readiness Anchor Standards for Reading states that "students should be able to: interpret words and phrases as they are used in the text, including determining technical, connotative, and figurative meanings, and analyze how specific word choices shape meaning or tone" (CCSSI, 2010, p. 10). One variable crosses all grade levels. Students must define, understand, and/or expand word meaning as the word is used in the text.

• Most words have multiple meanings, and choosing the correct meaning involves using the context of the passage. Teachers and coaches should teach the use of context as an aid to determining word meaning. They should make it a natural part of discussion.

• In selecting words to assess, choose words from the text in accordance with the dictates of the CCSS. Select important words that are essential to a reader's understanding of the passage. Consider using the Academic Word List (Coxhead, 2000) as a resource for word choice.

• Assessing words can be divided into two general categories: selected response and constructed response. Selected response takes the form of multiple choice. Constructed response involves use of context to determine word meaning: synonyms, antonyms, definitions, comparisons, and examples. It also includes usage or application of the word to a new context. A rubric can help the teacher to evaluate constructed response items.

• Application assessment activities include asking students to use the word in their own lives, matching parts of speech, and sorting words.

• Share with students the words that will be on the assessment. Explain how you will test their vocabulary knowledge. Make your assessment a parallel to class activities. Consider an open-book format for new and unfamiliar content.

• Instruct students how to infer word meaning from context and model the process for them.

Activities for Developing Understanding

• Locate and download the Academic Word List (Coxhead, 2000). Choose a selection from a social studies or science text at your level and examine it for inclusion of words on the list.

• Select a social studies or science text and identify words that you consider unfamiliar to students. Examine the various forms of context provided within the text.

• Examine the teacher's manual connected to a literature, social studies, or science text. Do you agree with the words that are signaled for instructional emphasis? What other words might you select and why?

• Select four words from a text and describe how you could instruct and assess these words in accordance with Standard 4.

Questions to Ask about Vocabulary Assessments

Published vocabulary tests are generally part of a complete assessment battery that can include decoding, fluency, and comprehension. A web search for terms that include "reading," "vocabulary," and/or "comprehension assessment" will lead you to many instruments both standardized and informal in nature. A search of publisher websites will also uncover example of vocabulary assessments. Your choice of a specific assessment depends primarily on your purpose. What do you want to know about a student or a class with regard to vocabulary?

- Is the instrument standardized, with student scores derived from comparison to a norm group? If the instrument is informal in nature such as an IRI, did the authors pilot and revise it prior to publication in order to adjust directions, choice of vocabulary words, and/or scoring? Piloted instruments are generally more reliable than those that were not piloted in any way.

- Is the instrument designed for a group or an individual? The format may affect both administration and scoring. A group vocabulary test has a selected response format; an individual vocabulary assessment may involve oral and constructed response answers. However, constructed response items are often difficult to score. Did the student offer an appropriate definition or synonym? A student's answer may not represent an exact match to the answer key; should it be marked wrong even if it seems to suggest some understanding of the word?

- How much time will it take to administer and score? This includes preparation time on your part involving reading directions, ascertaining that you understand them, and preparing for administration.

- Does this instrument focus on vocabulary alone, or is it part of a complete battery that focuses on other components such as decoding and fluency? If more than one area is addressed, does the instrument allow you to score each component separately?

- How does the instrument define vocabulary knowledge? In other words, how do students demonstrate their understanding of vocabulary? In this chapter, I discussed various ways in which a reader can indicate knowledge of a word and these are not all equal. Some are more difficult than others. Which form is employed by the test: synonyms, antonyms, associations, definitions, generation, and so forth? Is the question format selected response or constructed response? Most standardized and/or piloted instruments use selected response questions, which are easier and faster to score than constructed response. However, the ability to select an answer from four choices is less difficult than offering a synonym, explaining an association, or actually providing a definition. Another issue is the presence or absence of context. Recognition of word meaning is highly dependent on context. How much context does the test provide: a sentence, a paragraph, or a longer selection? An assessment that provides context is more closely allied with Standard 4 of the CCSS.

• What is the source of words chosen by the authors of the test? Most vocabulary assessments select words based on their frequency at different levels. They suggest a student's ability to provide meanings for such words; however, this does not mean that students will be equally successful defining content-specific words in their textbooks. Also, words take on multiple meanings depending on the context of the selection. For example, consider the word *feature*. It can refer to a part of a face, a prominent characteristic, an article in a newspaper or journal, and a geographical structure such as a canyon or plateau. A vocabulary test may suggest a student's ability to recognize and/or define in one context but not in others.

• What will a score on this measure tell you about individuals and about your class? Will it give you any specific suggestions for instruction? Does it categorize the word in any way and possibly identify a student's difficulty with prefixes, suffixes, and roots?

• Finally, and perhaps most important in this present educational climate, how is this assessment connected with the CCSS? Does the test in any fashion deal with technical, connotative, and figurative word meaning as stated in Standard 4?

CHAPTER 10

Comprehension of Text

How Can We Assess Understanding of Text?

The Role of Comprehension in the Reading Process

To state it simply, comprehension is reading. Without comprehension, there would be no purpose to reading words. Nobody ever curled up with a good list of words! Comprehension is what entices the reader to continue reading. Let's consider a familiar scenario. Picture yourself at 2:00 in the morning. You know you should be in bed, but you can't put down the novel you are reading. You only have 50 pages left, and you have to discover how it turns out. You know you will not get enough sleep and will probably wake up crabby, but you have to finish the book. This illustrates the power of comprehension. If you did not understand what you are reading, you would find it very easy to set the book aside and go to bed.

I remember working with Kellie, a middle school student who had few strategies for effectively analyzing unfamiliar words. As her skill in word identification improved, she was able to pay more attention to meaning, and for the first time she actually began to understand what she read. After reading a short article on her favorite singer, she commented, "You know, there was a lot of good stuff in here." Comprehension is the "good stuff"! Teachers and coaches need to know whether that good stuff is accessible to their students.

Comprehension is an active process. Good readers use the words of the author to construct a personal version of the text in their minds. This text is similar to what the author has written, but good readers supply additional details and make inferences that are not stated in the text. Remember the story of Taffy and Diane in Chapter 2, and all the things you did in your mind as you read? You understood information that was stated directly, such as the names of the characters and some of their actions. But you did much more. You created visual images. You made predictions and confirmed their accuracy. You asked questions and synthesized information. You drew on your knowledge of pet ownership to make inferences. You became emotionally involved in the fate of the characters. All of these actions are involved in comprehension. Good readers sometimes take comprehension for granted because it seems to happen so effortlessly.

Our ability to understand what we read is partially dependent upon the topic knowledge that we bring to the act of reading. If we know a lot about a topic, we use this knowledge to interpret the text, to make inferences, and to create visual images as you did when reading about Taffy and Diane. But what about your reading of the second selection on proving the continental drift theory? Was it as effortless? Probably not. Because you lacked knowledge of this particular topic, you found yourself asking more questions, drawing fewer inferences, and feeling considerably more uncomfortable with your ability to understand the text. In order for comprehension to occur, we need to bring some topic knowledge to the act of reading. A lack of this knowledge is what often makes some textbooks so difficult to understand. Until we develop knowledge of the topic (and this usually occurs as we continue to read about a specific subject), our comprehension is often limited.

Comprehension and the CCSS

Kintsch (2004) describes a text as made up of a series of ideas that he calls the *microstructure*. These ideas are organized in a variety of ways. They can be organized as a narrative, an explanation, a sequence of events, an argument, and so on. This organization is referred to as the *macrostructure*. The microstructure and macrostructure together form what Kintsch calls the *text base*. "Forming a text base is the first step in the comprehension process. . . . A good text base is representative of the meaning of the text and its structure" (Kintsch, 2012, p. 22).

Although readers must comprehend the text base, they move beyond it. Depending on their purpose, interests, and prior knowledge, they construct a *situation model*. You created a situation model of the Taffy and Diane scenario. You inferred, you questioned, you created images, you synthesized information, and you drew conclusions. In short, you created a situation model of the text. If you were a pet owner, your situation model probably looked very different from that of someone who has never owned or even wanted a pet.

Why have I inserted a paragraph on Kintsch's well-recognized and accepted theory of text comprehension? Because it is closely related to what the CCSS require. The Standards require readers to use the text base as the foundation for constructing their situation model, not their interests, opinions, or prior knowledge of the topic. In other words, readers must understand the author's ideas and how they are organized. "Readers need to get their mental arms around the text, to be able to retell it, to cite it, to ground anything they have to say about the text with textual references" (Calkins et al., 2012, p. 39). But where does reader prior knowledge come in?

We have tended to interpret prior knowledge in a somewhat narrow fashion as knowledge of the specific topic or content of the passage, what I referred to earlier as "topic knowledge." As a result, teachers have engaged in extensive pre-reading efforts to develop students' knowledge of a topic prior to reading. They often provide such information verbally, which rather negates the necessity for even reading the text. The Standards are quite definite in this regard. "Teachers should never preempt or replace the text by translating its contents for students or telling students what they are going to learn in advance of the text" (Coleman & Pimentel, 2011, p. 8).

This make a lot of sense if we accept the idea that prior knowledge is much more than knowledge of text content. Alexander and Jetton (2000) describe it as "a rich body of knowledge organized around pivotal concepts or principles" (p. 287). Prior knowledge includes linguistic knowledge of word meanings, sentence structure, and text structure. While it includes knowledge acquired in school, perhaps the largest component is the knowledge we attain from everyday experiences and from interactions with a variety of individuals. Readers construct a text base and a situation model using such knowledge even if specific information on the topic of their reading is relatively unknown. "Just as bridging inferences are required to form a coherent text base, world knowledge is often needed to form an adequate situation model" (Kintsch, 2012, p. 23).

There are three types of inferences that readers make as they construct a situation model: explanatory, predictive, and associative (Magliano, Trabasso, & Grasser, 1999). *Explanatory inferences* give reasons for an occurrence; they say how or why something occurred. Drawing *predictive inferences* involves inferring future consequences of an event. *Associative inferences* "enrich and fill in the detail" by providing information "on features, properties, relations and functions of persons, objects or concepts" (Trabasso & Magliano, 1996, p. 261).

Answering questions tied to the Standards involves drawing text-based inferences of all three kinds. The reader must search the text, identify relevant content, and select text components that generate or support a possible inference. For example, when asked to determine a central idea, the student must identify a topic either from a heading or from a repeated mention in the text. Then the reader must note what the author says about the topic, determine the author's overall purpose, discard statements that are irrelevant or unimportant to the topic, and combine all these in order to infer the central idea.

On the surface, the Standards seem to require different things; however, they are all really based on drawing inferences, albeit of different kinds. Standard 1 requires the reader to cite textual evidence for an inference. Drawing text-based inferences is the basis for the remaining Standards: determining central idea and themes (Standard 2); analyzing the development of individuals, events, and ideas (Standard 3); interpreting words and phrases (Standard 4); analyzing text structure (Standard 5); assessing point of view or purpose (Standard 6); interpreting content presented in diverse media (Standard 7); and evaluating and comparing arguments and claims (Standards 8 and 9).

There is another issue with regard to comprehension as defined by the Standards. Although the College and Career Readiness Anchor Standards for Reading "define general, cross-disciplinary literacy expectations" (CCSSI, 2010, p. 4) that pertain to both narrative and expository text, further iterations across specific grade levels wisely separate the Standards into narrative and informational categories. This is important because comprehension takes on different aspects depending on the type of text that is being read. Basically, comprehension of text, like text itself, is discipline-specific. What does this mean? "Disciplines of study such as social science, mathematics and science approach, represent and critique information in unique ways" (Shanahan, 2009, p. 240). Different disciplines are characterized by unique structures and content. History texts, for example, often take the form of chronological accounts and cause–effect relationships. Science text emphasizes procedures and explanations. Different disciplines also employ different forms of academic language. What is academic language? *Academic language* is impersonal, formal, and complex. It is also abstract, concise, and characterized by compression of ideas into as few words as possible (Nagy & Townsend, 2012). It contains words that are morphologically complex, that is, heavily dependent on Latin and Greek vocabulary. Contrast the academic language in a history or science text with the language in literature selections such as plays, short stories, and poems in which the meaning of text is often driven by the use of figurative and connotative language.

Of course, reading does involve some similar processes across various types of text. We identify words and attain some automaticity in doing so. We learn many and different word meanings. However, reading comprehension is truly "context-dependent and influenced in part by the kind of text that one reads" (Shanahan, 2009, p. 257). While we do recognize that a science passage is different from a short story or play, we have tended to assume that generic strategies such as note taking, graphic mapping, and paraphrasing can be effectively applied irrespective of the specific discipline. This may or may not be so. Conley (2009) suggests that generic strategies (note taking, paraphrasing, mapping, etc.) have been infused into different content areas "without considering what makes learning in content area contexts both diverse and often challenging" (p. 547). He suggests that the process needs to be reversed, that is, teaching and comprehension strategies should be germane to specific disciplines. Similarly, Moje (2008) suggests that disciplinary literacy should take preeminence over generic literacy practices because "knowledge is inherently different in different disciplines" (p. 99).

What does all this mean for assessment? Assessment of a student's ability in one discipline may not generalize to a different one. That is, a reading level obtained by reading and comprehending a short narrative may not transfer to a longer science passage. I am sure you became very aware of this when struggling with the continental drift theory after breezing through the tribulations of Taffy and Diane. Similarly, the ability to demonstrate mastery of the Standards in one content area may not transfer to a different area. Reading assessment like reading comprehension is heavily context-dependent.

Comprehension and RTI

The ultimate aim of any RTI program is growth in reading ability, and that includes growth in the ability to comprehend text. First efforts in RTI have emphasized the lower grades and the development of word identification skills. However, there is ample research to suggest that improvement in phonics "may not persist beyond second or third grade or generalize to comprehension" (Wixson, Lipson, & Johnston, 2010, p. 7). Therefore, RTI assessment and instruction should include a strong focus on comprehension.

The ultimate aim of any RTI effort is that the student "catches up," that is, returns to active and successful participation in his or her classroom activities. Therefore, RTI assessment and instruction must focus on the CCSS. If RTI instruction does not address the Standards, few, if any, students will be able to navigate a safe and successful return to their classroom activities. Standard 10 requires independent and proficient comprehension of grade-level text. If there is an unfortunate tendency to think that this goal is beyond the capabilities of RTI students, I believe thinking this way does the students and their teachers a grave injustice. The Standards aim high; we should do the same. Suggestions made in this chapter apply to all students.

Purposes of Comprehension Assessment

The CCSS require that, by the end of the academic year, students should be reading at their chronological grade level. A fourth grader should be able to read fourth-grade texts, a sixth grader should be able to read sixth-grade texts, and so on. A teacher or coach needs to know a student's level of comprehension. Is it at, below, or above grade level? Few students have a single reading level. How do their levels vary across the different disciplines? At what level can the student understand familiar narratives? At what level can the student make sense of expository selections? Is there a difference between a student's ability to comprehend social studies and science text? How does the student perform when faced with material on familiar and unfamiliar topics?

The teacher or coach also needs to know a student's strengths and/or areas of weakness with regard to the good reader behaviors and/or the Standards. Which represent a strength for the student? Which represent an area of need?

A teacher or coach can determine comprehension levels by using the informal reading inventory process with a published IRI or with classroom texts. Using classroom texts is more authentic than some published inventories because they assess within the context of the classroom. Many IRIs contain texts written specifically for the instrument; that is, the graded materials are not drawn from actual textbooks. This choice means that they may or may not be representative of what your student/s face each day.

Some caution must be exercised in using the IRI process. It provides two scores: a level for word identification accuracy and a level for comprehension. As noted in Chapter 5, the teacher or coach cannot assume that these scores will be identical for the same passage. Sometimes a student will demonstrate poor word identification accuracy but acceptable comprehension. This usually occurs with very familiar narrative text, in which the student can follow the story line and successfully infer answers despite difficulties with word identification. Some students display the opposite pattern of acceptable word identification accuracy and poor comprehension, which often occurs if a student focuses on saying the words as opposed to making sense of the selection. It also occurs when the student reads extremely unfamiliar text. The student can pronounce the words but does not know their meaning. Because word identification does not always suggest comprehension, the teacher or coach must not confuse the two.

Because comprehension is discipline-specific, the teacher or coach cannot assume that comprehension of familiar and/or narrative text will be the same as comprehension of unfamiliar and/or expository text. It is not expected that a busy teacher or coach will be able to use the IRI process to determine comprehension levels for all students in familiar, unfamiliar, narrative, and expository text. However, the teacher or coach must understand that comprehension varies across different kinds of selections and should not infer comprehension of other kinds of text from comprehension of one selection. For example, assessment of classroom activities and assignments may indicate that a student demonstrates acceptable comprehension when reading narratives. The teacher or coach cannot assume that the student will perform similarly when reading a science or social studies textbook. When one is talking with parents or writing reports, it is always wise to qualify statements about a student's comprehension by differentiating comprehension of narratives from comprehension of expository textbooks.

Assessing comprehension levels with the IRI process moves more quickly in the lower grades, where the passages are relatively short. Some published IRIs provide short passages for the upper grades, but these passages are not typical of what older students read. Administering the IRI process with longer passages is probably more authentic; however, it does take longer. Because of this time problem, many teachers and coaches of older students reserve the IRI process for students who are obviously struggling with class materials. For the majority of older students, a teacher or coach can use class activities and assignments to assess comprehension levels. In other words, if the student comprehends classroom texts and is successful in related activities, the teacher or coach can assume that the student is comfortable reading material at that grade level. This observation is obviously not the same as a formal evaluation of whether the student is reading at an independent, instructional, or frustration level, but it does indicate that the student can comprehend materials chosen for his or her grade level.

There are a variety of published test batteries, many of them standardized in nature, that designate a student's comprehension level. This level may or may not align with what you see in the classroom. It is important to carefully examine the passages used in the test battery. Are they similar to what your students read in the classroom? Some batteries use very short passages and assess comprehension by literal questions. If you decide to use a published IRI or a test battery, your primary consideration should be whether the test passages match the materials that your students read in the classroom. You should also be concerned about the match of test batteries to the Standards, that is, whether or not the types of questions and tasks match the Standards in any way. Appendix 10.1 provides questions that you should ask about any comprehension assessment.

Scores from group standardized tests can also be problematic. In Chapter 3, I discussed what such tests tell us and what they do not. The format of such tests is not a format that parallels typical classroom activities. Nor does it reflect authentic reading behaviors. That is, we do not ask students to read short passages on a variety of topics and genres and then ask them to answer multiple-choice questions. Nor do we do this in our own everyday lives! Therefore, the score on a group-standardized measure may or may not parallel classroom performance or reflect the intent of the Standards.

Comprehension is an extremely complex process, and a host of factors interact to facilitate or obstruct it. Although we know more about comprehension than we did in the past, we are still very far from effectively describing or even understanding exactly what goes on in the minds of readers as they interpret text. We know some of the things that good readers do during the act of comprehension, but we do not know all of them. Neither do we fully understand how these interact with one another, or which (if any) are most important to the comprehension process.

We have attempted to explain comprehension by breaking it into parts. We have listed myriad possible mental activities that readers perform when they comprehend. At one time, as I noted in Chapter 4, we arranged these activities into scope and sequence charts. Unfortunately, we went a bit too far by collecting more comprehension skills than any teacher or coach could realistically keep track of. Then we turned the scope and sequence charts into pupil performance expectations and continued to make the same mistake. The good reader behaviors listed in Chapter 2 are also attempts to explain the comprehension process, and they are more manageable than the number contained in most scope and sequence charts or lists of pupil expectations. And now we have the CCSS, nine standards that are directly focused on text comprehension. Many educators are not happy with the Standards for a variety of reasons; however, nine standards are certainly more reasonable than our past efforts in describing comprehension. "The Standards are high, clear, and few. . . . For educators who are accustomed to state standards that can't be contained within a huge bulging notebook and that ramble on endlessly, the design is impressive" (Calkins et al., 2012, p. 11). Teachers and coaches should feel comfortable with an emphasis on a few Standards. They are more manageable and allow teachers to better focus instruction and follow the progress of individual students. They also allow teachers to be more precise in their comments to parents as well as to students.

By the time the third edition of this book is published, standardized assessments of the Standards prepared by the Partnership for Assessment of Readiness for College and Careers (PARRC) and the Smarter Balanced Assessment Consortium (SBAC) will have been finalized and probably administered at least once. I suspect that the results of this initial administration will have a profound effect on literacy instruction. Of course these assessments focus on the Standards; however, they also focus on a student's ability to function successfully in grade-level or near grade-level text. These assessments move well beyond the typical selected response items. They include constructed response and open-ended assessments that move beyond the literal level. In short, students are asked to demonstrate their ability to meet the CCSS while reading grade-level text.

Assessing and Instructing Comprehension: Question Formation

The typical method of assessing comprehension has been for teachers and coaches to ask questions, questions, and more questions. However, this process has serious limitations. First, good readers ask questions of themselves and of the author as they read. It is questions that keep them up late to finish a book or chapter. Unfortunately, the heavy emphasis in our schools upon teacher questions tends to overshadow this role of the good reader. Students soon learn that teachers and coaches ask the questions, and that their job is to provide the answers. Teachers and coaches need to decrease the number of questions they ask and increase the opportunities for students to construct questions themselves and discuss possible answers. A second limitation involves the kind of questions teachers and coaches ask. Many educators, as well as authors of textbook manuals, ask questions that primarily assess literal comprehension. After all, they are much easier to construct and score. They seldom evaluate the higher-level comprehension processes that are the focus of the Standards. In order to assess and instruct students with regard to the CCSS, the teacher or coach will have to formulate questions that match the Standards.

Focusing on Question Stems

Questions begin with what we often call *question stems* such as *who, what, when, where, why,* and *how.* Question stems can also take the form of a direction: *Explain why . . ., Describe how . . ., Identify . . ., Defend . . ., Predict . . .,* and so forth. Question taxonomies use question stems to divide questions into various categories such as literal, inferential, and application. One of the first and perhaps the most well-known taxonomy of question types is that of Bloom and Krathwohl (1956) who divided questions into six categories: knowledge, comprehension, application, analysis, synthesis, and evaluation. Their original work was revised by Anderson and Krathwohl (2001) into remembering, understanding, applying, analyzing, evaluating, and creating. These taxonomies are based on what a reader must do in order to answer a question.

Grasser and Person (1994) based their question taxonomy on where the answer may be found, that is, "the nature of the information being sought in answer to the question" or what they term "question depth" (Grasser et al., 2010, p. 115). They list 16 different question types differentiated as shallow, intermediate, and complex. *Shallow questions* begin with *who, what, when,* and *where. Intermediate questions* focus on the understanding of quantity, quality, value, definitions, and comparisons. *Complex questions* center on data interpretations, causes, consequences, goals, instruments, procedures, resources, motivation, and values. According to the authors, this taxonomy correlates significantly with Bloom's original taxonomy. Mosenthal (1996) also differentiated questions based on the type of information needed to provide an acceptable answer. Identification of persons, animals, or things represents the easiest level. The second level asks for identification of amounts, attributes, time, locations, and types. The third level incudes identification of manner, goal, purpose, alternatives, and conditions. The fourth level focuses on identification of cause–effect and similarity, while the highest and most difficult level asks individuals to identify themes or indicate how things are equivalent or different.

So what does all this have to do with the CCSS? The Standards demand the high levels of comprehension identified by Bloom and Krathwohl (1956) as application, analysis, synthesis, and evaluation and by Anderson and Krathwohl (2001) as applying, analyzing, evaluating, and creating. The Standards address the intermediate and complex questions of Grasser and Person (1994) and the three highest levels of Mosenthal (1996).

If teachers and coaches are to assess which Standards their students have mastered and which ones still need instructional emphasis, they will have to match their questions to the Standards. At the present time, textbooks employ a variety of different question stems that are generally divided into literal and inferential. In the future, as publishers align their textbooks with the Standards, they may label questions as pertaining to specific Standards. However, until this occurs, the teacher or coach will have to match Standards to existing questions stems. I discussed this process in Chapter 4. You will probably also find that you will have to write your own questions and continue to do so until all textbooks are CCSS-friendly. Even at that point, you will probably have to compose questions for primary sources and other texts that do not come with attached manuals.

Let's begin by examining the question stems in the College and Career Readiness Anchor Standards for Reading. With the exception of *determine what the text says explicitly* and *cite specific evidence,* all question stems refer to components of higher-level thought processes identified by the previous question taxonomies. Simply use the stems that are present in the Standards to write your questions. While the question stems seem relatively clear, it may help to provide relevant synonyms. Such synonyms may aid in identifying questions in teacher manuals that match the Standards. Synonyms are provided in italics.

- Standard 1: determine (*decide; identify; explain*) what the text says explicitly
  make logical inferences (*conclusions; judgments based on evidence*)
  cite (*quote; refer to as authority*) specific evidence
- Standard 2: determine (*decide; identify; explain*) central ideas or themes
  analyze (*examine; explore; probe; interpret; evaluate; judge how and why*)
  summarize (*express concisely; condense*)
- Standard 3: analyze (*examine; explore; probe; interpret; assess; evaluate; judge how and why*)
- Standard 4: interpret (*explain; provide a meaning*) words and phrases
  determine (*decide; explain*)
  analyze word choice (*examine; explore; probe; interpret; evaluate*)
- Standard 5: analyze (*examine; explore; probe; interpret*)
- Standard 6: assess (*evaluate; judge*)
- Standard 7: integrate (*make into a whole; combine*) and evaluate (*judge; assess*)
- Standard 8: delineate (*define; describe; explain; present*) and evaluate (*assess; appraise; estimate; judge*)
- Standard 9: analyze *(examine; explore; probe; interpret; evaluate; judge how and why)*
  compare (*contrast; examine for similarity or difference*)

Questions are an integral part of the assessment process, and lack of student understanding of question stems will result in incorrect answers. You grasp the meanings of the above stems; do not assume that all of your students can do so as well. One of the first components of instruction should be to assess your students' understanding of such words as *analyze, interpret*, and the like. You can develop their understanding, if needed, by using question stems connected to familiar activities. For example, ask students to analyze why a particular play influenced the outcome of a game. Have them delineate the kinds of music played by different groups. Involve them in assessing the value of different computer games. Attaching question stems to familiar activities helps to clarify their meaning.

As mentioned previously, it is important that students ask as many or more questions than the teacher. They do not ask questions of the teacher. They ask questions of the text and of themselves. This is an important distinction. Standards-based comprehension is driven by what the text says and what the Standards expect the reader to comprehend and do.

Many students believe that it is the teacher or coach's role to ask questions. They do not really see themselves as questioners. In fact, some students avoid asking questions because they are afraid of looking dumb. As a teacher or coach, you can blend instruction and assessment by teaching students the different Standards, the question stems attached to these, and how they are answered differently. Have students generate their own questions using stems associated with the Standards and applaud and dignify their attempts to do so. Student ability to create such questions is a powerful indicator of their awareness of the Standards and what they should be looking for as they read. Students know why they are reading and what they are looking for when they read text they have chosen, that is, text that aligns with their specific interests. I recall a fourth grader who was passionately interested in weapons and wars and was eagerly perusing a book on great battles in history. When I asked him why he was reading this text, he immediately answered, "I want to see what kinds of weapons they had and how they worked." Students should approach their textbooks with the same aim, that is, know what they are looking for as guided by the Standards.

Joining Questions and Look-Backs

Looking back in a selection to find forgotten or unknown information is a common practice among good readers. Perhaps you are reading a novel that you have not picked up for several days. Before you begin reading again, you probably look back and skim the previous pages to refresh your memory about what happened. Perhaps you are reading a piece of nonfiction, and the author refers to a term or a process that you do not remember. What do you do? You look back in the text and locate where that term was defined or where the process was described. Do you remember when you were in college, and the instructor handed out a list of topics that just might be covered in an exam? Again, you looked back in the textbook to locate these topics and to reread the text sections that explained them. Because looking back and rereading for the purpose of comprehending are natural processes for good readers, you should encourage looking back to find answers to Standards-based questions. This practice allows you as a teacher or coach to differentiate between comprehension failure and memory failure. If a student fails to answer a question but can locate the answer after looking back, you have learned two things. First, the student is effectively using a good reader behavior and/or demonstrating ability to meet a Standard. Second, the initial failure to answer the question might have been due to memory lapse, not lack of understanding.

Unfortunately, many students do not spontaneously look back in the text to locate information. Many students unrealistically believe that one reading of a selection should suffice for answering questions or completing assignments. It is also unfortunate that many teachers and coaches assess comprehension without allowing students to look back in the text. Consider a typical classroom scenario. After the students have read a portion of the textbook, the teacher or coach begins to ask questions. If a student does not know the answer, the teacher or coach chooses another student and continues the process until a correct answer is given. Seldom does the teacher or coach suggest that the first student look back in the text to find the answer that was missed. It is even more unusual to find a teacher or coach who shows students how to do this by modeling the look-back procedure for them.

Good readers naturally employ the look-back strategy as a way of monitoring and increasing comprehension. Leslie and Caldwell (2011) noted that students with instructional reading levels of third grade and above could successfully engage in look-backs by skimming the text. Students with reading levels below third grade, however, tended simply to reread the entire text, beginning with the first sentence. The power of look-backs can be illustrated by contrasting a student's performance with and without look-backs. Using the IRI process, Leslie and Caldwell (2006) found that students uniformly raised their comprehension level after looking back in the text. Students at a frustration level moved to an instructional or an independent level. Students at an instructional level moved to an independent level. Because an assessment that does not allow for looking back tends to underestimate a student's comprehension level, Leslie and Caldwell (2011) strongly recommend that look-backs be a regular part of the IRI assessment process. A reading level based on a combination of questions answered with and without look-backs is more representative of what good readers do when faced with concept-dense and unfamiliar text.

Look-backs are a natural part of a good reader's repertoire of reading behaviors and they become even more important when dealing with Standards that "deemphasize(s) reading as a personal act and emphasizes textual analysis" (Calkins et al., 2012, p. 25). Look-backs are an integral part of "close reading" that I will discuss later in this chapter. It is important for teachers and coaches to model the look-back process as a form of instruction and to use it in assessment. Questions with look-backs can take two forms, oral or written. A teacher or coach can ask questions orally to an individual or to a group. However, when an answer is not known, the teacher or coach should suggest that the student and/or group should look back in the text to find the answer. Because the Standards are text-based, the answers must be based on text evidence.

If the student has difficulty looking back, the teacher or coach should model the process or ask questions that suggest look-back strategies.

"What are the key words in the question? Are you being asked to analyze, assess, interpret, delineate, or what?
Are you looking for a definition, a character, an event, a process, or something else?"

"Where in the selection might you find this information: the beginning, the middle, or the end?"

"How can the headings help you to decide where to look back?"

"If you are skimming the selection, what key words are you looking for?"

"Is there part of the text that you don't understand? Is it a word, a sentence, a concept?

As with all oral activities, the teacher or coach should keep a checklist handy to assess and record student responses. The teacher or coach can check whether a student answered a question after looking back in the text or demonstrated difficulty with doing so.

Written questions with look-backs are more controversial. We are talking about an open-book scenario in which students are allowed to look back in the text to locate answers to questions. Many content-area teachers and coaches frown upon this practice and require that students commit key concepts to memory. But reading teachers and coaches are not teaching content. They are teaching a process, the comprehension process. Therefore, it makes good sense for reading teachers and coaches to determine whether their students can employ the look-back process efficiently through writing. This process can be examined at your leisure and generally in more detail than oral look-back activities.

Assessing and Instructing Comprehension: Grade-Level Text

The first question asked by teachers and coaches when it is suggested that they use grade-level text is: "If they can't read it, how can I teach it?" Let's examine why use of grade-level text is important not only for meeting the Standards but also for moving students to grade level. This goes back to a concept that you probably encountered in a college psychology class, the concept of transfer.

Fostering Transfer to Grade-Level Text

Transfer is "the ability to use what was learned in new situations" (Mayer & Wittrock, 2006, p. 289). However, transfer between tasks occurs "as a function of the degree to which the tasks share cognitive elements" (Bransford, Brown, & Cocking, 2000, p. 65). In other words, understanding of literature passages will not transfer to science or social studies texts because the disciplines are so different. One possible explanation of the "fourth-grade slump" that occurs for both struggling and skilled readers may be that the focus on narrative text in grades 1–3 has not prepared them for reading expository selections that differ widely in vocabulary, structure, and conceptual demands (Kucan & Palincsar, 2011). I have administered the IRI process to many students over the years, and the majority demonstrated a wide gap between their instructional levels in narrative and expository text.

The accepted practice for struggling readers has been to identify their instructional reading levels and use these levels as the focus for instruction. The rationale has been that an instructional level represents the level at which they can succeed. While many of these readers demonstrate progress, few ever achieve at their chronological grade level (Johnston & Allington, 1991; Johnston, 2010). Results of the National Assessment for Educational Progress (NAEP) indicate that approximately two-thirds of our eighth graders do not read at a proficient level (Brozo, 2010). McCormick, Paratore, and Dahlene (2003) suggest that instructional-level text "may bar access to concepts and ideas otherwise acquired by reading grade-level texts" and "lack of exposure to grade-level concepts, vocabulary, and syntax may prevent children from acquiring information that contributes to their development of language, comprehension and writing" (p. 119). Gelzheiser et al. (2010) echo this viewpoint and suggest that if students "are not exposed to grade-appropriate vocabulary, their limitations in reading, language and knowledge grow even larger" (p. 224).

Basically, we need to teach students how to read grade-level material. The good reader behaviors and/or the Standards provide us with a blueprint for doing so. The Standards lay out nine activities that provide a foundation for both instruction and assessment. But let's return to the questions posed at the beginning of this segment. "If they can't read it, how can I teach it?"

Glasswell and Ford (2010) suggest that the teacher should offer instructional support for grade-level material through such practices as reading aloud and modeling strategies for analyzing text. The International Reading Association Committee on the Common Core State Standards (2012) states that use of challenging text "represents a major shift in instructional approach" (p. 1) and one that will require skillful scaffolding on the teacher's part. Such scaffolding includes reading aloud and extensive use of rereading, explanation, and encouragement. Shanahan (2011) emphasizes the need for teachers to identify what makes a book difficult and provide the motivation and support that students need to make sense of it. Some research actually suggests that grappling with difficult text may lead to more learning. McNamara and Kintsch (1996) examined the effects of prior knowledge on learning from coherent and less coherent text. Coherent text included such things as definitions, explanations, elaborations, sentence connectives, and the inclusion of numerous titles and subtitles. High-knowledge readers performed better on open-ended questions after reading the low-coherence text. Kintsch (2004) hypothesized that making things too easy may actually impede learning. Difficult text can stimulate deep processing if appropriately supported.

"Learners learning a new skill must have the opportunity to face difficulties and learn to repair mistakes" (p. 1314).

Remember that assessment and instruction are intertwined and that you assess as you instruct. As a teacher or coach, you can use several activities to guide development of the good reader behaviors and/or Standards in grade-level text, and at the same time effectively assess comprehension. These include engaging in read-alouds, fostering close reading of the text, and emphasizing summarization activities.

Engaging in Read-Alouds

We often read aloud to young students in order to expose them to text that they cannot read on their own. Why don't we read aloud to older students for the same purpose? I suspect we often assume that because they are able to read the text, they will be bored or even insulted by being read to. These assumptions may be woefully inaccurate. Many older students have instructional reading levels well below their chronological grade level. As a result they are unable to independently and successfully read their classroom texts. Many students reading at grade level might well appreciate being read to, especially if it helps them to better comprehend complex material. Adults obviously value being read to; audio books are extremely popular. So why should we hesitate about reading textbooks aloud and using this as a basis for discussing content and modeling comprehension strategies? You may say that you do not have time for reading aloud. However, the time spent reading aloud is probably no different than the time spent telling the students what is in the text and/or preparing them to read by engaging in lengthy prereading explanations of text content. In addition, it ensures that all students actually read the text. Assignments to read a chapter are, unfortunately, often ignored.

There are several keys to successful read-alouds. The first is the selection of the text and the second is the choice of Standard/s that you will emphasize. Seldom is an entire chapter the focus of a read-aloud. Select the most important parts of a chapter or sections or parts that you know will pose difficulties for the student. You want your read-aloud section to be relatively short in order to hold the students' attention. Using two or three short selections lets you avoid losing their focus, something that can easily happen during a longer read-aloud session. Another way to maintain attention is to have the students read along with you. You and the entire class can read together or you and a small group can do so. Do not ever ask students to take turns reading alone. This represents a boring experience for good oral readers and an often embarrassing one for poor oral readers. In addition, a focus on saying all the words correctly in front of their peers often ensures that little comprehension occurs. There are benefits to the process of you and the students reading together. Students are not troubled by having to perform in front of their peers and if they meet an unknown word, they hear a correct and fluent pronunciation. Reading with you focuses their attention; it is difficult to daydream when reading aloud. And you have the assurance that they have been exposed to the text, that is, they have read it.

The key focus during a read-aloud is not the oral reading itself but the Standards that you intend to emphasize during and after the process. Your focus is helping your students meet the Standards and there is no better way to do this than by combining the read-aloud with instruction in what to look for in order to answer a Standards-based question. "Discussion of specific reading techniques should occur when and if they illuminate specific aspects of a text. They should be embedded in the activity of reading the text rather than being taught as a separate body of material" (Coleman & Pimentel, 2011, p. 8). In a similar fashion, Johnston, Ivey, and Faulker (2011) suggest that classroom talk (including talk during read-alouds) should "turn students' attention to process" (p. 235). An emphasis on process dictates that you may read portions of the text several times as you and the students attempt to apply a specific Standard.

What processes should proficient readers engage in? Consider the Standards. Based on the text, they should draw inferences, determine main ideas or themes, explain and analyze text, determine the meaning of unknown words through context, recognize text structure, and understand author point of view. These are the activities that form the basis for read-aloud activities.

Read-alouds foster collaboration, which is a give-and-take proposition. Collaboration means that the teacher helps students find answers on their own instead of giving them the answers. Collaboration means that the teacher brings students into the process by asking them to identify areas of confusion and by pointing out textual clues that help them determine an answer. Collaboration does not mean giving students the answer. In a collaborative read-aloud, students ask as many or more questions than the teacher and they talk as much as the teacher.

Awkwardness is always part of engaging in a new activity, so expect to feel awkward at first. It will pass. A read-aloud does not take time away from content instruction. It involves helping students read text at a deeper level and showing them how to negotiate difficult parts. They will learn the content as they do this. Admit your own difficulties and how you resolved them. Students become aware that encountering problems during reading is a normal situation even for adults. It "changes the power dynamic" because you are not placing yourself above the students (Johnston et al., 2011, p. 232).

While the primary purpose of collaborative read-alouds is to help students meet the Standards, read-alouds serve a second and very important role. They expose below-level readers to the vocabulary, language, structure, and concepts of grade-level material. They provide direct and focused instruction in how to read such text. "By reading several challenging texts, students should build an infra-structure that enables them to approach new challenging texts with confidence and stamina" (Coleman & Pimentel, 2011, p. 8).

Fostering Close Reading

"Among the highest priorities of the Common Core State Standards is that students be able to read closely and gain knowledge from texts" (Coleman & Pimental, 2011, p. 6). Fisher and Frey (2012) define *close reading* as "an instructional routine in which students critically examine a text, especially through repeated readings" (p. 179). You engage in close reading when following instructions for filling out an income tax return or when assembling an expensive piece of electronic equipment. You do not skim. You read slowly. You reread multiple times, often word for word. You stop and tell yourself what you understand. You verbalize what you still find confusing. You move slowly through the text and do not proceed until you have clearly understood what came before. The instructional purpose of fostering close reading is "to build the necessary habits of readers when they engage with a complex piece of text" (Fisher & Frey, 2012, p. 179). It is not a quick fix. It involves engaging in multiple rereadings and paying attention to detail, two elements often ignored by students.

The basic component for effective close reading is choice of passage. Select short and relatively complex passages, what Fisher et al. (2012) describe as "worthy" (p. 108). This is necessary if students are to learn how to address difficult text. Do not tell the students what the text says. Students must use the close-reading process to determine meaning on their own. Provide a context by asking text-dependent questions that are based on the Standards and foster close reading through read-alouds, teacher modeling, and collaborative discussions (Fisher & Frey, 2012).

The key component of close reading is that students recognize what they do not understand and what they should understand. The Standards provide the structure for making this distinction. Students must become used to approaching a text in order to identify text evidence (Standard 1), recognize central ideas (Standard 2), analyze why and how (Standard 3), interpret word meanings (Standard 4), recognize text structure (Standard 5), and identify point of view or purpose (Standard 6). Reader confusion can lead to teacher modeling of various strategies such as breaking apart sentences, noting signal words, paying attention to headings, locating contextual clues, and restating content in different words. It should not involve the teacher or coach rephrasing content in simpler language or explaining content. The teacher or coach works with the students to build understanding of the text by rereading, examining sentences more closely, restating the text in their own words, locating context that offers clues to word meaning, describing what information is required by a Standard, and so on.

Approach close reading with questions that are focused on the Standards. Use the question stems that I discussed earlier. These stems represent what readers should ask themselves about the text. Students are not used to asking questions. From their viewpoint, questions emanate from the text or the teacher. Self-generated questions are the first step to effective close reading. What is the author's central idea? How does the author structure the text? What are some words that I have never met before? What is the author's point of view and what clues in the text suggest this? How does the visual help me to understand the text?

Taking notes in close reading is critical; offer students different options for doing this. Text annotation is an interesting option for close reading (Fisher & Frey, 2012). It involves marking the text using margin notes and various symbols to highlight major points. Zywica and Gomez (2008) describe *annotation* as a "structured way to mark up the text so it is more manageable" (p. 112). They offer 12 different annotation symbols such as placing a square around key vocabulary, circling headings and subheadings, double underlining of main ideas, and single underlining under supporting details. Of course text annotation also requires writing in books, which many teachers and school districts frown upon. However, the growing presence of e-books and electronic note taking make this an option worth pursuing.

A variety of books and websites offer specific suggestions for fostering close reading. You will find some of these useful. Others will seem too detailed and/or impossibly structured. Remember that while close reading can take many forms, it should be based on the Standards. Realize that there is no one form of close reading that works for all students and in all texts. Close reading is basically a work in progress; it is highly dependent on the nature of the text. It is difficult, it takes time, and it is not always enjoyable, but satisfaction comes with learning how to approach difficult text.

How do you assess close reading? You do this by assessing its product, that is, the answers provided to Standards-based questions, the notes taken by students, their annotations, and the like. You also do this by recording student behavior on your clipboard. You do this the way that good teachers have always assessed their students, by watching, listening, questioning, and using some device for remembering what they saw and heard.

Emphasizing Summarization

Good readers summarize and reorganize ideas in text. Accordingly, another assessment measure to gather evidence about a student's comprehension is asking the student to summarize, an activity specifically addressed by Standard 2. You will probably find that you will have to teach your students how to summarize, and, of course, some ongoing assessment of their progress is involved. Recent examples that I have read of student summaries by fourth-grade through high school students suggest that few students are able to construct a coherent and text-based summary.

Summary construction is a process in itself and one that requires reading, writing, rereading, and rewriting. Writing a summary is often more difficult than answering a content-based question. Question stems signal expectations for answers; however, the reader who summarizes must reconstruct the text on his or her own, selecting what is relevant to the intent of the summary and what is not. Crafting coherent and complete summaries is not an easy task, but helping students to summarize grade-level text serves multiple purposes. First, this specifically addresses Standard 2. Second, the process of writing a summary requires close reading. Third, if a student does not comprehend the text, the student will not be able to compose an adequate summary, so a summary is, in a way, a proxy for assessing text understanding. Teaching summarization through reading aloud and through close reading goes a long way to develop understanding of the language, structure, and content of the text.

Writing a summary of literature text is more straightforward than writing a summary of informational text. The structure of short stories, for example, follows a predictable sequence: setting, characters, goal and/or problem, a series of events in which one or more characters is trying to reach a goal or solve the problem, and a resolution. There are five possible structures that the summarizer of informational text may use: description, cause–effect, problem–solution, sequence, or comparison, and the choice of an inappropriate structure may negatively affect the coherence of the summary. Also a summary of informational text includes only the most relevant content about a specific topic (Ferretti & De La Paz, 2011), and selection of relevance is not always an easy task, especially in unfamiliar and/or difficult text.

Perin (2007) describes several steps for constructing an informational summary: delete unnecessary material; identify words, phrases, and sentences that can be removed; delete redundant material; replace a list of items with general words and actions; select a topic sentence; and if there is no topic sentence, write one. While these steps sound quite clear-cut, in reality, they often do not work for students. A passage may not contain lists of nouns or verbs that can be generically replaced. In addition, a key step is missing, that of *first* determining the central idea. Unless the reader is clear about what the author's purpose is or what the author has to say about the topic, it is extremely difficult to delete unnecessary material. It is the relationship or lack of relationship to the main idea that makes a text segment relevant or irrelevant. Helsel and Greenberg (2007) suggest crafting a summary on the main idea and details. Use the details to generate the main idea and to construct a main idea statement. Then, review the details and only select those that pertain most specifically to the main idea.

It is not easy to write a summary, and I strongly suggest that you construct the summary first before you ask students to do so and before you evaluate their work. You will be better able to understand the difficulties that your students may face. You can also construct the summary in front of the students using a SMART board. For informational text, identify the central idea and construct an introductory sentence. Then move through the text, cross out sentences, phrases, and/or words that are not related to the main idea and insert relevant descriptors (Caldwell & Leslie, 2013).

Evaluating summaries involves asking three questions. First, did the summary address and/or answer the question or the intent of the assignment? Did the assignment ask for a summary of an entire narrative or only focus on part of a text such as a summary of the process followed to ratify our Constitution or a description of proofs for continental drift? If so, did the student follow this direction and select text components that matched the intent of the assignment? Second, was the summary text-based according to the dictates of the Standards? This means that the contents of the summary must come from the text, not from student's prior knowledge of or opinions about the topic. Third, were the majority of summary components related to the content of the summary? If you have already written a sample of an acceptable summary, you can count the number of components in a student's summary that match your own and arrive at a fairly accurate estimate of summary quality.

Noting Student Progress in Comprehension

Noting progress in comprehension is crucial to students' development as good readers. As a teacher or coach, you can compare two performances of students or multiple performances. More is always better than less; multiple indicators offer a richer tapestry of student progress. Because of the many factors that can affect a student's performance on any one day, it is better to determine progress from multiple observations or activities. When doing this, be aware of the possible effect of such factors as the Standards that were emphasized, the text that was used, the discipline/s represented by the text, and the underlying concepts. Don't mix narrative and expository text. If the student's initial performance was in narrative text, assess later performances in narrative text to determine progress. Be wary of mixing Standards. Students may do better with one Standard as opposed to others. If assessments focus on different Standards, progress or lack of it may be a function of the Standards, not student ability.

During a single grading period, Garrett had multiple entries in his grade book. The grade-book entries represented different selections and activities, including performance during read-alouds, written summaries, activities that focused on specific Standards, and questions with look-backs. These involved reading both narrative and expository text. He coded each activity as SS for social studies, SC for science, and N for narrative. He coded each entry according the Standards (1, 2, 3, etc.) that were emphasized. He coded entries as oral (O) or written (W). This coding allowed Garrett to note progress and to evaluate performance in terms of possible contributing factors.

Summary

• Comprehension is an active process. Good readers use the words of the author to construct a personal version of the text in their minds. This text is similar to what the author has written, but good readers supply additional details and draw inferences that are not stated in the text.

• Kintsch describes comprehension as forming a text base from the microstructure (ideas) and the macrostructure (organization) of a text. Readers move beyond the text base to create a situation model. The CCSS require that readers use the text base as the foundation for constructing their situation model, not their interests, opinions, or prior knowledge of the topic.

• RTI students should also be exposed to comprehension instruction that is based on the Standards.

• Comprehension takes on different aspects depending on the text. Different disciplines represent information in different ways. Assessment of student comprehension in one discipline may not transfer to a different discipline.

• A variety of question taxonomies have grouped question stems according to level of difficulty and/or complexity. The CCSS address the higher levels of comprehension as described by several taxonomies.

• Questions are an integral part of the assessment process. The teacher or coach should use the question stems of the Standards to form their own questions. Students must understand the question stems, that is, what they are expected to do.

• Questions should be joined with look-backs. Many students do not know how to look back in the text to find answers. Look-backs are part of a good reader's repertoire of reading behaviors. They are particularly important because the Standards emphasize textual analysis.

- Teachers and coaches must learn a student's level of comprehension and how levels vary across disciplines. The teacher or coach must also know a student's strengths and/or weaknesses with regard to the Standards.

- The Standards require that by the end of the academic year, students are reading at their chronological grade level. Use of grade-level text is important for meeting the Standards and for moving students to grade-level competence. The use of grade-level text is based on the concept of transfer. An instructional emphasis on instructional-level text may bar access to the language, vocabulary, and concepts present in grade-level text.

- "If they can't read the text, how can I teach it?" Engaging in read-alouds in which the teacher and students read orally together is a strategy for making grade-level text manageable. The key focus during a read-aloud is not the oral reading itself but the Standards that are emphasized during and after the process. Read-alouds expose below-level readers to the vocabulary, language, structure, and concepts of grade-level text.

- Fostering close reading teaches students how to address difficult text. It can be easily combined with read-alouds. In close reading, students learn to use the Standards as their focus for comprehension. Taking notes is a critical concept of close reading. Text annotation is another way of making difficult text manageable.

- Writing a coherent summary is not an easy task. It can be made easier by first determining the main idea and by using this to select the relevant components of the summary. Summary evaluation involves asking three questions. Did the summary address the intent of the assignment? Was the summary text-based? Were the majority of summary components related to the purpose of the summary?

- Noting progress in comprehension means that grade-book entries should be coded to indicate differences in the text used and the Standard that was emphasized.

Activities for Developing Understanding

- Choose a selection and write a question for each of Standards 1 through 7. Compare these questions to those in the accompanying teacher's manual.

- Ask your students to define or explain question stems used by the Standards. Describe their understanding of specific stems.

- Ask students to answer questions first without look-backs and then with look-backs. What differences do you notice?

• Select a short text that you find difficult. Engage in close reading, taking notes, or annotating the text as you do so. What difficulties did you meet? Describe your success or lack of it. Which of the strategies that you used could you teach to your students?

• Write a summary of a story or a section of a social studies or science text. What difficulties did you encounter? How would you help your students to write an acceptable summary?

Questions to Ask
about Comprehension Assessments

There are many instruments that focus on assessment of comprehension. Some are standardized, some are informal in nature, and some are included as part of a teacher's manual. Published instruments change quickly; old ones are revised or dropped and new ones appear. A search using the following terms will call up more instruments than you may wish to consider: "reading inventories," "reading tests," "diagnostic assessments of reading," "comprehension tests," "tests of comprehension skills," "silent reading tests," and "reading mastery assessments." Also the websites of literacy publishers such as Pearson and Guilford offer numerous options for assessing comprehension. In addition, the web is full of individual teacher's ideas about how to assess comprehension in reading and in a variety of different disciplines. Your choice of a specific assessment depends primarily on your purpose for so doing. In other words, what do you want to get out of a specific comprehension assessment? Whether you are part of a group that is selecting an instrument for school or district use or choosing an instrument for personal classroom use, it is important to ask questions about any instrument and use the answers to direct your choice.

- Is the instrument standardized; that is, are student scores derived from comparison to a norm group (see Chapter 3)? If so, this means that you will have to administer it by strictly adhering to the directions regarding such things as passage choice and amount of time for administration.

- If the instrument is not standardized, did the authors pilot and revise it prior to publication? How extensive was the pilot? Piloting ensures that "bugs" are worked out prior to publication. Questions have been revised, scoring guidelines have been adjusted, and directions have been clarified. An informal instrument that has been piloted and revised may be more valid than one that was not piloted.

- Is the instrument designed for a group or an individual? IRI are all individualized in nature, as are other instruments that focus on individuals. Other comprehension measures such as the MAP mentioned in Chapter 3 are group-administered.

- What is the time element from your point of view? How much time will it take to administer and score the assessment? How much time will it take for you to learn how to do this? Time for assessment including preparation, administration, and scoring some instruments may be reasonable for a district assessment special-ist; it may not be practical for a classroom teacher or coach.

- Does this instrument focus on comprehension alone, or is it a complete battery that focuses on other components such as decoding, fluency, and vocabu-lary? If more than one area is addressed, does the instrument allow for separate scoring; that is, can you get a score for comprehension without administering the other subtests?

- How does the instrument define comprehension? I am not talking about a definition in the accompanying manual. I am talking about how the instru-ment specifically measures comprehension. Are the questions selected response or constructed response? Most, if not all, standardized and/or piloted instruments use selected response questions because the answer is either right or wrong and can be easily computer scored. Such instruments then "define" comprehension as the ability to select the correct answer out of three or four possibilities. I am not belittling selected response. I am only saying that the ability to select an answer may not transfer to the ability to construct an answer.

- How does the instrument define comprehension? Now I am talking about the nature of the passages. Are they narrative or informational in nature. Are they long or short? Do they resemble student passages in a basal reader, a social studies book, or a science text? In many cases you will find passages are relatively generic so a student's score is generic as well. It may or may not transfer to understanding of social studies, comprehension of a play or poem, or analysis of a science passage on an unfamiliar topic.

- What will a score on this measure tell you about individuals and about your class as a whole? Will it give you any specific suggestions for instruction? For example, if it is an assessment that is provided in the teacher's manual, does the manual offer any strategies for dealing with students who did not do well?

- Finally, and perhaps most important in this present educational climate, how is this assessment connected with the CCSS? Is there any match between the questions asked and the nine Standards? Is there any differentiation of the questions with regard to text structure, analysis, the recognition of central ideas or themes, etc.?

CHAPTER 11

Schoolwide Reading Assessment

How Can We Collect, Organize, and Present Classroom Data?

Overview of Classroom Assessment

A primary focus of this book has been classroom assessment of reading. Chapter 4 has addressed the issue of assessment as part of instruction, and subsequent chapters have explained various methods of assessing reading that can be employed by the classroom teacher or reading coach. Afflerbach (2004) lists several characteristics of effective reading assessment that can and should be addressed in the classroom. Reading assessment should be multifaceted; it should occur over time; it should measure a wide range of skills; and it should involve a variety of texts, formats, and purposes. Assessment should provide teachers and coaches with useful information about student progress. Such information should be aligned with and have an impact on curricula and instruction. Assessment should provide data

243

on student progress in meeting state and curricular standards—information that must be communicated to students, parents, and administrators. This chapter primarily addresses the last characteristic: providing and communicating data on student progress in reading.

Chapter 1 described four purposes for reading assessment: to identify good reader behaviors in students; to identify areas of weakness; to determine student reading levels; and to note individual student progress, as well as overall student progress in meeting state standards. In the current era of high-stakes testing and emphasis on accountability, this last purpose, noting student progress, must not only be emphasized but extended. We should not just identify student progress in meeting the CCSS across a school year, but we should communicate such progress to the external community—and, what's more, should present it as a viable addition to standardized test results presently being developed by PARRC and SBAC.

At the present time, our reporting of student progress in literacy is tied to two measures: a yearly standardized reading test (which may be replaced by the Common Core assessments designed by PARRC and SBAC) and report card grades. Both critics and supporters of high-stakes testing agree that such instruments should not be the sole measures of student progress. However, the public regards standardized measures as more important or meaningful than classroom assessment. This is not surprising. Data that are organized, reported, and annually shared with the public will naturally take on more significance than data that are not shared. But what about report card grades? Although they can have a profound influence on students and parents, they tend to be regarded as individual measures, and as such are not reported to the general public.

The richness of classroom assessment data on student reading performance remains largely unknown or unappreciated by the general public. Observing students, listening to them read, and talking with them about their reading can provide comprehensive and accurate pictures of their progress. However, such data are not accepted by public officials "as sufficiently 'controlled' or trustworthy to provide useful data for comparisons over time or across groups of students and teachers" (Enciso, 2001, p. 167). This may be because classroom assessment is extremely idiosyncratic. That is, individual teachers assess in different ways, with little consistency within a school or even a single grade level. Classroom assessment practices have been described as "highly variable and unpredictable" (Cizek, Fitzgerald, & Rachor, 1996, p. 159). This does not mean that the assessment is poor, but it does mean that, given such variability, it may be impossible to organize and report classroom data to the public in a clear and coherent manner.

Not only do assessment practices vary from teacher to teacher, but teachers' grading practices are also idiosyncratic. Allen (2005) believes that classroom grades as a measure of learning have low levels of validity, in that teachers assign grades based on a variety of nonacademic criteria such as effort, conduct, and attitude.

If classroom assessment of reading is to take on greater significance and be regarded as a possible addition to standardized high-stakes testing, it must change. There must be more consistency in reading assessment and grading practices across teachers, grade levels, and schools. Classroom assessments are very different from group standardized measures of reading, and criticism concerning their validity and reliability is common. The purpose of this chapter is to offer some viable suggestions for increasing the validity and reliability of classroom reading assessment and for reporting such assessments to the general public. If people begin to trust the soundness and the dependability of classroom assessments as indicators of student progress in meeting the literacy standards of their state, such assessments may some day be regarded as alternatives to standardized high-stakes test scores.

The Validity and Reliability of Classroom Assessment

It makes sense to begin a discussion of the validity and reliability of classroom assessment by describing a conversation with three fourth-grade teachers in an area school. I use this conversation to highlight the extremely idiosyncratic and inconsistent nature of classroom reading assessment. Although all were teaching the same trade book, it was quite clear that each teacher emphasized and assessed different components of reading, and did so in different ways. One teacher focused on literal understanding of the students through daily written quizzes and did not anticipate any final test activity. She felt that daily discussion was sufficient to evaluate overall student understanding of the text. However, she required each student to complete a project based on a character in the book. The second teacher combined literal and inferential selected response questions in a final written test that she designed. The test also included a short open-ended essay. The third teacher relied on a published test taken from the publisher's website and admitted that he had not analyzed the items as to what components of reading they assessed. Like the first teacher, he relied on discussion to evaluate student understanding.

Analysis of quizzes and tests focused on the number of right and wrong answers, with a literal item receiving the same point value as an inferential one. The teacher who assigned a character project used a rubric for evaluation, and she gave copies of the rubric to students before they began the project. The teacher who assigned a short, open-ended essay admitted that she did not use a rubric, but stated that she "knew what she was looking for." When I asked about grading, the first teacher said that she based final grades on the average of the quiz grades coupled with the grade on the character project. In addition, if students participated in the daily discussions, their grade could be raised. I asked if the quality of these discussions was assessed, and it was not; only participation and willingness to engage in discussion counted. The second and third teachers said that they assigned grades based only on the final test, but admitted that they included effort and behavior as components when finalizing grades for the report card.

I asked the teachers how they determined the grade level at which their students were reading. The first teacher used an IRI and attempted to assess each student at least twice during the year. She mentioned that it took a great deal of time, and she felt somewhat aggrieved that other teachers at her level were not doing the same thing. The second teacher indicated that if the students were successful in classroom activities, she assumed that they were reading at their chronological grade level. If students were not successful, she asked the school reading specialist to test them. The third teacher depended on data from a computerized system that assessed students after they read self-selected books at specific reading levels. If a student obtained an acceptable score on the book quiz, the teacher assumed that the student's reading level was the same as the book level.

Clearly, despite the fact that these teachers taught at the same grade level, were in the same school, had participated in the same district in-service training, and were required to meet the same state standards and curricular goals, there was little uniformity to their assessment practices. Subsequent conversations with teachers in other districts suggest that this disparity is symptomatic of classroom assessment, and research tends to support such a conclusion (Allen, 2005; McMillan, 2003; McMillan, Myran, & Workman, 2002; Cizek, 2000). Good things may be going on (I certainly hope they are in your classroom after you have read this book!), but teachers are generally "doing their own thing." This is not necessarily bad, but it does limit the extent to which classroom reading assessment data can be collected, organized, shared, and used as an alternative to high-stakes standardized testing scores. Unfortunately, the idiosyncratic and inconsistent nature of classroom reading assessment casts doubt upon its validity and reliability.

Classroom Assessment Validity

A *valid* test measures what it was designed to measure. Test validity is based on knowing the exact purpose of an assessment and designing an instrument that meets that purpose. Student assessment should "correspond to the type of learning behaviors being assessed" (Allen, 2005, p. 219). To return to the four steps of the assessment process described in Chapter 1, a teacher identifies what to assess and chooses an appropriate instrument for collecting evidence.

Teachers often are not specific enough with regard to the purpose of an assessment. I have made the case that it is important to tie assessment to the good reader behaviors and the CCSS. There is a vast difference between calling an assessment a measure of reading and calling it a measure of determining the central idea or theme of a text (Standard 2). Two of the teachers in my example clearly differentiated between literal and inferential comprehension but had not considered more specific aspects of inferential comprehension as delineated in the Standards and good reader behaviors. Sometimes educators choose published instruments that may not accurately reflect what has been emphasized in the classroom. This might have been the case with the third teacher I interviewed: items on his published instrument may or may not have paralleled classroom discussion.

All assessments should adequately reflect the skills, behaviors, or content to be measured. For example, if a test reflects what was demonstrated and studied in the classroom, it possesses validity. However, if the teacher emphasizes student understanding of the characters' thought processes and why they behaved as they did, but asks students to recall literal items such as names, places, and sequence of events, the test is not valid. Teachers who write their own classroom tests "should make sure that items on the test correspond to what was covered in class in terms of content, behaviors and skills" (Ravid, 2000, p. 264).

Assessment validity can also be weakened by scoring practices such as using a single score to represent performance on very different skills and abilities. Marzano (2000) offers the example of a math quiz with completion items and word problems that addressed four distinct numerical skills. A single score on the test would be ambiguous; two students might receive the same number of correct answers but demonstrate very different patterns of mathematical learning. The teacher who combined literal and inferential selected response items lowered the validity of the measure by not differentiating between the two question types when assigning a grade. One student might answer the literal questions and miss the inferential ones, while another could demonstrate the opposite pattern. However, because all items were awarded 1 point each and because a single grade was awarded, a valid analysis of student performance was not possible.

Classroom Assessment Reliability

A *reliable* test is consistent; that is, it yields similar results over time with similar students under similar situations. A reliable test would be scored similarly by all teachers in the district, and two students of similar ability would receive similar scores. This may be the case for objective measures such as multiple-choice and other selected response tests, but what about essay tests and class projects? We inherently understand test reliability. All of us have taken essay tests or completed various class projects for which we questioned the fairness of the grading procedure. College students often seek out certain teachers because of their reputation as high or easy graders. I suspect that experiences with the poor reliability of classroom tests may be one reason why the public regards standardized measures as more fair and scientific. To return to our three teachers, what if another individual scored the open-ended essay designed by the teacher who "knew what she wanted"? Would students receive the same scores? Maybe not. However, in the case of the character project accompanied by a rubric, there might be a better chance for reliability across different scorers.

Any discussion of classroom assessment reliability must involve attention to teacher grading practices. Individual assessments all receive grades, and these are somehow grouped into a report card grade. Marzano (2000) questions the reliability of classroom grading and cites several concerns. In particular, teachers consider factors other than academic achievement when assigning a grade (Allen, 2005; McMillan, 2003; McMillan et al., 2002). They may raise or lower a grade based on subjective elements such as perception of student effort, participation, and behavior. Brookhart (1997) found that teachers paid attention to two forms of effort in assigning grades: mental effort (how hard a student tried) and overt effort (the amount of work actually completed); however, some emphasized one more than the other. Although academic learning is clearly the most influential factor in assigning grades, McMillan et al. (2002) determined the following to be other important contributors to the grading practices of elementary teachers: student effort, student ability level, student attention and participation, inclusion of zeros for incomplete assignments, and improvement of performance since the beginning of the year. Of course, this also represents an issue with validity. If a test is supposed to measure reading comprehension, doesn't the insertion of effort or behavior lower its validity? Another factor that weakens the reliability of classroom assessment is how teachers weight different classroom assignments in determining the report card grade. One teacher may attach more importance to one assignment, while another teacher may emphasize something different.

Teacher grading practices have been called a hodgepodge of achievement, effort, and attitude (McMillan, 2003). Teachers vary in how they handle academic achievement versus student effort in assigning grades, and there is much variation in how they weight each factor. Measures of effort, motivation, and attitude are very subjective. Although they are no doubt important, Allen (2005) does not believe that they should be combined within a single grade but should be designated separately. Many districts require a single report card grade for each academic subject, and teachers attempt to communicate multiple pieces of information in a single grade. For example, what does a grade of A in reading actually mean, given the multifaceted nature of the reading process? What does it communicate about student strengths and areas of need? Did that grade include the subjective factors of effort and attitude? Including multiple sources of information in a single grade renders such grades "so imprecise that they are almost meaningless" (Marzano, 2000, p. 1).

Classroom assessment is a powerful tool for identifying the good reader behaviors and for identifying strengths and weaknesses with regard to the Standards, for noting student progress, and for determining reading levels. Such assessment tells us much more than any standardized test score can. But while classroom assessment possesses many benefits, it also has serious defects. It is probably impossible to eradicate all assessment flaws. There is no such thing as a perfect test, and this is true of standardized high-stakes measures as well. However, classroom assessment can and should be improved.

Raising the Validity and Reliability of Classroom Reading Assessment

How can we raise the validity and reliability of classroom reading assessment measures? And why should we even want to try? The answer is to recognize the skill and knowledge of teachers and to use their judgment to provide additional information on student progress. It is not enough to criticize standardized instruments; we must provide options to the prevailing view that only formal testing instruments provide meaningful results. The option I am suggesting is to rework classroom reading assessments to make them more valid and reliable than they are at present. Much improvement can occur if we do several things: pay careful attention to the four steps of the assessment process as described in preceding chapters; set school policies for grading guidelines; and choose consistent assessment instruments across a single grade or multiple grade levels. I am not suggesting that these are easy tasks, but they can be completed by collaborative and dedicated educators who want to do more than just criticize standardized instruments and maintain the status quo.

Pay Careful Attention to the Four Steps of the Assessment Process

First, identify what to assess in as specific terms as possible; that is, pinpoint the good reader behaviors and/or Standards that you are teaching and assessing. If you prefer not to use the good reader behaviors, you may begin with the Standards themselves and match these to your instruction and assessment. Clear delineation of the purpose of your instruction and assessment helps to establish its validity, but more is needed.

If you have clearly defined the purpose of your instruction and assessment and the attendant target behaviors, you will more easily move into the second step, which is to collect evidence. But the evidence you collect must be appropriate to what you are assessing. It can take the form of observation, selected response answers, essay questions, or projects of some sort, but it must be appropriate to the targeted purpose. For example, asking multiple-choice questions may not be as sensitive a measure of whether a student understands the structure of a narrative or expository selection (Standard 5) as asking the student to fill out a structure map or diagram (Caldwell & Leslie, 2013). Similarly, a multiple-choice test is not an appropriate measure for assessing student summarization skills (Standard 2) or for determining whether a student can analyze specific components in a text (Standard 3). Appropriateness of the match between assessment purpose and assessment format increases the validity of the assessment process.

The third step is to analyze the evidence. Here is where differentiating types of test items and assigning different point totals to different types of items comes in. Here is where rubrics raise their interesting heads. I have heard teachers protest that designing a rubric takes too much time. However, it has been my experience that the time taken in rubric construction is made up many times over during the correction cycle. And if the rubric is shared with the students, it results in improved performance. The use of rubrics not only makes grading easier, but it increases the reliability of your assessment.

Finally, you make a decision about each student's literacy performance and the effectiveness of your instruction. At this point, you will probably assign a grade. Ideally, that grade will reflect the student's literacy learning and not the student's effort, behavior, or perceived motivation. If you include effort or behavior as part of a grade, you introduce an element of unreliability because your perception of an individual student's effort may be very different from that of another teacher. Removing such perceptions from the grading criteria and basing it upon literacy performance will enhance reliability.

In summary, you can increase the validity and reliability of your classroom reading assessment by specifically identifying what you are instructing and assessing; by choosing assessment formats that are appropriate to your identified purpose; by using such analysis tools as rubrics and differentiated point totals; and by basing grades on literacy performance, not on perceptions of motivation and effort.

Set School Policies for Grading Guidelines

Given the recommendations made above, it is important that schools address the imprecise and subjective nature of grade assignment. This applies to all subject areas, not just assessment of reading performance. The purpose of a grade is the same: to indicate whether a student has met the district and/or state curriculum standards. If course, it should also involve whether a student has met the CCSS for English Language Arts and Literacy in History/Social Studies, Science, and Technical Subjects. However, if classroom grades are to provide alternatives to standardized scores, their validity and reliability must improve. This means that teachers should discuss how and why they grade as they do. As collaborative professionals, they should come to some consensus regarding important implications of grading. Why should they do this? Let us consider a fictional but quite realistic example.

Let us suppose that a family has three students in the same local elementary school. Two of the children are fraternal twins and, at the parents' request, are in separate third-grade classrooms. The third child is in fifth grade. The twins both receive a B for reading. The first twin is struggling with reading; if an IRI was administered, he would probably score slightly below grade level, with fluency a decided concern. But this child works very hard, hands in all assignments, pays attention in class, and endeavors to please the teacher in every way. The teacher notes this by assigning a grade of B, even though his reading performance would suggest a C grade. The second twin is a very good reader, probably well above grade level. However, she often neglects to turn in assignments and seldom completes homework. She rarely participates in class activities, preferring instead to draw in her notebook. Her reading performance is of A quality, but the teacher lowers her grade to reflect what she perceives as lack of effort and attention. And what about the fifth grader? His teacher recognizes that he is a fine reader, but he has never turned in a major project. Because the teacher's grades represent the average of all work recorded in the grade book, he receives a grade of B.

So all three children in our fictional family receive a report card grade of B. The parents will probably interpret these as meaning above-average performance in reading. Even if the teachers write comments on the children's report cards commending the first twin for his diligence, berating the second twin for her inattention, and noting the missing assignment for the fifth grader, will the parents truly understand that these features were responsible for raising or lowering the grades? Unless the teachers specifically describe their grading practices during a parent–teacher conference (which may or may not be attended by the parents), I suggest that the report card grades do not present a clear picture of the three children's literacy skills.

What consensus about grading should teachers reach? First, they should agree to separate literacy achievement from effort and behavior. Simply put, students who are better readers should receive higher grades. "Grades are supposed to reflect a student's level of success in learning the required material" (Stiggens, 1994, p. 369). Student achievement is the most prized product of schools. If students achieve, schools are perceived as efficient. Confusing the issue by using effort, behavior, attendance, missing work, or other factors to raise or lower the grade renders the grade suspect as a measure of reading performance.

Can't teachers agree to assign two grades, one for reading and one for effort and behavior? Admittedly, it is difficult to assign an A to a troublesome or seemingly unmotivated student, but if that student is a superlative reader, doesn't he or she deserve it?

I found myself in just such a quandary in a graduate-level research class. One student was habitually late. She sat in the back of the room with a scowl on her face, tended to take an adversarial position in class discussions, and was rather insensitive in her relationships with peers. However, her written work was excellent, and the quality of her final research project was superb. Should I lower her grade because I perceived her as unmotivated and somewhat unpleasant? My role was to judge her knowledge of research design—not her time sense, her personality, or how she related to others. But I will admit it was hard to write an A on the grading sheet. I might have found it equally difficult to assign a grade of C to a student whose work merited a C, but who came to class on time, participated in class discussions, and interacted positively with peers. So the first area of agreement should be to separate achievement and effort, no matter how difficult this may be. Cross and Frary (1999) found that 81% of teachers agreed that grades should only reflect performance. However, 39% admitted that they included effort and behavior in their grades. Could this be because it is so difficult to assign a high grade to a student who is perceived as unmotivated or whose behavior is questionable?

This leads to another issue: the role of missing work. It just does not make sense to use missing work as a statement about an individual's performance. How can you judge performance from something that does not exist or something you have not seen? Missing work, whether it is homework or a major project, should be assigned to the effort side of the ledger. I know of one teacher who refused to give a report card grade until all work was turned in, which proved to be a powerful motivator for students and parents alike! Another teacher wrote *Incomplete* instead of a grade and explained that she was unable to judge the student's progress from the small amount of work that had been submitted. Won't this mean that the report card will have to be revised to include two grades? Yes, it probably will. In this age of standards-based assessment, many schools and districts will need to revise report cards, so it may be the perfect time to make changes.

Another issue for teachers to discuss is what assignments and activities should be included in a report card grade and how they should be weighted. Some assessments are obviously more important than others. Should a short quiz count as much as a final chapter or book test? Should daily written class activities count as much as a major paper or project? I am not suggesting that teachers should all give the same assessments. This would be impossible. Teaching is an intensely personal and individual activity, and teachers have different styles of teaching and assessing, which should be respected. However, if teachers would agree to include only important items in a report card grade or to attach different weights to items of greater and lesser importance, the validity of grading across a grade level and school would be enhanced.

I do not suggest that such agreements will be easy to come by, but it is definitely worth the effort. If the validity of classroom grades increases, we can communicate these grades to the community. I am not suggesting that we communicate the grades of individual students, but we can offer a description of the spread of grades as an indicator that students have met the Standards. However, we can only report this information if we agree on those factors that should be included or excluded from a grade.

Choose Consistent Assessments across a Single Grade or Multiple Grade Levels

Standardized tests are consistent; that is, all students receive the same test at the same time, and their answers are scored in the same way. It is easy to report such results and use them to compare schools, districts, and states. Now consider the three fourth-grade teachers who taught the same trade book but assessed student literacy learning in very different ways. There was no consistency, and it would be difficult if not impossible to communicate such results across a grade level in a simple and direct way. If we are to use classroom assessment as alternatives to standardized scores, we must have some consistency in the kind of assessments we use.

In order to have consistent assessment, we must have a consistent curriculum. I suspect that the CCSS will be a strong force in curriculum reform. Of course states have curriculum standards but some are so broad that almost anything can be justified as meeting a standard. Some schools have uniform textbooks or common trade books taught at an agreed-on grade level; within this framework, however, teachers are free to emphasize very different components, and different teachers may emphasize different things at the same grade level. Schmoker (2006) recommended that teachers collaborate to create a common set of curricular standards. This has basically been done for us in the guise of the CCSS. A consistent curriculum is the first step to consistent assessment. And consistent assessment is absolutely necessary if we are to move beyond standardized scores for reporting school progress in meeting the standards.

But won't this destroy the creativity of teachers? I do not think so. Suppose a fifth-grade team agrees to emphasize Standard 2: determining central ideas and/or themes and summarizing during the first 2 months of the school year. There are many ways to do this and many kinds of texts that can be used. All fifth-grade teachers do not have to use the same books, articles, or other media. They do not have to use the same instructional strategies. Within the framework of teaching students to identify central ideas and themes and to summarize, there is much room for creativity during discussion, in classroom activities, and through the construction of projects. However, if all teachers are focusing on synthesis, the culminating assessment can be the same for all classrooms.

Let's use another example. Recognizing the structure of a text is an important good reader behavior that is addressed in Standard 5. All third grade teachers can agree to teach recognizing structure through narratives, and fourth-grade teachers can agree to teach it through expository text. The exact nature of the chosen text is up to each teacher, as is the presentation of the instruction. Some teachers can use idea maps or structure grids (Caldwell & Leslie, 2013), while others can teach structure through writing. Teacher individualism is limited only to the extent that teaching text structure is the ultimate aim of the instruction and the focus of the assessment.

Schools are beginning to realize the value of similar assessments across a single grade level or across several grade levels. Many schools are purchasing test batteries that are administered to all primary or elementary students. Some schools administer running records, curriculum-based measurement (CBM) segments, or IRI passages to all students at least once, and in some cases two or three times, a year. This consistency allows the school to report student scores across all grade levels.

Assessments designed, chosen, or agreed upon by teachers possess qualities that standardized tests do not have. First, they tend to be more "user-friendly" and may not produce the anxiety that often accompanies standardized assessment. Second, they may more accurately reflect the real reading process by asking students to engage in more authentic tasks than answering multiple-choice questions. Third, if well designed, they offer much more information about an individual student's reading strengths and needs. Fourth, they can truly have an impact on instruction, in ways that a standardized measure cannot do.

Schmoker (2006) suggests that regular assessments focusing on an agreed-upon curriculum can provide much information to teachers. He believes that regular meetings by teacher teams to discuss curriculum, design uniform assessments, and review student performance on these assessments would result in "serious improvements in teaching and learning" (p. 130). Consistent assessments across a single grade or spread of grades would also allow the school to report student scores in a relatively uncomplicated fashion. Of course, students would not be identified by name; their scores would be reported in a group format. Instead of indicating that Jonas attained a rating of Highly Proficient on a specific Standard, the school would report the number of Highly Proficient scores at Jonas's grade level.

What kind of consistent assessments can be chosen? These can come from any of the assessment techniques that I have described in this book. They can be designed by teachers or form part of published assessment batteries. Many published reading series come with their own assessments. A school or district that decides to use such measures should be very careful that the instruments actually match the CCSS as discussed in Chapter 2.

An IRI is another option for such alternative testing and reporting. The IRI can be a published document, or it can be one designed by the school or district. A district in my area chose passages that were representative of what students should be able to read and comprehend at each grade level. The teachers wrote questions to accompany the passages and decided whether the passages would be read orally or silently. They administered the passages in January and June. It took a lot of work, and perhaps it would have been easier to have chosen a published IRI. However, the district was quite pleased with its "homemade" assessment, and the results were communicated to all parents in the district. If this district is still using their assessment, it will probably have to be revised in order to address the CCSS.

Some schools have uniform book units across a grade, as our three fourth-grade teachers did. If this is the case, another option would be to design a consistent way of assessing student understanding of the book by designing a task that matches one or more CCSS. Some schools have uniform assignments or projects at a single grade level. In this case, teachers could design a uniform rubric to evaluate student achievement and use the rubric score for reporting purposes. If teachers improve the validity and reliability of classroom assessments, if they agree on grading criteria, and if they select or design common assessments, then they are in a position to take the next step: organizing the data and reporting it to the community.

Organizing and Reporting Classroom Literacy Data

Let us assume that you and the other teachers at your grade level (fourth grade, let's say) have agreed to focus on a specific good reader behavior and/or Standard for 2 months. Working together, you have designed a cumulative assessment to determine the extent to which students can perform this behavior. You give the assessment to all the fourth graders at the same approximate time. You and your peers use a rubric or an agreed-on set of grading criteria to evaluate student performance, and you assign a score or grade to each student. What is the next step? Now you group the scores. If your grading designations were Highly Proficient, Proficient, and Not Proficient, you tally the numbers of fourth graders who received these scores and report them to your community. This step may sound easy, but in reality it represents a major change to the typical assessment process, and several important caveats and guidelines must be addressed.

Report Grouped Scores

Most of the data collected and analyzed by teachers are individualized in nature. In fact, the assessment strategies described in this book center on individualized assessment techniques such as running records, IRIs, phonological awareness tests, and measures of word identification. Schmoker (2006) suggests that teachers "tend to evaluate students individually and reflect on how to improve class performance less frequently" (p. 37). That is, teachers primarily focus on individual students' performance, not the performance of the classroom group. I am not suggesting that we should give up our emphasis on individuals, but I am suggesting that we should broaden our focus to include grouped data that can be reported to the community. As discussed throughout this book, the purposes of reading assessment are to identify good reader behaviors and/or ability to meet the CCSS, identify areas of weakness, determine student reading levels, and document student progress—purposes that demand an individual focus. We would never report individual scores to the community, as this would be a serious breach of student privacy. However, we can group individual scores and report such anonymous data. Such data can inform the community of the extent to which students are meeting standards.

Recognize the Risks of Reporting Grouped Data to the Community

If the majority of students at a certain grade level received a rating of Highly Proficient or Proficient, reporting such data is easy. Obviously they indicate that students are learning to read and making progress toward meeting the Standards. But what if the majority of students received a score of Not Proficient? You still report your data, even if they are not as good as you had hoped. Reporting disappointing data, accompanied by an explanation of how your school intends to remedy the situation, is as useful to parents and the general public as reporting high scores for all students. Recognizing a need in students and being able to address it with specific instructional interventions are the marks of professional educators!

Let us be frank. Data can be threatening to teachers. Standardized test data have been used inappropriately to identify poor teachers, which should never occur. The same holds true for classroom data. Schmoker (2006) emphatically states several guidelines for choosing and reporting classroom data: teachers should have autonomy in selecting the kinds of classroom data that will be collected and reported; classroom data should be collected and analyzed collaboratively and anonymously by grade level or school, never by classroom; and classroom data should not be used as an indictment of teachers. The purpose of reporting such data is to show that students in a school or at a specific grade level are meeting the Standards. If the data are reported by classrooms, it would be very easy for someone to compare classroom data and come to the erroneous conclusion that some teachers are ineffective. Unfortunately, teachers themselves could come to this same conclusion. Therefore, it is important for classroom data to be grouped anonymously, or teachers will resist reporting it. And who can blame them? Classrooms vary widely within a school, and factors other than instruction can affect student performance. The identification of poor teachers is not the purpose of reporting classroom data, nor is it the job of the community.

Set Guidelines for Reporting

What guidelines should you follow if you intend to report classroom assessment data to parents and the community? The most important rule is to keep it simple! Complex tables of numbers or intricate charts and graphs do not work. The majority of people do not have the background to interpret them or the time to do so.

Organize your data as simply as possible, and avoid trying to include too much information in one presentation. For example, resist the temptation to include student and school demographics with your performance data. Focus on the accomplishments of the students; they are of primary interest to parents and the general public. I am not saying that demographics are unimportant, but put them in a separate table and on a separate page. Showcase your student achievement in simple but direct terms. You can report the exact number of students who achieved a specific grade, or you can use percentages. If you wish to use a graph, a simple bar chart is sufficient. Before you distribute your data, ask someone who is not an educator whether the data arrangement makes sense to him or her. Some of the published assessment programs provide extensive data analysis for you. If you choose to use these features, make certain that they retain simplicity and clarity.

Data should be accompanied by an explanation or a description of the assessment. Briefly and clearly, explain the good reader behavior and/or Standard that was the focus of the instruction, and describe how you and your peers assessed student performance. After presenting the scores, explain simply and clearly what you are going to do as a result of student performance on the assessment.

Use existing instruments for your first efforts at reporting. For example, many schools send out monthly or bimonthly newsletters to parents. Such a newsletter would be a perfect vehicle for reporting consistent assessment data. Eventually, schools can design assessment summaries to distribute to parents and school board members at regular intervals. Unfortunately, examples of such data summaries and reporting instruments are rare, but some do exist (Schmoker, 2006).

In a way, this reporting of classroom data is uncharted territory. Why should reading teachers and coaches venture into it? However, there are reasons. First, we need alternatives to standardized measures, which are increasing in importance every day. Second, we need to dignify the role of teachers/coaches and the classroom assessment process. Third, we must contribute to the recognition of the professional status of teachers. Darling-Hammond and Goodwin (cited by Schmoker, 1996) believe that the key to professional status is accountability, involving the relationships between teachers and students and between teachers and the society at large. Reporting classroom literacy data would be a giant step toward improving accountability.

Calhoun (2004) provides a variety of templates for reporting different sets of data, such as grades, reading attitudes, and standardized and criterion-referenced measures. The following example of data reporting may also offer a workable template for you to use. It is simple, I admit; you might be tempted to say that it is too simple. However, my answer would be that beginning efforts demand simplicity. If data are reported simply, there is a greater chance that teachers, parents, and the general public will understand and appreciate them. Once basic understandings are in place, you can gradually increase the complexity of your reporting.

Example of a Group Data Report

Description

In May, all third- through fifth-grade students in Mountain View School were administered an IRI to determine their reading level. They silently read a grade-level narrative selection and answered literal and inferential questions. If their comprehension was above 75%, they read a higher-level selection, and the same process was followed.

Analysis

The majority of students in all three grades are reading at or above grade level in narrative text in accordance with Standard 10 of the Common Core State Standards. The reading specialist will conduct additional assessment of those reading below grade level to determine appropriate plans for intervention. Of the five students who were not tested, three were special-needs children, and two were English language learners who had not yet achieved proficiency in spoken English.

Group Data 1

	Grade 3	Grade 4	Grade 5
Number of students at grade level	50	44	46
Number of students above grade level	18	14	18
Number of students below grade level	5	8	8
Number of students not tested	2	3	0
Total number of students	75	69	72

A similar template can be used to compare levels obtained in September and May.

Group Data 2

	Grade 3, Sept.	Grade 3, May	Grade 4, Sept.	Grade 4, May	Grade 5, Sept.	Grade 5, May
Number of students at grade level	30	50	37	45	35	46
Number of students above grade level	10	18	9	14	10	18
Number of students below grade level	33	5	21	8	27	8
Number of students not tested	2	2	3	3	0	0

Summary

• Reporting of student progress in meeting state standards is presently tied to yearly standardized tests and report card grades. The richness of classroom assessment data on reading performance remains largely unknown and unappreciated by the general public.

• If classroom assessment is to take on greater significance, it must change. In particular, there must be more consistency in reading assessment and grading practices across teachers, grade levels, and schools.

- At present, classroom reading assessment is extremely idiosyncratic, with little uniformity even within a single grade in the same school.

- Teacher grading practices are also idiosyncratic, and different teachers use different factors to assign grades.

- Validity and reliability of classroom reading assessment can be improved if teachers pay careful attention to the four steps of the assessment process, set school policies for grading guidelines, and design consistent assessments across a single grade level or multiple grade levels.

- In reporting classroom data, educators should follow several guidelines: report grouped data, not individual scores; recognize and accept the risks of reporting group data; do not group data by classrooms; and focus on simplicity in reporting and presenting data.

Activities for Developing Understanding

- Interview teachers in your school about the factors that they include in their report card grades. To what extent are these factors alike or different?

- Interview teachers at your grade level about their assessment practices. What measures do they use? Do they tie their assessments to the good reader behaviors or to the Standards?

- Examine your grading practices. How can you change them to make them more meaningful?

- What grouped classroom assessment data might you report to parents? How could you set these data up in a clear but simple format?

General Summary

Assessing the Good Reader Behaviors and the Common Core State Standards

Reading Standards: Foundational Skills K–5. Know and apply grade-level phonics and word analysis skills in decoding words.

Good readers use letter and sound patterns to pronounce words accurately and fluently.

Early Literacy

- Pay attention to oral language development.
- Observe students' concepts of print.
- Assess word and syllable awareness.
- Administer measures of phonological awareness.
- Determine known alphabet letters.
- Take running records.

Word Identification

- Administer the informal reading inventory (IRI) process.
- Listen to students read orally.
  - —Graded passages
  - —Graded word lists
  - —Nonsense words

- Observe students sort words on the basis of letters and sounds.
- Analyze miscues.
- Ask students how they identify words.

Fluency

- Determine reading rate as both words per minute (WPM) and correct words per minute (CWPM).
- Use curriculum-based measurement (CBM).
- Use timed administration of a word list.
- Use a checklist to assess intonation.

Anchor Standard for Reading 4: Interpret words and phrases as they are used in the text, including determining technical, connotative, and figurative meanings, and analyze how specific word choices shape meaning or tone.

Good readers learn new words and extend the meanings of known ones.

- Select words to assess from classroom texts as opposed to word lists.
- Select important words, that is, words essential to text meaning.
- Assess students' ability to use context to determine word meaning.
- Assess constructed response vocabulary items with a rubric.
- Assess word knowledge by asking students to put a word in their lives.
- Assess word knowledge by asking students to match a word with a noun, a verb, an adjective, or an adverb.
- Assess word knowledge by observing students as they sort words on the basis of meaning.
- Share the words that will be on an assessment with your students.
- Explain how you will assess vocabulary knowledge.
- Make assessment a parallel to class activities.
- Consider an open book format.

Anchor Standard for Reading 1: Read closely to determine what the text says explicitly and to make logical inferences from it; cite specific textual evidence when writing or speaking to support conclusions drawn from the text.

Anchor Standard for Reading 3: Analyze how and why individuals, events, and ideas develop and interact over the course of a text.

Good readers determine what is important in the text. They ask questions and read to find answers. They draw inferences.

- Construct and/or select questions that focus on these behaviors.
- Use the IRI process to assess reading levels.
- Assess students' understanding of question stems.
- Assess students' ability to construct questions.
- Join assessment of question formation and question answering to text look-backs.
- Assess students' understanding by engaging in read-alouds.
- Assess students' understanding by fostering close reading.
- Ask students to look back in the text to make inferences or to locate clues for inferences.
- Include inferring as a heading on a checklist or rubric.

Anchor Standard for Reading 2: Determine central ideas or themes of a text and analyze their development; summarize the key supporting details and ideas.

Anchor Standard for Reading 5: Analyze the structure of texts, including how specific sentences, paragraphs and larger portions of the text (e.g., a section, chapter, scene, or stanza) relate to each other and the whole.

Good readers recognize the structure of the text. They summarize, synthesize, and reorganize ideas.

- Ask students questions that focus directly on this behavior: "What are the parts of narratives?" "What pattern is the author using?"
- Ask students to look back in the text to locate narrative parts or to identify expository patterns.
- Ask students to retell or summarize; focus on text structure when you are assessing this.
- Include text structure as a heading on a checklist or rubric.
- Include synthesis on a checklist or rubric.

Anchor Standard for Reading 6: Assess how point of view or purpose shapes the content and style of a text.

Anchor Standard for Reading 8: Delineate and evaluate the arguments and specific claims in a text including the validity of the reasoning as well as the relevance and sufficiency of the evidence.

Anchor Standard for Reading 9: Analyze how two or more texts address similar themes or topics in order to build knowledge or to compare the approaches the authors take.

Good readers form and support their opinions.

Good readers recognize the author's purpose/point of view/style.

- Ask questions that focus directly on these behaviors: "What was the author's purpose in writing this?" "What does the author believe about . . . ?" "Why did the author choose this style?"
- Ask students to look back in the text to determine purpose or point of view.
- Ask students to use the text as a support for their opinions.
- Include forming and supporting opinions on a checklist or rubric.

Good readers monitor comprehension and repair comprehension breakdowns.

- Ask questions that focus directly on this behavior: "What don't you understand?" "Where in the text might you find the answer?"
- Ask students to look back in the text to clear up misunderstandings.
- Focus on noting understanding or lack of understanding during look-backs, read-alouds, and close reading.

References

Adams, M. J. (1990). *Beginning to read: Thinking and learning about print: A summary.* Urbana–Champaign: University of Illinois, Center for the Study of Reading.

Adams, M. J., Foorman, B. R., Lundberg, I., & Beeler, T. (1998). *Phonemic awareness in young children.* Baltimore: Brookes.

Afflerbach, P. (2004). *National Reading Conference policy brief: High stakes testing and reading achievement.* Oak Creek, WI: National Reading Conference.

Alexander, P. A., & Jetton, T. L. (2000). Learning from text: A multidimensional and developmental perspective. In M. L. Kamil, P. B. Moesenthal, P. D. Pearson, & R. Barr (Eds.), *Handbook of reading research* (Vol. 3, pp. 285–310). Mahwah, NJ: Erlbaum.

Allen, J. D. (2005). Grades as valid measures of academic achievement of classroom learning. *The Clearing House, 78* (4), 218–223.

Allington, R. L. (2001). *What really matters for struggling readers.* New York: Addison Wesley Longman.

Anderson, K. L. (2010). Spotlight on the interactive strategies approach: The case of Roosevelt Elementary School. In M. Y. Lipson & K. K. Wixson (Eds.), *Successful approaches to RTI: Collaborative practices for improving K–12 literacy* (pp. 66–87). Newark, DE: International Reading Association.

Anderson, L. W., & Krathwohl, D. (2001). *A taxonomy for learning, teaching and assessing: A revision of Bloom's taxonomy of educational objectives.* New York: Addison, Wesley Longman.

Applegate, M. D., Quinn, K. B., & Applegate, A. J. (2002). Levels of thinking required by comprehension questions in informal reading inventories. *The Reading Teacher, 56,* 174–180.

Au, K., & Raphael, T. (2007). Classroom assessment and standards-based change. In J. R. Paratore & R. L. McCormack (Eds.), *Classroom literacy assessment: Making sense of what students know and do* (pp. 306–432). New York: Guilford Press.

Ball, E. W., & Blachman, B. A. (1991). Does phoneme awareness training in kindergarten make a difference in early word recognition and spelling? *Reading Research Quarterly, 26*, 49–66.

Baumann, J. F., Edwards, E. C., Font, G., Tereshinski, C. A., Kame'enui, E. J., & Olejnik, S. (2002). Teaching morphemic and contextual analysis to fifth-grade students. *Reading Research Quarterly, 37*, 150–176.

Baumann, J. F., Ware, D., & Edwards, E. C. (2007). "Bumping into spicy, tasty words that catch your tongue": A formative experiment on vocabulary instruction. *The Reading Teacher, 61*, 108–122.

Bear, D., Invernezzi, M., Templeton, S., & Johnston, F. (2011). *Words their way: Word study for phonics, vocabulary, and spelling instruction* (5th ed.). New York: Pearson.

Beck, I. L., McKeown, M. G., & Kucan, L. (2013). *Bringing words to life: Robust vocabulary instruction* (2nd ed.). New York: Guilford Press.

Billmeyer, R. (2001). *Capturing ALL of the reader through the reading assessment system.* Omaha, NE: Dayspring Printing.

Bloom, B., & Krathwohl, D. (1956). *Taxonomy of educational objectives: The classification of educational goals.* New York: Longmans Green.

Bradley, L., & Bryant, P. (1983). Categorizing sounds and learning to read: A causal connection. *Nature, 30*, 419–421.

Brady, S. (1997). Ability to encode phonological representations: An underlying difficulty of poor readers. In B. A. Blachman (Ed.), *Foundations of reading acquisition and dyslexia: Implications for early intervention* (pp. 21–47). Mahwah, NJ: Erlbaum.

Bransford, J. D., Brown, A. L., & Cocking, R. R. (2000). *How people learn: Brain, mind, experience, and school.* Washington, DC: National Academy Press.

Brookhart, S. M. (1997). A theoretical framework for the role of classroom assessment in motivating student effort and achievement. *Applied Measurement in Education, 70* (2), 161–180.

Brozo, W. G. (2010). The role of content literacy in an effective RTI program. *The Reading Teacher, 64*, 147–150.

Burke, K. (2005). *How to assess authentic learning.* Thousand Oaks, CA: Corwin Press.

Burke, K. (2006). *From standards to rubrics in 6 steps.* Thousand Oaks, CA: Corwin Press.

Byrne, B., & Fielding-Barnsley, R. (1991). Evaluation of a program to teach phonemic awareness to young children. *Journal of Educational Psychology, 83*, 451–455.

Caldwell, J. S. (2008). *Comprehension assessment: A classroom guide.* New York: Guilford Press.

Caldwell, J. S., & Leslie, L. (2004). Does proficiency in middle school reading assure proficiency in high school reading? *Journal of Adult and Adolescent Literacy, 47,* 324–335.

Caldwell, J. S., & Leslie, L. (2013). *Intervention strategies to follow informal reading inventory assessment: So what do I do now?* Boston: Pearson.

Calhoun, E. (2004). *Using data to assess your reading program.* Alexandria, VA: Association for Supervision and Curriculum Development.

Calkins, L., Ehrenworth, M., & Lehman, C. (2012). *Pathways to the Common Core: Accelerating achievement.* Portsmouth, NH: Heinemann.

Cangelosi, J. S. (2000). *Assessment strategies for monitoring student learning.* New York: Addison Wesley Longman.

Carlisle, J. F. (2010). Effects of instruction in morphological awareness on literacy achievement: An integrative review. *Reading Research Quarterly, 45,* 464–487.

Carver, R. B. (1990). *Reading rate: A review of research and theory.* San Diego, CA: Academic Press.

Ciardiello, A. V. (1998). Did you ask a good question today?: Alternative cognitive and metacognitive strategies. *Journal of Adolescent and Adult Literacy, 42,* 210–219.

Cizek, G. J. (2000). Pockets of resistance in the assessment revolution. *Educational Measurement: Issues and Practices, 19* (2), 16–24.

Cizek, G. J., Fitzgerald, S. M., & Rachor, R. E. (1996). Teachers' assessment practices: Preparation, isolation, and the kitchen sink. *Educational Assessment, 3,* 159–179.

Coleman, D., & Pimentel, S. (2011). *Publishers' criteria for the Common Core State Standards in English, language arts and literacy.* Retrieved from *www.corestandards.org* .

Common Core State Standards Initiative. (2010). *Common Core State Standards for English language arts and literacy in history/social studies, science, and technical subjects.* Washington, DC: National Governors Association and Council of Chief State School Officers. Retrieved June 21, 2011, from *www.corestandards.org* .

Conley, M. W. (2009). Improving adolescent comprehension: Developing comprehension strategies in the content areas. In S. E. Israel & G. G. Duffy (Eds.), *Handbook of research on reading comprehension* (pp. 531–550). New York: Routledge.

Cowley, J. (1999). *Mrs. WishyWashy.* New York: Philomel.

Coxhead, A. (2000). An academic word list. *TESOL Quarterly, 34,* 213–238.

Creech, S. (1994). *Walk two moons.* New York: Harper Trophy.

Cross, L. H., & Frary, R. B. (1999). Hodgepodge grading: Endorsed by students and teachers alike. *Applied Measurement in Education, 12,* 53–72.

Cunningham, P. M. (1992, October). [Presentation given at West Bend, WI, school district.]

Davidson, M., & Myhre, O. (2000). Measuring reading at grade level. *Educational Leadership, 57,* 25–28.

Davis, F. B. (1968). Research in comprehension in reading. *Reading Research Quarterly, 3,* 499–545.

Dorn, L. J., & Henderson, S. C. (2010). The comprehensive intervention model: A systems approach to RTI. In M. Y. Lipson & K. K. Wixson (Eds.), *Successful approaches to RTI: Collaborative practices for improving K–12 literacy* (pp. 88–120). Newark, DE: International Reading Association.

Ebro, L. C., Borstrum, I., & Petersen, D. K. (1998). Predicting dyslexia from kindergarten: The importance of distinctiveness of phonological representations of lexical items. *Reading Research Quarterly, 33,* 36–60.

Ehri, L. C. (1991). Development of the ability to read words. In R. Barr, M. L. Kamil, P. Mosenthal, & P. D. Pearson (Eds.), *Handbook of reading research* (Vol. 2, pp. 383–417). White Plains, NY: Longman.

Ehri, L. C. (April 1997). *The development of children's ability to read words.* Paper presented at the convention of the International Reading Association, Atlanta, GA.

Ehri, L. C., Nunes, S. R., Willows, D. M., Schuster, B. V., Yaghoub-Zadeh, Z., & Shanahan, T. (2001). Phonemic awareness instruction helps children learn to read: Evidence from the National Reading Panel's meta-analysis. *Reading Research Quarterly, 36,* 250–287.

Enciso, P. E. (2001). Taking our seats: The consequences of positioning in reading assessments. *Theory into Practice, 40* (3), 166–174.

Ferretti, R. P., & De La Paz, S. (2011). On the comprehension and production of written texts: Instructional activities that support content-area literacy. In R. E. O'Connor & P. F. Vadasy (Eds.), *Handbook of reading interventions* (pp. 326–412). New York: Guilford Press.

Fisher, D., & Frey, N. (2012). Close reading in elementary schools. *The Reading Teacher, 66,* 179–188.

Fisher, D., Frey, N., & Lapp, D. (2012). *Text complexity: Raising rigor in reading.* Newark, DE: International Reading Association.

Flynt, E. S., & Brozo, W. G. (2008). Developing academic language: Got words? *The Reading Teacher, 61,* 500–502.

Flurkey, A. (2006). What's "normal" about real reading? In K. S. Goodman (Ed.), *The truth about DIBELS: What it is, what it does* (pp. 20–49). Portsmouth, NH: Heinemann.

Fry, E. (1998). The most common phonograms. *The Reading Teacher, 51,* 620–622.

Fuchs, L. S. (1992). Identifying a measure for monitoring student reading progress. *School Psychology Review, 21,* 45–59.

Fuchs, L. S., & Fuchs, D. (1999). Monitoring student progress toward the development of reading competence: A review of three forms of classroom-based measurement. *School Psychology Review, 28,* 659–672.

Fuchs, L. S., Fuchs, D., Hosp, M. K., & Jenkins, J. R. (2001). Oral reading fluency as an indicator of reading competence: A theoretical, empirical and historical analysis. *Scientific Studies of Reading, 5,* 239–256.

Gelzheiser, L. M., Scanlon, D. M., & Hallgren-Flynn, L. (2010). Spotlight on RTI for adolescents: An example of intensive middle school intervention using the interactive strategies approach—extended. In M. Y. Lipson & K. K. Wixson (Eds.), *Successful approaches to RTI: Collaborative practices for improving K–12 literacy* (pp. 211–230). Newark, DE: International Reading Association.

Glasswell, K., & Ford, M. P. (2010). Teaching flexibly with leveled text: More power for your reading block. *The Reading Teacher, 64,* 57–60.

Glickman-Bond, J. (2006). *Creating and using rubrics in today's classrooms: A practical guide.* Norwood, MA: Christopher-Gordon.

Goetze, S. K., Scanlon, D. M., & Ehren, B. J. (2010). RTI for secondary school literacy. In M. Y. Lipson & K. K. Wixson (Eds.), *Successful approaches to RTI: Collaborative practices for improving K–12 literacy* (pp. 173–210). Newark, DE: International Reading Association.

Good, R. H., Kaminski, R. A., Smith, S., Laimon, D., & Dill, S. (2001). *Dynamic Indicators of Basic Early Literacy Skills.* Eugene: University of Oregon.

Goodman, D., & Hambleton, R. K. (2005). Some misconceptions about large-scale educational assessments. In R. P. Phelps (Ed.), *Defending standardized testing* (pp. 91–110). Mahwah, NJ: Erlbaum.

Goodman, K. S. (1969). Analysis of reading miscues: Applied psycholinguistics. *Reading Research Quarterly, 5,* 9–30.

Goswami, I. (2000). Phonological and lexical processes. In M. L. Kamil, P. B. Moesenthal, P. D. Pearson, & R. Barr (Eds.), *Handbook of reading research* (Vol. 3, pp. 251–267). Mahwah, NJ: Erlbaum.

Gough, P. B., & Juel, C. (1991). The first stages of word recognition. In L. Rieben & C. A. Perfetti (Eds.), *Learning to read: Basic research and its implications* (pp. 47–56). Hillsdale, NJ: Erlbaum.

Grasser, A., Ozuru, Y., & Sullins, J. (2010). What is a good question? In M. G. McKeown & L. Kucan (Eds.), *Bringing reading research to life* (pp. 112–141). New York: Guilford Press.

Grasser, A. C., & Person, N. K. (1994). Question-asking during tutoring. *American Educational Research Journal, 95,* 524–536.

Greenwood, S. C., & Flanigan, K. (2007). Overlapping vocabulary and comprehension: Context clues complement semantic gradients. *The Reading Teacher, 61,* 249–254.

Halladay, J. L. (2012). Revisiting key assumptions of the reading level framework. *The Reading Teacher, 66,* 53–61.

Harmon, J. M., Hedrick, W. B., Soares, L., & Gress, M. (2007). Assessing vocabulary: Examining knowledge about words and about word learning. In J. R. Paratore & R. L. McCormack (Eds.), *Classroom literacy assessment: Making sense of what students know and do* (pp. 135–153). New York: Guilford Press.

Hasbrouck, J. E., & Tindal, G. A. (1992). Curriculum-based oral reading fluency norms for students in grades 2 through 5. *Teaching Exceptional Children*, Spring, pp. 41–44.

Hasbrouck, J. E., & Tindal, G. A. (2005). *Oral reading fluency: 90 years of measurement* (Tech. Rep. No. 33). Eugene: University of Oregon, College of Education, Behavioral Research and Teaching.

Hasbrouck, J. E., & Tindal, G. A. (2006). Oral reading fluency norms: A valuable assessment tool for reading teachers. *The Reading Teacher, 59*, 636–643.

Helsel, L., & Greenberg, D. (2007). Helping struggling writers succeed: A self-regulated strategy instruction program. *The Reading Teacher, 60*, 752–760.

Hirsch, E. D. Jr. (1987). *Cultural literacy: What every American needs to know.* Boston: Houghton Mifflin.

Hirsch, E. D. Jr., Kett, J., & Trefil, J. (1998). *The dictionary of school literacy: What every American needs to know.* Boston: Houghton Mifflin.

Huey, E. B. (1968). *The psychology and pedagogy of reading.* Cambridge, MA: MIT Press. (Original work published 1908)

International Reading Association. (2012). *Literacy implementation guidelines for the ELA Common Core State Standards.* Newark, DE: International Reading Association. Retrieved from *www.reading.org* .

Johns, J. L., & Berglund, R. L. (2006). *Fluency: Strategies and assessments.* Dubuque, IA: Kendall/Hunt.

Johnson, M. J., Kress, R. A., & Pikulski, P. L. (1987). *Informal reading inventories* (2nd ed.). Newark, DE: International Reading Association.

Johnston, P. H. (1997). *Knowing literacy: Constructive literacy assessment.* York, ME: Stenhouse.

Johnston, P. H. (2010). A framework for response to intervention in literacy. In P. H. Johnston (Ed.), *RTI in literacy: Responsive and comprehensive* (pp. 1–9). Newark, DE: International Reading Association.

Johnston, P. H., & Allington, R. (1991). Remediation. In R. Barr, M. L. Kamil, P. Mosenthal, & P. D. Pearson (Eds.), *Handbook of reading research* (Vol. 2, pp. 984–1012). New York: Longman.

Johnston, P. H., Ivey, G., & Faulkner, A. (2011). Talking in class: Remembering what is important about classroom talk. *The Reading Teacher, 65*, 232–237.

Juel, C. (1988). Learning to read and write: A longitudinal study of 54 children from first through fourth grades. *Journal of Educational Psychology, 80*, 437–447.

Kame'enui, E. J., & Simmons, D. C. (2001). Introduction to this special issue: The DNA of reading fluency. *Scientific Studies of Reading, 5*, 203–210.

Kintsch, W. (2004). The construction–integration model of text comprehension and its implications for instruction. In R. B. Ruddell & N. J. Unrau (Eds.), *Theoretical models and processes of reading* (5th ed., pp. 1270–1328). Newark, DE: International Reading Association.

Kintsch, W. (2012). Psychological models of reading comprehension and their implications for assessment. In J. P. Sabatini, E. Albro, & T. O'Reilly (Eds.), *Measuring up: Advances in how to assess reading ability* (pp. 21–38). Lanham, MD: Rowman & Littlefield Education.

Klenk, L., & Kibby, M. W. (2000). Re-mediating reading difficulties: Appraising the past, reconciling the present, constructing the future. In M. L. Kamil, P. B. Moesenthal, P. D. Pearson, & R. Barr (Eds.), *Handbook of reading research* (Vol. 2, pp. 667–690). Mahwah, NJ: Erlbaum.

Kucan, L., & Palincsar, A. S. (2011). Locating struggling readers in a reconfigured landscape. In M. L. Kamil, P. D. Pearson, E. Birr Moje, & P. P. Afflerbach (Eds.), *Handbook of reading research* (Vol. 4, pp. 341–358). New York: Routledge.

Kuhn, M. R., Schwanenflugel, P. J., & Meisinger, E. B. (2010). Aligning theory and assessment of reading fluency: Automaticity, prosody and definition of fluency. *Reading Research Quarterly, 45*, 230–251.

Leslie, L., & Caldwell, J. (2006). *The Qualitative Reading Inventory 4.* Boston: Pearson.

Leslie, L., & Caldwell, J. (2011). *The Qualitative Reading Inventory 5.* Boston: Pearson.

Leslie, L., & Caldwell, J. S. (in press). *Content area reading assessment.* New York: Pearson.

Lundberg, I., Frost, J., & Peterson, O. (1988). Effects of an extensive program for stimulating phonological awareness in preschool children. *Reading Research Quarterly, 23*, 263–284.

Magliano, J. P., Trabasso, T., & Grasser, A. C. (1999). Strategic processes during comprehension. *Journal of Educational Psychology, 91*, 615–629.

Marzano, R. J. (2000). *Transforming classroom grading.* Alexandria, VA: Association for Supervision and Curriculum Development.

Marzano, R. J., Kendall, J. S., & Gaddy, B. B. (1999). *Essential knowledge: The debate over what American students should know.* Aurora, CO: McRel.

Mayer, R. E., & Wittrock, M. C. (2006). Problem solving. In P. A. Alexander & P. H. Winne (Eds.), *Handbook of educational psychology* (pp. 287–303). Mahwah, NJ: Erlbaum.

McCormack, R. L., Paratore, J. R., & Dahlene, K. F. (2003). Establishing instructional congruence across learning settings: One path for struggling third-grade readers. In R. L. McCormack & J. R. Paratore (Eds.), *After intervention, then what?: Teaching struggling readers in grades 3 and beyond* (pp. 117–136). Newark, DE: International Reading Association.

McKenna, M. C. (1983). Informal reading inventories: A review of the issues. *The Reading Teacher, 36*, 670–679.

McMillan, J. H. (2003). Understanding and improving teachers' classroom assessment decision making: Implications for theory and practice. *Educational Measurement: Issues and Practice, 22* (4), 34–43.

McMillan, J. H., Myran, S., & Workman, D. (2002). Elementary teachers' classroom assessment and grading practices. *Journal of Educational Research, 95* (4), 203–213.

McNamara, D. S., & Kintsch, W. (1996). Learning from text: Effect of prior knowledge and text coherence. *Discourse Processes, 22,* 247–288.

Moje, E. B. (2008). Foregrounding the disciplines in secondary literacy teaching and learning: A call for change. *Journal of Adolescent and Adult Literacy, 52,* 96–107.

Mosenthal, P. (1996). Understanding the strategies of document literacy and their conditions of use. *Journal of Educational Psychology, 88,* 314–332.

Nagy, W. E. (2010). The word games. In M. G. McKeown & L. Kucan (Eds.), *Bringing reading research to life* (pp. 72–91). New York: Guilford Press.

Nagy, W. E., & Townsend, D. (2012). Words as tools: Learning academic vocabulary as language acquisition. *Reading Research Quarterly,* 91–108.

National Assessment of Educational Progress. (2011). *Reading: Summary of major findings.* Retrieved February 21, 2013, from *http://nationsreportcard.gov/reading_2011/summary.asp* .

National Institute of Child Health and Human Development. (2000). *Report of the National Reading Panel: Teaching children to read: An evidence-based assessment of scientific-based literature on reading and its implications for reading* (NIH Publication No. 00-4769). Washington, DC: U.S. Government Printing Office.

Northwest Evaluation Association. (2013). *Measures of Academic Progress (MAP).* Retrieved December 22, 2013, from *www.nwea.org.*

Nunes, T., & Bryant, P. (2011). Morphemic approaches for reading words. In R. E. O'Connor & P. F. Vadasy (Eds.), *Handbook of reading interventions* (pp. 88–112). New York: Guilford Press.

Paris, S. G. (2010). Thinking straight about measures of early reading development. In P. H. Johnston (Ed.), *RTI in literacy: Responsive and comprehensive* (pp. 103–114). Newark, DE: International Reading Association.

Pearson, P. D., & Hamm, D. N. (2005). The assessment of reading comprehension: A review of practice—past, present and future. In S. G. Paris & S. Stahl (Eds.), *Children's reading comprehension and assessment* (pp. 13–70). Mahwah, NJ: Erlbaum.

Pearson, P. D., Hiebert, E. F., & Kamil, M. (2007). Vocabulary assessment: What we know and what we need to learn. *Reading Research Quarterly, 42,* 282–297.

Perfetti, C. A. (1985). *Reading ability.* New York: Oxford University Press.

Perfetti, C. A. (1988). Verbal efficiency in reading ability. In M. Daneman, G. E. MacKinnon, & T. G. Waller (Eds.), *Reading research: Advances in theory and practice* (Vol. 6, pp. 109–143). New York: Academic Press.

Perin, D. (2007). Best practices in teaching writing to adolescents. In S. Graham, C. A. MacArthur, & J. Fitzgerald (Eds.), *Best practices in writing instruction* (pp. 242–264). New York: Guilford Press.

Pflaum, S. W., Walberg, H. J., Karegianes, M. L., & Rassher, S. W. (1980). Reading instruction: A quantitative analysis. *Educational Researcher, 9,* 12–18.

Popham, W. J. (2001). *The truth about testing: An educators' call to action.* Alexandria, VA: Association for Supervision and Curriculun Development.

Pressley, M. (2006). *Reading instruction that works: The case for balanced teaching* (3rd ed.). New York: Guilford Press.

RAND Reading Study Group. (2002). *Reading for understanding: Toward an R&D program in reading comprehension.* Santa Monica, CA: RAND.

Rasinski, T. V. (1986). Repeated reading naturally. *The Reading Teacher, 39,* 244–245.

Rasinski, T. V., Reutzel, D. R., Chard, D., & Linan-Thompson, S. (2011). Reading fluency. In M. L. Kamil, P. D. Pearson, E. B. Moje, & P. P. Afflerbach (Eds.), *Handbook of reading research* (Vol. 4, pp. 286–319). New York: Routledge.

Ravid, R. (2000). *Practical statistics for educators.* Lanham, MD: University Press of America.

Risko, V. J., & Walker-Dalhouse, D. (2010). Making the most of assessment to inform instruction. *The Reading Teacher, 63,* 420–422.

Roskos, K., & Neuman, S. B. (2012). Formative assessment: Simply, no additives. *The Reading Teacher, 65,* 534–538.

Santa, C. M., & Hoien, T. (1999). An assessment of Early Steps: A program for early intervention. *Reading Research Quarterly, 34,* 54–79.

Scanlon, D. M., & Anderson, K. L. (2010). Using the interactive strategies approach to prevent reading difficulties in an RTI context. In M. Y. Lipson & K. K. Wixson (Eds.), *Successful approaches to RTI: Collaborative practices for improving K–12 literacy* (pp. 20–65). Newark, DE: International Reading Association.

Schmoker, M. (2006). *Results now.* Alexandria, VA: Association for Supervision and Curriculum Development.

Shanahan, C. (2009). Disciplinary literacy. In S. E. Israel & G. G. Duffy (Eds.), *Handbook of research on reading comprehension* (pp. 240–260). New York: Routledge.

Shanahan, C., Shanahan, T., & Misischia, C. (2011). Analysis of expert readers in three disciplines: History, mathematics and chemistry. *Journal of Literacy Research, 43,* 393–429.

Shanahan, T. (2011). Common Core Standards: Are we going to lower the fences or teach kids to climb? *Reading Today,* August/September, pp. 20–21.

Sireci, S. G. (2005). The most frequently unasked questions about testing. In R. P. Phelps (Ed.), *Defending standardized testing* (pp. 111–121). Mahwah, NJ: Erlbaum.

Spear-Swerling, L., & Sternberg, R. J. (1996). *Off track: When poor readers become "learning disabled."* Boulder, CO: Westview Press.

Stahl, S. A. (1986). Three principles of effective vocabulary instruction. *Journal of Reading, 29,* 662–668.

Stahl, S. A., & Fairbanks, M. M. (1986). The effects of vocabulary: A model-based meta-analysis. *Review of Educational Research, 56,* 72–110.

Stahl, S. A., & Hiebert, E. H. (2005). The "word factors": A problem for reading comprehension. In S. G. Paris & S. A. Stahl (Eds.), *Children's reading comprehension and assessment* (pp. 161–186). Mahwah, NJ: Erlbaum.

Stahl, S. A., Heubach, K., & Cramond, B. (1997). Fluency-oriented reading instruction. In *Changing reading instruction in second grade: A fluency-oriented approach* (pp. 420–422). Athens: National Reading Research Center, University of Georgia.

Stahl, S. A., & Nagy, W. E. (2006). *Teaching word meanings.* Mahwah, NJ: Erlbaum.

Stanovich, K. E. (1980). Toward an interactive–compensatory model of individual differences in the development of reading fluency. *Reading Research Quarterly, 16,* 32–71.

Stanovich, K. E. (1986). Matthew effects in reading: Some consequences of individual differences in the acquisition of literacy. *Reading Research Quarterly, 21,* 360–407.

Stanovich, K. E. (1988). *Children's reading and the development of phonological awareness.* Detroit, MI: Wayne State University Press.

Stanovich, K. E. (1991). Word recognition: Changing perspectives. In R. Barr, M. L. Kamil, P. Mosenthal, & P. D. Pearson (Eds.), *Handbook of reading research* (Vol. 2, pp. 418–452). New York: Longman.

Stanovich, K. E. (1993–1994). Romance and reality. *The Reading Teacher, 47,* 280–291.

Stanovich, K. E. (2000). *Progress in understanding reading.* New York: Guilford Press.

Stein, N. L., & Glenn, C. (1979). An analysis of story comprehension in elementary school children. In R. O. Freedle (Ed.), *Advances in discourse processes: New directions in discourse processes* (Vol. 2, pp. 53–120). Norwood, NJ: Ablex.

Stiggens, R. J. (1994). *Student-centered classroom assessment.* New York: Merrill.

Sweet, A. P. (2005). Assessment of reading: The RAND Reading Study Group vision. In S. G. Paris & S. A. Stahl (Eds.), *Children's reading comprehension and assessment* (pp. 3–12). Mahwah, NJ: Erlbaum.

Taylor, B. M., Pearson, P. D., Peterson, D. S., & Rodriguez, M. C. (2010). Reading growth in high poverty classrooms: The influence of teacher practices that encourage cognitive engagement in literacy learning. In P. H. Johnston (Ed.), *RTI in literacy: Responsive and comprehensive* (pp. 44–79). Newark, DE: International Reading Association.

Tierney, R. J., & Thome, C. (2006). Is DIBELS leading us down the wrong path? In K. S. Goodman (Ed.), *The truth about DIBELS: What it is, what it does* (pp. 50–59). Portsmouth, NH: Heinemann.

Trabasso, T., & Magliano, J. P. (1996). Conscious understanding during reading. *Discourse Processes, 21,* 255–287.

Trice, A. D. (2000). *A handbook of classroom assessment.* New York: Addison Wesley Longman.

U.S. Department of Education. (2004). *Building the legacy: IDEA.* Washington, DC: U.S. Government Printing Office. Retrieved from *http://idea.ed.gov* .

U.S. Department of Education. (2005). *Testing for results.* Retrieved from *www2. ed.gov/nclb/accountability/ayp/testingforresults.html* .

Valencia, S. (2007). Inquiry-oriented assessment. In J. R. Paratore & R. L. McCormack (Eds.), *Classroom literacy assessment: Making sense of what students know and do* (pp. 3–20). New York: Guilford Press.

Wixson, K. K., & Lipson, M. Y. (2012). Relations between the CCSS and RTI in literacy and language. *The Reading Teacher, 65,* 387–391.

Wixson, K. K., Lipson, M. Y., & Johnston, P. H. (2010). Making the most of RTI. In M. Y. Lipson & K. K. Wixson (Eds.), *Successful approaches to RTI: Collaborative practices for improving K–12 literacy* (pp. 1–19). Newark, DE: International Reading Association.

Yopp, H. K. (1992). Developing phonemic awareness in young children. *The Reading Teacher, 45,* 696–703.

Yopp, H. K. (1995/1999). A test for assessing phonemic awareness in young children. *The Reading Teacher, 49,* 20–29.

Yopp, H. K., & Yopp, R. H. (2000). Supporting phonemic awareness development in the classroom. *The Reading Teacher, 54,* 130–143.

Zeno, S. M., Ivens, S. H., Millard, R. T., & Duvvuri, R. (1995). *The educator's word frequency guide.* Brewster, NY: Touchstone Applied Science.

Zywica, J. K., & Gomez, K. (2008). Annotation to support learning in the content areas: Teaching and learning science. *Journal of Adult and Adolescent Literacy, 52,* 155–165.

Index